Being a Boss doesn't make you a Leader

First published in Great Britain 2018

Published by MSG, Baginton, UK

UK with Amazon CreateSpace

Copyright Martin Goodyer & MSG 2018 ©

ISBN:
978-1723413315

I0481931

Please forward any feedback to martin@martin.coach

Being a Boss doesn't make you a Leader

*** To Rachel ***

for keeping the faith, and being 'the half' I need to stay whole

Being a Boss doesn't make you a Leader

*"Those Greeks and Romans, they are so overrated. They only **said** everything first. I´ve said just as good things myself. But they got in before me"*

Sir Winston Churchill

Being a Boss doesn't make you a Leader

CONTENTS

Preface

"If a leader can figure out how to consistently and positively change people's behaviour to match the needs of the business, get the most from them, and simultaneously help them to be successful in their own right - then he or she will have cracked it."

Martin Goodyer

What do Confucius, Plato, and The Buddha etc., have to do with leadership today?

The short answer is "Oodles", but I'm guessing on its own that response isn´t overly convincing, nor particularly eloquent. Okay, so, in no particular order here are 10 good reasons to ponder - 10 reasons that form the tip of what might just be an 'oodles' iceberg:

1. **Blame.** When all is said and done, without a healthy bottom line a business isn't sustainable. Bosses and leaders know this, however, bosses look to blame when things don't go as planned, whereas leaders are as pragmatic as some of the earliest shapers of modern thinking and seek to collaborate and find ways to get back on track.

2. **Clarity and vision.** Leaders familiar with the thinking of those who've shaped the scientific and artistic landscape we enjoy today, know that without a clear image of success it is almost impossible to gain the commitment, enthusiasm, and combined energy of a workforce. However, the typical response from a 'boss' charged with achieving such clarity is to order

9

posters with a printed 'mission statement', and for employees to be told to learn it.

3. **Communication:** The complexity, unpredictability, and dynamic nature of today's world requires leaders to communicate on multiple levels. A boss communicates in ways which she or he feels 'comfortable'. Leaders who've learned from the best thought leaders in history communicate so that their message is heard, and then acted upon.

4. **Fear of being 'let go'.** It wasn't so long ago that only soccer team managers were judged on the smallest time frames regarding their success or otherwise. These days the head of an organisation may have a similar slippery grip on tenure. The characteristic of 'a boss' is to respond badly, their emotions coming to the fore - making them a nightmare to work with however good or bad the results. A leader who's learned from those philosophers 'keeping their heads' during the warring states period of ancient Chinese history, know that calmness and clarity of vision are better tools than rampant emotion.

5. **Lack of accountability.** While every manager reporting to them will have measures, key performance indicators, and calibrated outcomes, the head person probably does not. A person seeing themselves as 'the boss' uses this lack of accountability to pressure employees to do more and work harder. Yet, a Leader following in the footsteps of early thought-leaders will use their privileged position to absorb the accountability of all their managers, and share in the commitment to reach successful outcomes, judging themselves as harshly as anyone in their service.

6. **Lack of goal alignment** - is common when the top people in an organisation worry more about their own 'slice of the cake' than the whole tray of baking in the oven. 'Bosses' brush aside the needs of the organisation in favour of attempting to be a 'star' in their own little corner of their business universe. Leaders who've been exposed to the earliest thinkers who've explored the concept of a 'joined up world' know how short sighted those bosses are being - and instead ensure that the same 'my bit of the pie' thinking doesn't happen with managers reporting to them. The results are almost always that they outperform even the most egotistical 'boss'.

7. **Sagging self-belief.** When someone with a 'boss' mentality makes it to the top it's likely they put on a good front. Sadly, beneath that fragile veneer a bubbling cauldron of doubt is always close to bursting through. On the other hand, leaders with the high levels of self-awareness that come from a good grasp of successful thought-leader approaches, are far less likely to suffer from imposter syndrome than their 'boss' counterparts.

8. **Superficial 'trust'.** Of course, there's no such thing, but superficial trust is how bosses tend to behave - attempting to appear trustworthy but failing miserably. Leaders aware of what it takes to be trusted may have learned such skills by asking themselves how men without the aid of a PR department, Social Media gurus, or TV and the Press, came to have so many believing and trusting in them.

9. **Talking a 'good game'.** Perhaps the ebullient Cuba Gooding Jn. had it right in the old movie 'Jerry McGuire', with his catch-phrase *"show me the money"*

- it's certainly a position many early philosophers would recognise (and a repeated theme), as their patrons and supporters often needed evidence or to have person enlightenment experiences themselves. 'Bosses' may feel the need to 'oversell' themselves and then live in fear of being found out. Leaders like those early thought-leaders know that words alone won't cut it - and hence focus on real outcomes that can be delivered.

10. **The way we do things around here** - aka 'company culture'. 'Bosses' shake their heads in defeat, complaining that change can only come from some place other than where they are at. Leaders who've listened to the words of wisdom from philosophers and world leading thinkers from millennia ago know that change 'starts right here'. They also know it takes courage, commitment, and creativity to begin wherever they find themselves - but they do it anyway - and are almost always successful.

The list doesn't end at number 10 - but I think ten is enough to make the point that there *is* something here for aspiring leaders to learn. These issues are as obvious as the poor morale suffered by millions of employees in businesses large and small, the often unbelievably poor productivity of those same businesses, and the revolving door for senior business managers and so-called leaders - as increasingly the workforce have no sooner learned who they are, before they're fired and replaced.

'Being a Boss doesn't make you a Leader' is all about looking back - in order to see forward with increased clarity. In fact, it doesn't just look back, it looks way, way back. You see, I believe that there's quite enough people

'selling' leaders their idea of what great leadership is and is not - and as someone working with senior leaders (who are sometimes just 'big bosses') I'm heartily fed up of hearing the same message packaged a zillion ways. Which is why I've written this; there are no words of wisdom from Martin Goodyer about what makes or does not make a good leader. Instead, this is a book based on facts but with a good sprinkling of imagination to (hopefully) bring it to life. These are not my ideas but the ideas of 22 of the earliest people from modern history who've contributed to shaping the way we all think today. They are genuine, honest to goodness thought-leaders. As such, they have something to say or contribute to the way business leaders of today might think.

The common theme underlying blame, clarity, communication, fears about being sacked, lack of accountability and of aligning goals, sagging self-belief, and sad, superficial levels of trust while talking a good game, and then pretending problems are caused by the history of a corporate culture is that of *changing the way people behave'*. Therefore, each of the 22 is re-imagined as a leader today and asked to pose questions to help an employee become desirous of positive change.

I hope you end up liking these characters and what they have to say as much as I have.

Martin Goodyer

December 2018

PS If you are only interested in knowing about the philosophers and not about applications etc. then go straight to page 65!

Being a Boss doesn't make you a Leader

CHAPTER 1: A THINKING MANAGER'S' GUIDE TO LEADERSHIP

LEADING PEOPLE IS NOT A 'PROBLEM' TO FIX, BUT A PHILOSOPHY TO FOLLOW

Leading = people following

People following = manifesting new behaviours

Manifesting new behaviours= thinking differently

Thinking differently = having a philosophy to follow

Thinking differently, being willing and able to stay laser-focused on a goal despite the temptation to 'do what you always did' separates great leaders from the rest of the pack. Being a boss does not automatically confer the attributes of a leader and adopting the term 'leader' or 'leadership' does not suggest the ability to 'think like a leader' – particularly when ascribing the term to people who have challenged the thinking-status quo and led the rest of us to change the way we think too.

Picture this ...a meeting, not just any meeting but one where the message must land with your audience - if the team don't hustle for more business and savings then soon none of them, including the boss, will have a job. Sound familiar? Maybe not exactly, but hasn't something similar happened to you, some situation where it's important to get other people to change what they're doing, and change quickly?

Eek! No matter how senior or experienced you may be, it's easy to be a little on edge? Perhaps a tiny bit stressed? So, what would you say to them? Would you explain the importance and critical nature of the situation? If you did, will that work? Do people really respond to logic, or do they secretly, (or not so secretly) harbour resentment at being criticised? Do people listen to logic despite how they feel, or do feelings affect the way they respond?

Let's face it, have you ever seen a group of people leap up from a meeting like that saying "Wow, I didn't realise the company wanted more from us, now that I know I will work much harder!" ...is that really what happens? I don't think so. Maybe you wouldn't simply explain the situation, perhaps you'd try to 'sell' them on the idea that producing better results is good for everyone? Well, it sounds plausible, but does it work? Do team members silently nod in agreement and then smile at the new realisation that improved performance is a good thing? Again, I don't think so. Isn't it more likely that they'll be chatting away silently in their head, saying something like 'here we go again...same old, same old...'? Or let's suppose you prefer the 'direct approach' of simply telling them what they need them to do because after all, you're the boss, how might that work out for you? I'm guessing that some people may bend to your will, others may cower, and do as they're told ....at least, for the time being, but at what cost? Is that approach sustainable? Yet again, I don't think so. Rather, isn't it true that often the best people won't put up with that rubbish approach to management, simply 'walking' as soon as they're able, leaving only the poor performers behind who'd basically stumble through anything they're told to do because they know they're unlikely to get a job elsewhere?

So, what's left? Could you ask them questions that engage and inspire and encourage participation? Hm... maybe you could? But, here's the thing; what questions do you ask? How do you find questions that get past barriers like beliefs about already doing 'everything they can'? How do you formulate questions that demonstrate you understand how they might be feeling? In short, where do you get inspiration and advice for how to ask better questions that generate even better results, and help make even better decisions? There's no easy answer, but there's no doubt that learning from 'genuine thought-leaders' who've been successful in getting people to change behaviours must be a good start. Aren't those people who shaped the society we live in as good a choice as any? This book is about two things; philosophers - firstly, how they might have thought and what might have shaped them to think that way. Secondly, what questions they might have asked if they were in our shoes. How can we use their thinking and apply it in our real-world - right here, right now to become one of those leaders that produce the very best results? A genuine, honest to goodness 'coaching-leader'.

According to Socrates, people like us - like you, because you've picked up this book - are likely to be interested in 'thinking' and using those thoughts to help make the world a better place. While other people are wading their way through yet another self-help book on meditation and mindfulness, you'll be adding to your tool-kit of knowledge by doing something different. Again, Socrates would say, and I agree wholeheartedly that we are making a valuable contribution to the life and well-being of far more people than we might realise. Learn to think more effectively and you'll inevitably act more effectively. One doesn't come without the other.

It might be more accurate to turn this on its head and say that people who don't stop and think about what they're doing before they do it add to the damage and chaos in the world around us. For example, so-called 'leaders' who tweet knee-jerk thoughts at 3am to the workforce don't inspire confidence. As opposed to those who take time to think about what they want to achieve and engage their key team players in that goal, encouraging everyone else with a stake in the ventures to support it. They're the ones who end up achieving the most. I'm going out on a limb here, but I'm guessing there won't be too many ego-maniacal' leaders' seeking this out if they don't have the patience, time, or opportunity to read it. I've written this for aspiring leaders and managers who want to be better managers and leaders, managers and coaches who want to be more effective coaches and coaching managers, managers who also want to use those same skills at home or for other reasons than 'be a better leaser'. They might be mums or dads wanting to connect more with their kids. They could be doctors who lead teams of staff as well as patient care who want to cut to the chase while staying rapport. They could be anyone desirous of helping another person change their behaviour for good. In fact, anyone who recognises that being a coaching-leader is going to help them do better in whatever they do.

How can a book applying philosophy to management be useful to all these people? Well, think about how managers get their job and start their journey toward leadership. Managers are promoted because they're good 'decision makers'; they wouldn't get a seat at the table if they couldn't figure out answers to problems and get things done, - it goes with the territory. The notion that because a manager is a good problem solver, he or she is also a 'good' manager seems natural, and yet, it's not. Many of them don't get that not everything that needs to change is a problem per-se, certainly not when it comes to people needing to behave differently - these are not problems for them to solve. People are NOT a 'problem', they are a something else entirely. Their behaviour may cause problems, but that's a different issue; a person may leave the bath water to overflow, causing damage to the floor below. The overflow and damage may be problems, and the forgetfulness of the person leaving it running may have caused the *problem*, but the 'person' who left it running is not the problem, are they? That person is much more than the problem of causing the overflow; he or she has strengths, experience, attributes and skills, as well as weaknesses and blind-spots. You can't lump all this together and call that person a 'problem'. They are not the problem - changing their behaviour so they don't let the bath overflow again is a goal, a positive change, and a benefit to them as well as anyone living beneath the bathtub.

So, if it's a good idea to ensure that person doesn't do it again, then something must be done. Adopting a problem-solving approach with that person by identifying what went wrong, what can be done instead, and telling them to be careful next time guarantees nothing. Zip. Nada. Every manager I've ever met knows this to be true. However, in the place of a workable alternative they try the same thing over and over. As Einstein famously pointed out, all they do is drive themselves nuts. Their problem-solving skills are a tool. A good set of wrenches are useful when a wrench is called for, but what if the thing that needs altering can't be altered with a wrench? What if the tool required is a screwdriver? What if it's not just any old screwdriver that's needed but one with a special shape? How useful are the wrenches then? You see, no matter how wonderful the wrench-set is, it's about as useful as a baron of beef at a vegan banquet; wonderful if that's what's needed but just 'wrong' if it's not. What you'll read in here are those new tools; different ways of thinking, so you ask yourself better questions and get better results.

There's no doubt that some situations are problems that require solving: a delivery hasn't arrived, insufficient staff have been scheduled for an event, a machine has broken down, and so on. However, if a situation requires a person to change their mind, be persuaded to do what you want them to do, or to stop doing something they're doing then this 'change of behaviour' is NOT a problem, even though we so desperately might want it to be! As I've said, it's something else entirely, but that something else isn't so easy to figure out. With problem-solving we can be taught a set of rules to follow, but with this, all we get to learn is how to ask better questions, - then it's up to you to find the right one at the right time. You'll read later about one of our team of philosophers who demonstrated his skill as a philosopher when visiting Rome, by arguing convincingly for a set of behaviours that all citizens of the Roman Empire should adhere to. He had crowds cheering and calling for him to come back and speak again the very next day. He did. This time he argued just as eloquently and with as many powerful questions for the crowd, but against the exact thing he'd rallied them for the day before. They found themselves wanting to do what he extolled even though it was in direct opposition to the things he'd got them to agree to the day before! The Roman authorities were less than pleased, but from our point of view he demonstrated a powerful leadership skill; not to negatively manipulate their workers, but to 'frame' whatever is going on so that the behaviour of the people they care for changes to support the best outcome.

If you are an experienced leader, you already know that no matter how painstakingly patient you've been in explaining the 'need' to change, a person only changes their behaviour if they want to. It's not logic that causes a person to change, it's emotion every time. Think about it; how many times have you done something just because you 'wanted' to do it, even though you knew it may not be the best course of action? If you are human, the answer will be 'lots of times'! That's why finding the 'right' question to ask at the 'right' time is so very, very important; questions stimulate emotions, and a good question pushes the right buttons so that a person changes, even when you didn't think they ever would. Managers and people who lead may be prone to leap into every situation assuming there is a problem to be solved, - and that they're the obvious person to solve it. This applies to almost every manager I've met, so anyone with that job title would do well to take note; Socrates would say that we who plan what we are going to do and say are the highest of achievers, and the ones who realise the potential of human potential most fully. Philosophers may not have answers, but they sure do know how to ask better questions!

The thing about people is that they haven't changed much in thousands of years, they're not so different today than they ever were. Technology and life's circumstances are very different, but the flesh, bone, and brains of people two or three thousand years ago are indistinguishable from those of people today. So, it makes sense that their understanding of the world is as useful now as it ever was. As insights are discovered, rediscovered, and reinterpreted, isn't it simply logical to seek out those who have already asked great questions, so we might do the same? Anyone interested in improving their own performance (or anyone else's) at work or in life more generally, may already know that it is a good question that causes them to stop and think. Therefore, it makes sense that the better the question the more likely the change. So, it follows that improvements in performance are almost always preceded by asking a good question, a better question, one that causes a person to start the process of change in their own behaviour. Smile and people are more likely to smile back, become a 'moaner' and you'll be avoided, or get angry and the first person you frustrate is yourself. These facts are true for us all and have been since humans began communicating. By now, surely humanity must have developed the means to overcome these problems, at least you'd think so? Well, it turns out we have, but that each generation has a short memory and so much of what's been learned gets forgotten, only to be rediscovered - and then turn up in a self-help book on the virtual shelves of Amazon. So, if the knowledge is there, the experience is evident, and the communication of 'how' is accessible, then changing behaviour to achieve better results should be a synch, shouldn't it? Sadly, it is not that easy. How do you change what you might believe can't be changed? What do you do when someone else's beliefs just won't change - no matter how logical and persuasive you try to be?

It's a tough situation, and there is no simple step-by-step guide for leaders, which is why there's a plethora of books claiming to be the 'next big thing' in leadership. It might be why the same issues of getting people to listen, and buy-in to necessary change, is just as prevalent now as it ever was. These 'truths' are why I've taken a different route - one that looks backwards in the hope of finding something useful for now and in the future. Rather than 'guess' what might be useful in helping bosses become the very desirable coaching-leader organisations look for today, I've looked for solid evidence of what has worked in the past. I've gone back to rediscover the thought-leaders of yesteryear and learn something useful from them. I sought out individuals who's impact on the way people think has stood the test of time. People whose wisdom has either been dumbed down into a social-media meme or might have been forgotten altogether. Many of the names that follow may be familiar, and others less so, but they all share one defining characteristic - if they had been 'bosses' in their time, their colleagues would have seen them as a leader. I accept that looking back at what's been successful once doesn't guarantee that it'll be as successful now. However, if there is a better chance of succeeding, even if it's not guaranteed it'd be crazy not to think about it, wouldn't it? I'd like to think that was so but, it may not be, which may explain why in all my time studying as a manager in the UK, the US and Canada, and there was never a mention of anything I've included in this book. There was plenty of received wisdom from the gurus of the day. There were plenty of theories, and plenty of how to-guides, all of which were updated and replaced by new (and different) how-to guides as the years passed. Looking back, it was bonkers because even when it was clear that something wasn't working, it took years for text books to be updated. Is it any wonder then, that the would-be-leaders of today are left scratching their heads? They rely instead on their personal experience, and it is that rather than empirically tested best-practice that becomes the 'success map' they then advocate to their juniors.

It's a clear case of emotion trumping logic. I can't believe anyone would argue that one person's experience can be applicable to everyone. Logically, personal experience can't be the best way to lead even if only for the fact that we are all different, we all pull different things from our experiences, and we all know that works for us may not work for someone else. The experience of one boss passed down to a subordinate is unfortunately all too common. A best-case scenario might be that the boss in question has taken steps to be the best leader they can be, has been educated in leadership best practice, and has extensively read around the subject to pass down leadership gems. In the worst-case, they assumed their own relatively poor experience to be good and have passed down flawed advice to unsuspecting up-and-comers. Therefore, sadly it's more likely that shared personal experience might 'on balance' be more damaging than helpful.

However, experience gleaned from people to whom the title thought-leader has been applied and has been earned is a different matter. The experience of those people is way more valuable than opinions from the average (or often below average) leader. It's common practice to seek out 'great leaders' – people like wartime leaders or contemporary business leaders, and to be fair, sometimes there is value in understanding what and why they did what they did. The trouble is, very often these same people fall out of favour; public opinion changes about those same wartime leaders and business organisations that were once at the top of their game inevitably fall from grace – and along with them those same once hero-worshiped leaders, slip into quiet obscurity. Sad, but true. Yet, being open to adapting our own thinking when it's based on highly successful thought-leaders who've stood the test of time is bound to be a good thing; something that's likely to add lasting value, something that might make us better at leading simply by learning from them how they came to think differently, and something that might help change an ordinary boss into a potentially extraordinary leader. Thought-leaders who have stood the test of time despite the ongoing experience of global cultural changes, have remained a source of inspiration for a reason – what they had to say, the way they chose to think, and the insights they left behind are evidence of the value they still hold.

Unfortunately, up to now there hasn't been a single source of that information. There hasn't been a guide to look at leadership from a different perspective, to see it from a different angle, to describe it differently, ...and then to ask better questions that help us become better leaders. If the bad news is that this is hard, then the good news is that the fact people have already pondered these things, have already come up with good ideas, and have already prepared the ground for improved leadership by utilising what they've spent lifetimes trying to master.

CHAPTER 2: LEADERS ASK BETTER QUESTIONS

BOSSES DO NOT

'If the know-how to get people to change has been around for millennia, how come most of us don't know what to do, say, or ask?'

Without getting too 'heavy', just look at the well-publicised productivity problems all around the world. Just ask yourself – do these results suggest that 'leadership' isn't as good as it could be? Duh. Don't get me started with the anecdotes I've heard every time I mentioned this book title – seriously, every single time someone has piped up with their own experience of a terrifying boss and dreadful leadership.

Now, I'm not saying that all 'bosses' are terrible leaders, just that too many of them may well be. Aristotle is credited with saying *"the unexamined life is not worth living"*, in other words, the more we 'think' the better results we get. Therefore, unthinking bosses - those who blindly follow bad rules, those who aren't considerate of feelings, and those who have ego's preventing them from being genuine leaders all have one thing in common - they just don't think enough. Perhaps we need a new saying – something like *'the unexamined leader ought not be leading'*?

I'm no spring chicken and can personally testify to experiencing years of awful, terrible, bossy, grumpy, and non-thinking leadership - including once upon a time and to my great shame, from myself. Not that I, nor any of the people I worked with back then tried to be less than brilliant 'leaders' on purpose, quite the opposite; I think people have tried hard to be good at leadership. They've learned lots of 'techniques and tools' but have been shoe-horned into a system that doesn't support 'free' or 'creative' thinking. So, I forgive them (and hope I can be forgiven too) for doing the best they could with what they were told they had, and rather than being all holier-than-thou about it would prefer to take a lighter approach:

In that light-hearted vein, here's a rubbish joke that starts to unwrap what I mean by 'free' and 'creative' thinking;

Difficult people will keep on pushing-back until you ask a better question:

"Old George walked into an antique store dragging a plank of wood. The owner heaved a huge sigh. He'd seen George before - he was always trying to palm off junk as antiques. "Ah ha!" Said George with a toothy grin, "Today, I have for you ...this!" and heaved the plank onto the counter. "Yeees," said the owner politely but, with more than a hint of exasperation. "This my dear chap," continued George in a fake upper-class British accent, "may look like any old plank, but it is in fact from one of the lifeboats from none other than ...the Titanic itself!" The owner, not wanting to appear rude, said he needed a second opinion. He turned toward the rear of the store and shouted "Cosgrove! I need a second opinion on this plank of wood from the lifeboat of the famous Titanic". Although a little deaf, old Cosgrove knew what was expected. He took out a magnifying glass, gave the plank a thorough look over and then sighed wearily. "Yes sir, this is indeed from one of the lost lifeboats of the Titanic..." With that George grinned from ear to ear, hardly believing his luck. "...but" continued Cosgrove, "I'm afraid the lifeboat is no longer lost as we purchased the rest of it just last week ...and so this small

piece is of no interest to us now". Crestfallen, George heaved the plank off the counter and shuffled out of the shop. A little while later, much to the annoyance of the shopkeeper, George appeared again, this time dragging behind him the branch of a tree. "Ah ha!" he said, "I have something you can't turn down this time!" "Yeees, what is it" replied the shopkeeper politely. "This... I say, THIS... all the way from India... is none other than a branch from the Olive tree under which the Buddha sat when having his divine inspiration!" Without missing a beat, the owner replied, "Ah-hem, I think I need a second opinion... COSGROVE... could you come out here a moment please... this 'gentleman' is with us again, ...this time with a branch from the Olive tree under which Buddha once sat." Cosgrove dutifully shuffled out with his magnifying glass and painstakingly looked over the branch from end to end, before declaring. "Yes, indeed... I do believe this IS such a thing..." Again, George looked on wide-eyed with hope. "However, I strongly suggest the gentleman hangs onto the item for at least another decade, as I'm aware the rest of the tree has recently been discovered and so this is worth very little right now". Ushering the disappointed George out of the shop Cosgrove and the shopkeeper conspiratorially raised their eyebrows and returned to work. To both their surprise, George returned for a third time later that day carrying a small bag. "Yeees..." said the shopkeeper wearily. "Ah-ha!" said George, "...I have something amazing for you this time... I bet you haven't seen anything like this?" and with that reached into the bag and slammed onto the counter a golf-ball sized rock. "This... THIS... is nothing less than the mummified remains of Emperor Napoleon's right testicle!" Then, before the shopkeeper could say a word, he rushed on... "AND before *you call that old fool Cosgrove..."with which he slammed a second ball shaped rock on the counter... "there's his LEFT one!"*"

Groan if you must! It may not be the best funny story in the world (and I did warn you), but it does demonstrate that even against the odds, a person prepared to think on their feet, ask themselves a better question, question their surroundings, and question the people they are with, will always stand a better chance of success than those who don't. Thinking freely and creatively doesn't guarantee success, but NOT doing it does guarantee having less chance of being successful. Who is the hero of the story? Is it George for being relentless in his dynamic and changing approach to making a sale? Or, was it the shopkeeper for maintaining his calmness in the face of such obvious absurdity? Or, perhaps it was Cosgrove for creatively putting off George with his explanations without being offensive? Hm… or could it be that all of them had something to learn? If George had asked himself better questions, might he have put his efforts into finding 'real' antiques? If the shopkeeper had asked himself better questions might he have saved himself wasted time and the use of his labour? What if Cosgrove had asked himself better questions, and rather than assuming his role was to creatively outwit the would-be customer had clarified with George what a real antique is and what it is not? Of course, it wouldn't have made for a very humorous story, but I hope you get the idea. Asking better questions is a sign of thinking; it's what each one of the ancient philosophers became known for but asking questions alone won't cause anyone to become a better leader.

Here's the thing, a typical boss and leader I'm talking about here sees the 'boss' as concerned with being 'right' and the leader as more concerned with being successful. By freely and creatively thinking that typical 'boss' might get better at leadership. It's not guaranteed and it's a tough journey, but by following in the steps of great thinkers it should make it a little easier. It's not easy; it takes practice because it requires the boss to re-pattern their unconscious and the way they process information. Bosses are all about 'ego', whereas leaders are all about 'outcomes'. Bosses are unconsciously driven by fear, while leaders are resilient. Bosses want to blame the person responsible if something goes wrong, but leaders are drawn to praise the person doing the most to rectify whatever needed fixing. Yet, both bosses and leaders have something in common - they both act without thinking. It all happens in the unconscious. Both bosses and leaders develop patterns and then act without thinking. To think differently they must develop a new pattern of 'thinking differently'. That's what this book is all about - developing those new patterns by a) learning something interesting about 'names' you may only vaguely recognise, and b) allowing their approach to thinking to influence the way you unconsciously think about leadership.

Uh-oh, I can almost hear ... 'Say what?'. Fear not, trust me I'm not about to launch into some psychobabble about the unconscious. What I mean is if you want to unconsciously think differently then there must be a new framework for how you 'think'. If it sounds a bit 'out there' then don't worry, I promise it'll become clearer, and that by the end of the book you will take away something new and useful, because in the words of Yoda you'll learn something new and, "...*you cannot unlearn what you have learned*".

Here's a bit of reflection: On a plane coming back from successfully helping a group of bosses become better leaders, I started to think how I'd explain what had happened to them if I only had, let's say less than thirty seconds. What could I say that was meaningful and made sense to describe what'd happened? Saying *"they changed their behaviour toward subordinates"* might have been accurate but wasn't the whole story. First, it suggested there'd been something wrong with them or they'd been 'broken' before attending - which simply wasn't true. Most were there because they were 'good' bosses not bad ones; their teams produced good results, and they were probably rising stars in their organisations. They'd been with me to push themselves and achieve even better results, to find ways to get their colleagues, employees, and even their customers to succeed more. If that meant moving from boss to leader then they were up for it. My job had been to use tried and trusted 'scientific' approaches to help them get those results.

So, there I was on the plane, wondering how to say what had happened before getting to thirty seconds, what it all boiled down to and what had they been doing that was so successful? Hm… had they really shifted from bosses to leaders in one fell swoop? Of course, I wanted to say "Yup, that's exactly what happened", but, nah, - that wasn't it. Sure, they'd all left the session happy; their wishes (for now) fulfilled and were excited to be applying newly discovered techniques and approaches. I tried this; 'they had been reminded that people are not machines, and that to help them lead more effectively they needed to behave differently by applying leadership tools and techniques'. Well, that may be true, but it wasn't all that had happened, and it was awfully bland. In fact, I tried

31

over and over to come up with a form of words that expressed what they'd done, but no matter how I tried, I couldn't escape a nagging sense I might be missing something. Something was going on that was more than just psychology and willingness to achieve more.

Fair enough, the information comes from solid sources, and many of the 'tools' I'd had a hand in developing, so no worries on that score - I believed they'd had great stuff to engage with; tools and approaches that are contemporary, practical, and pragmatic. It was something else bothering me. I found myself asking what was the true source of these ideas I'd spent the week sharing? What if there was something obvious but forgotten? Could it be true that only now, after hundreds of thousands of years in human development it's only now that we've discovered ways to think more clearly about leadership? I wondered if it could really be true that psychologists in the 50's, 60's, and 70's were the first to think about 'thinking differently'? I quickly realised this just couldn't be true. After all, human beings had been interacting and working together for millennia. Great leaders had come and gone, led fabulous civilisations, and been honoured by the people they were leading. People had been creatively thinking long before we've given our ancestors proper credit. The 22 ancient philosophers I'm talking about here are by no means the only free thinkers in history. How surprised would you be if I told you that a prototype steam engine wasn't the work of a top-hat wearing Victorian, but a Greek engineer called 'Hero' (great name by the way), who invented a toy steam engine over 2000 years ago? What about computers, who do you think invented that concept? My first answer was 'Turing', but nope I was wrong. It seems that some relatively unknown person from at least as long ago as 100

BCE created something called the *'Antikythera mechanism'* - which is an actual basic working computation device. Who knew? Not me, for sure. So, while I didn't doubt that post Second World War psychologists had done a good job in pulling useful information together, I also guessed that whatever they'd 'found out' might be a modern repeat of something discovered way earlier.

I knew from the deep dive reading I'd been doing for a PhD[i] that there was an uncanny similarity between modern 'coaching' concepts and philosophical thinking from way back when. Maybe then, my less than thirty second explanation was that..."*they had moved from successful bosses to even more successful bosses -that were now thinking like successful leaders; asking better questions, thinking without so much constraint, and with more creativity*". Yes, that sounded much more like it. Not perfect by any means, but better. All those exercises, learnings, and conversations they'd had over the week had 100% left them thinking, questioning, and acting in a different way. Ha! Who needs thirty seconds to explain, - I'd just cracked it in less than ten!

This got me thinking; what if the best thinkers of their time could be transported into today's world and asked to coach someone? What would they say? I started to wonder what might transpire if those philosophers were to step into my coaching-shoes and were to meet with a high-flying executive desirous of achieving more. What would they ask her? I began to wonder if the problems faced by people today are so very different from those of a couple of thousand years ago. Did people have difficult relationships back then, did they have workers that needed to be motivated, did they have deadlines to meet, did they have issues with self-esteem, self-worth, and self-direction just like today? The more I thought about it the more I realised that with the exception of technology, not a lot has changed; there are still people in charge who make awful decisions, still politicians that can't be trusted, still bankers who'd take the shirt from your back, still people who fall in love when they shouldn't, still otherwise sensible people who act recklessly when they ought not to, and still people who behave poorly when they could easily have made better choices. There are just as many dictators, poor leaders, bad managers, difficult employees, stroppy teenagers, drunks, idiots and fools as there ever were, even if nowadays they happen to own an iPhone, Sat-Nav, and 52-inch TV! That's where this chunky little book started. I started searching for the true source of 'wisdom'- and found so much material that what we think might be 'modern' has in fact got its roots firmly in the past. Not just a recent past but a past from long, long ago. At first, I thought I'd pick out a few of the better-known philosophers and that'd be that, but it didn't work out that way. The more I looked, the more surprised I was to learn about people who'd clearly fallen through the cracks of my education. I 'discovered' people who three thousand years ago had been thinking about similar things to those that still fascinate leaders today. Clearly, there's no way of having these guys step into my shoes, so it seemed both appropriate and obvious that I should find a way to step into theirs.

Okay then, here we go; my attempt to walk in the sandals of some seriously smart people, men who might be amused that a psychologist and coach in 2018 should attempt to imagine what it's like to think like them, look at the world like them, and ask questions as if I were them.

34

CHAPTER 3: WHY PHILOSOPHY?

WHAT DO 'THE CLASSICS' HAVE TO DO WITH MOVING FROM BOSS TO LEADER?

My official disclaimer! Do you know what the number one fear is among senior executives... the fear they 'confess' when comfortable enough to be honest? Believe it or not, it's the fear of *being found out* - but found out about what exactly? Technically, it's known as *imposter theory* because the person feels like an imposter in their own role. They'll say things like *"sometimes I wonder if anyone knows how easy this job really is... I'm not sure if I deserve the position I have"* or words to that effect. The thing is, in majority of cases they don't deserve to feel that way. Most of the time they've worked hard to get where they are, and it's only because they're so experienced that they do things without thinking - things that other people simply could not do. However, I must be honest and say that's not me right now because the fact is, I AM an imposter in the world of philosophy. My background and training are in business and psychology, but sadly not philosophy - so what the heck am I doing writing this? I hope you agree that my answer is a good one (here goes); I believe I'm the right person to be writing this precisely **because** I'm not a classics scholar and hence, I'm more interested in what to 'do' with this philosophy than necessarily in philosophy for philosophy's sake. I'm an honest imposter, interested in helping people do better with what they have. Okay? Good, now we've got that cleared up, let's get going;

Philosophy; the root of the word comes from 'Philo' meaning *to love*, and 'Sophia' meaning *wisdom*. What a great combination because who wouldn't want to fall in love with wisdom, eh? Hm... if my experience is anything to go by, most of us. You see, unfortunately for the most part the people I've engaged with in my life have rarely if ever used philosophy as a foundation for their own thinking. They clearly do not love wisdom enough to base their way of life on it, nor I hasten to add, did I. Unfortunately, I too was one of those people, who until relatively recently woke up to the fact that being smart is less about reinventing wheels, and much more about rediscovering things - then wheeling out very clever stuff that's been long forgotten.

There is a downside to recognising the reality that recent generations were not the inventors of all things clever; it meant that I went from feeling modestly smug about my own contribution, to feeling distinctly less than average about any tiny effort I'd made to improve the 'lot' of humanity. Any warm, fuzzy feeling of a job well done does tend to pale when your own work becomes a grain of sand in comparison to the mountains moved by the big brains of the past. I suppose a good dose of reality doesn't do any harm. It was during years of research as a PhD candidate into the *'effectiveness of coaching in the workplace'* that I noticed how 'thinking' has evolved. Of course, it is both obvious and well understood that academic research always builds on the work of others - and evolves. But I'd only thought about that evolution in terms of learning about facts, observations, or other forms of empirical and testable evidence. I'd sort of fallen into the trap of lumping academic studies together and treating them differently to the modern cut and thrust of leadership activity. I know I can't be alone - I can't be the only person to have witnessed a capable and effective leader, apparently lose their common-sense after being immersed on an academic

MBA, can I? It doesn't happen to everyone, but it is something caused by this imaginary dichotomy between the real world and academia. As a mature student I had to learn to think in terms of asking 'so what?' and 'says who? 'to conform to academic requirements, and not - who thought of that in the first place, or how did that person come to think of that? So, I hadn't thought about the development of coaching in the workplace in terms of ways and means of 'thinking'. Looking back, I can see how naive that must sound, but there it is, I admit it, and I don't appear to be alone in that naivety; the assumption that a great idea came from the writers of a scientific paper, or the interpreters of experiments now feels just a bit silly. I'm left wondering if it is ever so slightly arrogant for people like me to imagine that suddenly, after thousands of years, our snapshot of humanity comes up with brilliant insights that alluded all who came before?

Now, forgive me if you happen to be a scholar of philosophy, but you're a rare breed in the big scheme of things, even though I know there are many of you in the cluster of your field. When it comes to ordinary 'Joes' like me, we see you as a rare beast in a society more interested in how many 'likes' they get on Facebook than learning how the world around them works. Such is life I suppose. On a very personal note, I was surprised to learn that my son-in-law had graduated in Philosophy. Not because of anything negative, just that I don't know many managers who chose philosophy at university. I think that's a shame because if there were more philosophy grads in leadership roles there'd possibly be a better understanding of EQ[ii] than I've experienced. Clearly, I like my son in law, which may be why I've attributed his love of wisdom as the defining factor that shaped him into someone my daughter fell in love with. Yet, in conversations about challenges within the workplace he made it clear that a gap exists between *'knowing about philosophy'*, and *'applying what's known about philosophy'* in a meaningful way - particularly when faced with office politics and a difficult boss. So, what came next was obvious - a recognition that learning *'how to think'* has evolved but utilising this evolution to make better sense of the modern world of leadership simply hasn't.

My day job isn't writing books; I'm a psychologist coaching people to change their behaviour. As such, I constantly seek to ask better questions- all of which goes with the territory of coaching. Therefore, I imagined that if I could step into the shoes, sandals, or slippers of one or two of these progressive thinkers and formulate 'coaching questions' based on the way they might be thinking, I'd hopefully stimulate new or better questions to add to my own coaching approach. I began to think that the evolution of 'how to think' might be helped along by for once looking backwards at what had been done and forgotten, rather than constantly looking forward for something new. I shared this thinking with colleagues and they agreed it was interesting. Well, at least they didn't say I was crazy- so that was encouraging. To be fair, they were genuinely interested. That's how and why this book came about. That's why a psychologist has ended up writing about philosophy. Here's what I did; first, I spent some time researching early philosophers, then I followed a time-line of development that began with the earliest references I could find and went from there. I was amazed because the more people I 'discovered', the more there were to be found. Soon, I realised that there are far more interesting characters to talk about than I'd initially

38

imagined. Instead of skipping from the sixth century BCE right up to the seventeenth century, and the emergence of those big-named guys recognised as fathers of modern science and philosophy all in one go, I've chosen to present them in groups. I've started with the earliest, crossing continents as required. Then from that first group I've chosen a set that stood out as thinking differently. Their unique 'take' on how to think about dealing with other people and the world more generally means that they'd probably formulate their own 'coaching questions' with a unique or unusual spin. They knew how to change how people thought about the world. They knew what to say to cause people to change their behaviour. They'd proved that, so, with a little imagination plus as many facts as I could find, it turned out there's plenty for us to learn about shifting from being a boss to becoming a leader.

Now, with all due respect to the many wonderful people who've committed their lives to studying philosophy, I couldn't help but notice that sadly, the subject is often presented in a very dry manner - (sorry and all that, but bluntly it's just boring). It's either written in academic jargon that takes a while to get used to, or lectures that go on for hours -Zzzzzz... So, it required numerous cups of strong coffee to stay focused. Which is why I've kept the language here as 'everyday' as I can. I've tried not to assume any prior knowledge on the part of the reader, without I hope being patronising nor overly simplistic, and have taken a light-touch to the explanation of who each person is, and how they came to be chosen as worthy of inclusion. After the titles, I included an additional subheading to the book - *'The thinking manager's guide to leadership'*, I did that because learning to think differently is what turns bosses into leaders. It won't be the only guide, because there was no way I could get everything useful in here - the number of great philosophers who've had a big impact on thinking are more than I can squeeze into this book. However, let me be 'real' about this, I'm a coaching-psychologist drawn to notice ways in which these people thought relevant to causing change; it's inevitable (or at least likely) that my approach to understanding these ancient philosophical thinkers is going to be from a 'coaching-leadership' point of view. Therefore, I acknowledge up front that I've probably missed unrelated (but probably interesting) elements in their stories. I'm only interested in how to **apply** their thinking in ways that work for a leader today. Hence, my internal voice constantly *asked, 'what would they ask if they were a leader coaching one of their team today'?* - I know that moving from boss (not-so-good leader) to leader (or better still, great leader) must include asking better questions - in other words becoming more of a 'coach'.

What follows asks how each of these 'thinking-greats' might they use their take on the world to make it easier to help people behave differently and achieve better results. To get into the mindset of each philosopher what follows is presented in structured way. It goes like this - after introducing each 'thinker' and un-wrapping them as best I can, I suggest some insightful questions I hallucinate they'd ask if their goal was to help improve someone's performance. In other words, I imagine them as a modern-day coaching-leader intent on facilitating behavioural change.

Coaching-leaders are always asking great questions because I believe that, like me they believe that *"coaching hasn't happened unless behaviour has changed"*. They know that a good coaching conversation is one that causes a person to reflect, engage with their 'ultimate-goal', and then change their behaviour to move them a little closer toward it. That's as true for a leader effecting improvement as it is to a professional coach like me. With each re-imagining of these great philosophers as a coaching-leader, better questions have emerged, - questions that will help dodgy bosses become terrific leaders. These guys were very smart and there is a lot for us all to learn, but let's not pretend this is new. We've been lifting aphorisms from the great and the good since terms like leadership and coaching were coined; you can't scroll through most leadership or coaching websites without finding plenty of quotes like this:"*I hear, and I forget. I see, and I remember. I do, and I understand*". Quotes like this are great, and to be fair, in most cases the first two elements of Confucius's lesson are taken care of in any book; we can't help 'hearing' what we read with that little voice in our head, and we can't help seeing what we see, after all it is a book. Yet, most books don't do the third part very well - getting you to 'do' something. I know from my own experience that buying a book with little exercises after each chapter can be helpful, but sadly, doesn't mean the exercises will get done. Good intentions don't always equal good results, and little exercises only work when the reader wants to do them. There's a time and place for them, but this isn't it. I don't believe anyone will admit to being one of those bosses I've talked about (not openly anyway), so they're not going to do little exercises. However, I'm certain that most of us know someone who fits the description of 'boss' and would like to help them become a leader.

Therefore, instead of exercises, the 'understanding' comes at the end of each chapter where you'll find a set of immediately useful questions; questions that anyone can use straight away, useful questions that I promise developing leaders will want to use. Even leaders who know they're already good at leadership will recognise something in those questions that can help them move from good to great. Hence, as Confucius pointed out will cause people to 'do', and so 'understand'.

CHAPTER 4: WE MEET AGAIN MY SCEPTICAL FRIEND, WHAT SAY YOU?

HOW CAN ARISTOTLE, CONFUCIUS, AND THE BUDDHA HELP ME MOVE FROM BOSS TO LEADER?

Four years ago, in *'How to be a Great Coach'*[iii] I introduced my rather sceptical 'friend'[iv] and we talked about what it takes to have a great coaching conversation. He wanted to get over his scepticism about coaching -"...*it's just another fad, isn't it something I've always done naturally, just another thing for companies to waste money on...*"etc. He is a manager who wanted the people in his team to be better at their jobs and he thought he knew what they needed to change, but try as he might, he wasn't getting anywhere. Does that sound familiar? It should do, because it's something almost every boss has experienced at some time in their career. Despite misgivings, my 'friend' asked for help. He decided to learn to become a coaching-leader himself, to incorporate the skills into how he led his people and to do it without feeling like he was using a sledgehammer to crack a nut.

He was sceptical if coaching could deliver changes in behaviour as quickly and easily as I'd said they could; after all, if it was so easy, then why wasn't everybody doing it? But as sceptical as he might have been, he didn't want to miss out of there is something 'in it'. I'd like to think that by the time we'd finished, his mistrust or feeling of 'faddishness' had gone away. He'd learned that a coaching approach wasn't some 'off the cuff' chat, but had a structure underpinning it. He now knew that, if done well it could lead to a person changing their behaviour. He had learned that coaching could delivered hard, tangible

43

results. He knew that a good coaching conversation **always** led to positive changes because it applied a scientific-method. Rather than some 'chat over a coffee' he'd imagined coaching to be before-hand he now knew better. He also now knew that coaching has a much better chance of achieving a result than trying to convince someone ever can. Coaching was already helping him move from being a boss to a leader, which is precisely why he wanted to know more. Therefore, we were about to meet again, this time to talk specifically about a different way of formulating ways to ask great coaching questions - this time, questions that come from some of the greatest minds from human history. Here's how it went:

"ᵛHi, so here we are again. It's been a while. How've you been getting on with coaching?
Okay, yeah - pretty good thanks - but I can't promise I remember everything we talked about, ...and yet,I've got to admit things have been different.
Different?
Hm...yeah, I think you brain-washed me! I find myself 'thinking' differently now, and there are times when I notice myself asking myself questions before opening my mouth. To be fair, it's saved me from saying things that might have been a bad idea.
So, was it a useful conversation?
You know it was! Okay, I was a bit dubious about it, but I can see that using coaching is a good way of thinking, ... and I'm not just saying it because we are here again... it was helpful - honestly.
Well, proof of the pudding and all that, - you're back, so if it was helpful last time then I'm guessing there's more you'd like to know if it'll be even more useful?

Sure, but like I said, I don't necessarily remember everything...

That's fine. May I ask you a question?

Okay.

What was it that's prevented you from reflecting on it and reading it enough, ...so that you do end up remember it all?

I see what you've done there; I did buy the book, but I only read it once! I'm not sure why. Life kind of takes over and it gets pushed back to the bottom of the proverbial pile ...stuff happens, and then 'here we are'.

Hmm... So, what would you like this time if you're only going to read it once?

That's a good question; Okay... I'm fascinated that you think the classics can help with a coaching conversation, so I do want to know more about that ...and I want it to be interesting and 'fun' to remember.

Okay, I can do that, - what else do you want?

Hm...the biggest thing is putting what you talk about in to action. I get the idea that asking a better question will always achieve a better conversation ...and hopefully, a better outcome, but I get stuck about what question to ask.

Great. I can help with that too.

How?

I've delved into up to 3000-year-old literature to find out how great thinkers figured out how to ask better questions. I know it's difficult enough to know what to ask, and even more difficult to come up with the right question just at the very moment you need it, and that about what you could have asked, or should have asked five minutes too late isn't helpful.

You are not kidding. I did buy a book on 'good questions to ask'. There are quite a few available and I had a peek, but I'm afraid all the ones I could find were confusing. They don't explain the thinking that must have gone on behind the formulation of the question, and I just couldn't hear myself using them.

What do you mean?

They seem to assume that the suggestion of a question in one circumstance makes it transferrable to another, and I don't think that is true. They make up 'categories' that don't have any relevance to the real world.

In what way were they confusing?

Well, I know from the last conversation we had that being a 'coach' and being a 'problem-solver' are opposites, or at least very different approaches, ...and that kicking off what should be a coaching conversation with 'data-gathering' questions is to fall into that problem-solving trap. Yet, in the books there are loads of data gathering questions! Questions like 'what have you done so far?' seem to be for the benefit of the person asking and don't add any insight to the person being asked. As I said, it's confusing.

I hear what you are saying. The answer is to find the 'right question' in the 'right place'. It's all about positioning; if a question causes someone to recognise possible barriers in their way, then it is a good question, but if the same question adds no insight, gathering information for the benefit of the questioner then it's a bad question. Let me give you an example; if I ask you what you have done so far that hasn't worked, I'm causing you to reflect on the reality of your situation and forcing you to gain insight into your actions so far. Whereas if I simply ask you what you've done up until now, all I may do is cause you to tell me your 'story', waste time and add little value. Do you see what I mean?

Sort of? No, not really.

OK. Have you ever talked to anyone and they've told you they've tried 'everything' and nothing has worked?

Yes, regularly!

Well, asking what specifically hasn't worked, or what were the last hundred things they attempted, or what they did that they've done before and knew didn't work back then, may all be ways of causing the person to engage with their situation and think about it differently. It all depends on the context of the specific situation.

That's my problem, how do I figure out if the same question is going to be a good one or a bad one?

Are you just asking, or do you really want to know?

I really want to know!

I'm not being intentionally difficult, it's just that this book is the answer to your question. It's a collection of questions that come with deeper thinking in multiple contexts, collected from the re-imagined minds of brilliant thinkers. I know that sounds a bit weird, but I have stepped into the shoes, sandals, and bare-foot patterns-in-the-dirt of these guys and asked questions as if I were them.

Why am I not surprised! [Laughs] But seriously, philosophy, it sounds kind of heavy to take onboard. I realise that getting to understand this stuff takes time, and I do want to ask better questions, but are you sure this will help me?

I promise. Look, the more you read about the old guys, the more able you will be to put together your own 'better questions'.

That makes sense.

OK. Let's start with a story; I'm taking you on a journey that starts in Ancient Greece around six-hundred years before our modern calendar began, and I'm going to introduce great thinkers from those times, learn from them how they formulated their thoughts, and try and figure out what they'd ask if they were modern-day leaders. As we travel through time, we will re-imagine each person we meet as a coaching-leader and ask them not only how they came to be such a leading thinker and philosopher, but what great questions they might ask someone who wants to improve their life circumstances and their performance at work.

How did you ask dead people?

Good question! ... as I said, I'm mentally stepping into their imaginary shoes and allowing myself to think like they did. I dug out as much information as I could find, applied a psychological model to make stepping in those shoes easier, and then figured out what they'd ask. Okay, before we begin in earnest let me give you a taste. There's a terrific story that'll give you a feel for what's to come:

One day, some of the greatest philosophers of the ancient world were gathered together discussing the concept of something called 'ontology', which means the understanding of how things came to be. They were in deep discussion, trying to figure out what makes a person a 'person'. In other words, how to define 'being human' as opposed to being 'something else' and trying to uncover distinctions that would determine once and for all an irrefutable definition of a human being. The story goes that they settle on the statement... that a human being is a *'featherless bipedal animal'*. They test each other trying to think of any other creature that is both a biped and has no feathers and apparently, they can't think of any. Then, suddenly, a scruffy looking character called Diogenes bursts in clutching a plucked chicken, crying 'Behold! Here is a human being!"

Ha! What? A chicken?

Yup, a chicken! I'm guessing they were more than a little irritated, not just because their thinking was so obviously flawed, but that it had been shown up as such by someone like Diogenes.

Now, Diogenes wasn't a joker per-se, but was an unusual character; he's known as one of the first 'cynics', a word that comes from the Greek meaning 'dog-like' because Diogenes made a point of living life much like a dog. He'd noticed that dogs seem to have a pretty good life, with few worries and plenty of time to chill, so adopted that style of living himself. He would lie down under the sun in the marketplace, be content to eat from scraps thrown to him from the table of others and then settled down to sleep at night in an empty bath tub. He wasn't interested in the world values of those around him because he was content with the 'least necessary' for him to live. A sort of extreme minimalist.

I'm picturing some wild-eyed dude living under railway arches - the kind who scares the pants off-of most people!

That may not be far from the truth! History tells us that he was certainly interesting - though he must have been more than a vagrant because he's not just a footnote in history but a memorable figure of his time. It seems that while most people probably thought him crazy, there were more than a few that liked the idea of scaling one's needs down to the bare minimum and using only the minimum of resources to live.

It does sound like they were minimalists, - there are plenty of people today that try to live without many possessions?

Yes, I guess so, but extreme. The cynics like him had their own philosophy, but the concept of living simply isn't unique to them. Anyway, Diogenes was at his peak at the time of Alexander the Great, and apparently was such a well-known and much talked about character that even the great king himself had heard of him. There's a story that Alexander took a liking to him and made a point of meeting him when in Athens, and in a good-natured jokey way said, *"If I was not Alexander, I should like to be Diogenes!"* To which Diogenes replied, *"If I were not Diogenes, I too should like to be Diogenes!"*

Wow, now there's someone with confidence!

I suppose if you are stripped down to having no material goods and not knowing where your next meal is coming from, confidence might be a necessity. Anyway, he was known by some as a figure somewhat like 'Socrates-gone-mad'. He saw his purpose as being 'free to think' and ask questions that were unencumbered by the cluttered thinking of his contemporary society. Which may be why, while the more established and more civilised thinkers had concluded that a human being could be defined as a featherless bipedal animal and were congratulating themselves on the cleverness of their succinct academic definition, he asked himself a better question. They were asking, 'does nature manifest any other featherless bipedal animal than a human being?', he was asking 'if I had to create a featherless bipedal animal using what nature has provided, what might I do?' Diogenes' answer must have come to him quite quickly, because even though plucked chickens were as common back then as they are today, he must have nipped out quickly while they were in conversation to get back in time to make his point. This raises an interesting question; what prevented the collective 'best-minds' of the ancient world from coming up with the same critical thinking as someone *their world* considered a wild maverick, and who most people assumed was more than just a little 'bonkers'?

So, what are you saying? Must I become even more cynical and a bit bonkers to ask good questions?

I wouldn't go quite that far, but you do need to think differently, just like Diogenes did. At least, in the sense of divesting your thinking of all the 'fog' that might be getting in the way of thinking clearly. You see, by stripping everything away except the bare bones of whatever is being focused on it is much easier to find the most appropriate insightful question to ask yourself, or to ask anyone else.

Is the moral of the story to keep in mind what you are trying to achieve and not get caught up in the 'noise' that might get in the way?

In many ways, it is. Until I started to think about writing a book about great questions I was as guilty as anyone for 'inauthentic thinking', and as ignorant as this group of ancient philosophers were before being confronted with the stark pragmatic reality of Diogenes. I won't bore you with my own story, but suffice it say that twenty years ago when I began to earn a living as a full-time professional coach no one was paying too much attention to the academic underpinning of coaching.

"The Wild West of coaching, eh?"

Yup, a bit like that yes. I know, and freely admit that I'm by no means the only coach who 'fell' out of corporate leadership and operational management into this thing we now call coaching. Nor am I the only coach whose early training and learning about coaching was, well the best word I can come up with without being overly rude to anyone is 'sketchy'. My ignorance was at times as powerful as the indignation I felt toward many of the unscrupulous providers of so-called professional training who were no more 'qualified' to talk about the effectiveness of coaching than those poor souls (pun intended as the training was always expensive) were after receiving their 'certificate of competence'.

Not carrying a grudge at all then? Ha!

Very funny. Not a grudge per se, just an irritation!

Are saying you were starting to think like Diogenes?

Maybe, just a little. Let me explain; asking 'better' questions can be the difference between helping a person deal more effectively with the stress of their situation or not, and so it matters how good a coach is at thinking differently and that he or she has the tools to laser-guide their question and be the most effective possible in the time available. Sometimes a coach may only have a few minutes with a client on a subject, particularly if they've held back from mentioning something serious until the very end of a session.

What do you mean?

Typically, if something unexpected and serious has happened in their home life the client won't lead with it in a work-related coaching session, yet it often the single biggest issue that's causing them stress. If they don't mention it until five minutes before the end of a session, then that's all the time the coach must find the 'right' questions and ask them.

That's a bit unreasonable isn't it? How can anyone do that?

Well, is it really? Did Diogenes have warning about what Alexander was going to say to him? Of course not, you see, the only way anyone comes up with something 'that works' on the spot is to be constantly ready to think in a way that makes it easy to do that.

Okay, I buy that; if I think like this guy thinks then I might automatically ask a question like he would?

Absolutely. Therefore, if the job of a coaching-leader is to make it easier for a person to 'change what they do' and improve their 'well-being' and 'performance', then the leader must be able to think in a way that makes this 'normal'.

Change what they do? Improve well-being and performance? Is that what I'm trying to do?

It might not seem like it, but you are. Think about one of the situations you've experienced since we last spoke.

Alright, I had a situation where one of my team was being difficult because she thought she should have been promoted, - to the position I'd just been given. She wasn't being overtly passive-aggressive, but neither was she giving her all.

What did you want to happen?

Isn't that obvious? I wanted her to get over herself, do her job, and stop being a pain in the proverbial derrière.

If I may rephrase what you just said; you want her to change her behaviour, her well-being and that of the rest of the team will improve when she does change her behaviour and accept the new situation, and her performance will improve as a result. Is that right?

Yes, I guess it is.

The ultimate measure of an effective question must be the benefits accrued from it by the person you're speaking to. That means the completion an academic course 'about' coaching is not the same as being able to 'do' coaching and ask great questions that change behaviour.

It sounds like I'm not the only one who ends up struggling for the right question then, eh? I'm frustrated enough that having talked to you it still isn't easy, but if I'd paid out for a training course and still had trouble, I think I'd be mightily upset!

The key here is expectation. If you attend a course and **expect** to learn something about what being a coaching-leader is, the methods some people use to apply it, and **expect** that you won't necessarily be able to do it yourself, then that's fine.

Ha! No one would go on a course like that!

That's my point. My take on it is that unfortunately leadership coaching may have become something of a gravy-train. What follows in these stories about philosophy is the opposite of that, - no gravy, no train, no dressing things up to sound more complicated than they need be, - just plain and simple, straightforward useful questions.

OK, but I have two questions of my own for you; I remember you talking before about the fact that 'coaching hasn't happened unless behaviour has changed', and that there are plenty of coaches that don't pass that base-line test. Sorry to have to ask, but is this just a rant or can you back it up, and will this help?

Now, those are both good questions! Indeed, I can back it up; having now undertaken extensive research into workplace coaching I'm able to state with confidence that ignorance isn't unique. In my early years as a coach I spent a small fortune on attending various 'courses' and emerged full of confidence. Feedback from my equally ignorant clients had been okay, so when I was faced with doing a short 'example' session in front of a panel of experts I was as confident as confident could be, having no clue how badly I was crashing and burning! Afterwards I was angry and frustrated to be told that my conversation may well have been helpful but was not what they considered as coaching. It was a severe ego-bruising!

Oops...didn't get the gig then I guess?

I'm afraid not. This was one of those *'WTF just happened moments'*[vi] that led to me eventually distilling the experiences of other people into a book, one with the intent to help people ask themselves better questions and make better decisions about how they behave.

Another book 'plug'?

Ha! I can't help myself. Anyway, for weeks I was seething after getting that feedback. Instead of asking myself a better question I was reflecting only on what I knew, rather than what I hadn't thought about yet. Eventually, I calmed down enough to become a little more Diogenes-like - not that I started living in a bath tub, but I did open my eyes to what was needed, and to make new choices - rather than delude myself that my old choices were the only ones available.

Doesn't everyone experience something like that in a successful career?

Yes, I guess so. Anyway, eventually this realisation led me to teaching coaching-skills to leaders, coaching-science to leaders, and coaching-philosophy to leaders. It led me to ask more and better questions of myself before asking questions of anyone else. As for your second question, will this help? Well, ... you must be the judge of that!

Which is of course, why I'm here! I want to get better at asking those questions. Yet, I don't just want a list of someone else's questions, or questions out of context, or to be told just trust myself - because I've tried all that.

Forgive me, but if you have tried everything we spoke about last time, are you honestly saying that none of it has helped?

No, of course it has helped! Just not as much as I want it to. I want to be more like one of those great coaches you talk about. I want my questions to come naturally and to find the right words coming out of my mouth as a matter of course, and for it to feel easy.

You aren't asking for much!

Is that sarcasm, or are you being Diogenes-like and cynical?

Honestly? I think what follows will help. You do have to practice, but this will give you plenty to practice with. So, are you ready to take on board different ways to think about the world and what questions to ask?

I'm ready, let's give it a whirl..."

Chapter 5: Joining the Mental Dots

How to step into the shoes of dead people

Are you ready for a little time-travel? Here's how this is going to work: I'm going to say a little about each philosopher and great thinker by re-imagining them based on what little we know from history. I'm using the hierarchical levels of thinking (more about that in a moment), to help figure them out in the best way I know how; I'll start with saying something about where they were born, who they were born to, and the environment in which they spent their formative years – we all know that there's a bit of nature and nurture shaping us all, and that was as true two or three thousand years ago as it is today.

Next I'll imagine what it might have been like to live as they did and what expectations that society would have had of me, what I might have been allowed to do or say, if I had money and resources to do what I pleased or was forced to earn my own living, and what affect my personal circumstances might have had on how I was expected to behave. It's not hard to use modern day comparisons to suggest that a person born to a wealthy family in the so-called free world has a very different world view and behavioural expectations than a similar person born into abject poverty in a war-torn, highly regulated, and controlled state – their choices would obviously be different, but so too would be their expectation of what was acceptable or not before any choice was made. The same was true back then. Hence, to have any chance of understanding why and how one person became a great thinker and another of their contemporaries did not, it's essential that these behavioural expectations be examined. However, that's just where the investigation starts - their background and behavioural expectations are merely the foundation for the thinking that followed. The investigation continues with figuring out what education, training, skills, and attributes each person had been born with or acquired.

It's obviously from our own time that having a 'skill' doesn't guarantee it'll be usefully applied. Knowing something is not the same as using that same thing - just look around at how many people 'know better' than what they do - I'm sure it was the same back then. Therefore, counting skills alone won't get us 'under the skin' of these ancient thinkers. For that to happen, it's necessary to establish what they were equipped with *before* they began to make a unique contribution of their own; their experiences, learning, and the way in which they saw the world.

Insights into their origins, expectations, and education provide a good start in understanding why these individuals might have stood out from the crowd, and why they might have been perceived as different to their contemporaries. Therefore, I delved into evidence about what their beliefs and values might have been. Clearly, I can't know for sure if my evaluations are correct, but I did my best to read as much as possible about what they did, how they went about doing it, and what else apart from their well-known philosophies might be known about their lifetime activity. Some were written about more than others, and a few might have been the subject of wishful thinking on the party of their biographers – yet, whatever the information available, I used it to imagine being them and adopting the values and beliefs they might have held.

There are two more steps in the construction of this hierarchy; the first is that of the identity (both public and private) that each person adopted as their own. In many cases this might have been different from their public perception - I attempted to get a sense of what label they might ascribe to themselves, and hence how that label might have shaped the way they both thought and acted. I freely admit that the higher up this hierarchy I travelled, the more likely I was to use my imagination more than simply transcribe the often rather dry descriptors of historians. I hope you agree that having a 'stab' at their identity provided insights that might otherwise have alluded me and that are useful in understanding how they came to leave their various legacies. Finally, the cherry atop the cake of what causes a person to shape their thinking is the life-purpose that person adopts as their own. Of course, I could only make an educated guess at the purpose for each of them. I based these guesses on whatever they had achieved – if their success in being remembered had to be in some way linked to what they left behind, what they did, and what they achieved, then my guesses can't be too far off the mark. I hope.

Forgive me from pressing this point, but I need to be clear that my aim has not been to produce a history book on philosophy. There are plenty of those already, written by eminent scholars who know far more about each of these guys than I do. I am a psychologist looking at them through the lens of psychology, hence I apologise in advance if my interpretation doesn't necessarily match the accepted norm - but then no one truly knows how each person would have sounded or precisely how they might have unwrapped their own situation, which I suppose means my interpretation might be considered as good as anyone's. At least, I believe it is for the purposes of using their thinking to demonstrate how being a boss doesn't make anyone automatically a leader, but that new and improved thinking will start them on the right road to becoming one. I also apologise for the fact that they are all 'guys'. My own take on this is that there must have been as many women over the last couple of millennia that were just as capable as men of thinking big thoughts and learning to think differently. If only they'd been given as many opportunities as the men, they might have been included in this collection. It's sad that we don't know about them, but I'm afraid that's just the way it is, or at least, how it was.

Without the aid of a time machine and with but a few contemporary accounts of the life and times of each of our creative thinkers, the structure I've outlined was necessary to formulate a foundation and then construct a persona to inhabit, before attempting to imagine them as a coaching-leader. While there is no blueprint for stepping into the body of an ancient philosopher, there are ways to re-imagine how a person might have been thinking – and the approach I've outlined is one such approach. It is a framework that separates those 'levels' I mentioned into a hierarchy; meaning that thinking is always governed, controlled, or at least influenced by what sits above it. The structure suggests that rather than every thought being equal, some hold more importance than others; a person from a particular background might well have been influenced by that experience, but the beliefs and values they adopted will make use (or not) of that start in life in a different way depending on what they are – the person who believed 'anything is possible' will have lived a very different life to the one who accepted that 'I have my place and I will stick with it'. Similarly, the identity a person adopts will use that start in life, their experiences, and their beliefs and values in very different ways

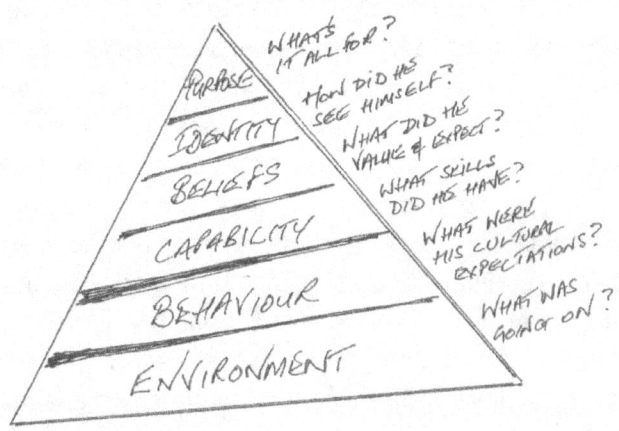

depending on what it is. The 'level' at which a person thinks determines what a person might be thinking. So, while the environment in which they lived might have been their foundation, their beliefs might have come from all manner of sources and would have become more important to them than the environment or culture from which they hailed, - similarly their purpose in life would eventually have guided all of their decisions and actions once they'd engaged with it. This structure was the obvious choice for me as an approach and as I said earlier is a hierarchical set of thinking levels commonly referred to as 'logical thinking levels'[vii].

These levels don't necessarily predict the way a person would have behaved, or might behave now, but they do provide insights into how a person learned to be the renowned thinker they became. The framework does this because it's applicable to all, and the fact that a single framework can be applied in every case significantly reduced any chance that I might let my imagination get the better of me. I must admit, it was tempting to make up 'stuff' about them and start getting all 'romantic' about the lives they lived. However, the thinking levels framework held me in check. At least, I did my best to make it so. Therefore, while I can't guarantee there isn't any romanticising, the fact that I was having to relate everything back to a base-level did keep me grounded. It allowed me to pick through researched evidence about each person layer by layer, knowing that the hierarchical construct of these thinking levels makes each higher level more likely to have influenced the way they behaved. I don't pretend that it's a perfect methodology, but it is better than just having a good guess. They each have their story, a personal tale that includes information about the environment within which they lived and worked. That's the base level of learning and the lowest logical level of thinking response they will have had.

Even having outlined it, I must point out that it is to some extent somewhat counter-intuitive; can a person's belief in themselves and their self-styled purpose in life overcome the inevitable moulding of their environment or their inherited DNA? Popular belief would have us accept that some choices are not ours to make, however the logical thinking level structure flies in the face of such received wisdom. The suggestion that people are not necessarily shaped by their environment but by the way in which they

62

respond to it may be controversial, but for the purposes of this particular 'exercise' did go some way to explaining how it was that these sometimes very unlikely characters ended up shaping the thinking of millions of people, thousands of years after their death. Their environment may have acted as a baseline but that's all it was. The person they ended up becoming was informed by the levels of thinking that take place above it; their behavioural expectations of that time and of those circumstance, the skills and capabilities they acquired, the values and beliefs they held, the identity they forged for themselves - and finally their raison d'être, whatever it was they accept as their purpose in life. To re-imagine them and think now what it might be to think like they might have thought was a challenge to say the least. To then take on the mantle of a coaching-leader, asking a few questions in the style they might have used might have been ambitious, but I gave it a go! Of course, I've used my own words and the questions have always been contextualised by a coaching-leader situation where a person requires help in thinking through an issue or assistance in coming up with new insights.

All in all, I'm not too worried about contradiction, after all the latest of these philosophers died over a thousand years ago, and the earliest has been dead for around two and half thousand years. They are not around to say I'm either right or wrong, and when all is said and done, does it really matter? What is important is that there are insights to be gained about how anyone from any background or start in life, can become a thought-leader and leave the world a better place than they found it. My fervent hope is that by getting under the skin of these long-dead thought-leaders that it inspires people to step up and become one themselves. Being a boss doesn't make anyone an instant leader, but it most certainly does provide an opportunity to lead – and that's all that's necessary. Where's there's the will there is a way and understanding a little more about how these guys made it happen for themselves might just make it a little easier for any boss of today to follow suit.

CHAPTER 6: #1 THE FIRST PHILOSOPHER

THALES OF MILETUS

His Claim to Fame: He was a thought-leader who might just have changed the way everyone thinks today. Yup, everyone – you, me, everyone.

You see, Thales is known as the first in the tradition of Greek philosophers. He was a polymath with special interest in geometry and astronomy who had been to Egypt to study – clearly, he'd had a good start in life to have been funded on what must be one of the world's earliest gap-years. Apparently, he was gifted with an insatiable curiosity and could well have been the most attractive of all the early philosophers, at least if his images and busts are anything to go by.

Thales is depicted as a strong, square jawed, handsome chap with plenty of thick wavy hair -even some of the statues of their gods don't look as good as he did. It's because he happens to have been rich and well-travelled that it's tempting to assume that he picked up some specialised knowledge and skills while in Egypt. Over there, they may not have had a tradition of philosophy as such, but they were well into astronomy, had their own explanations for how the 'world works', and may even had themselves inherited deep-knowledge from even earlier civilizations. He came back with more than a few tricks up his proverbial sleeve.

For example, in 585BCE he amazed the people of Miletus by correctly predicting a solar eclipse, which to them must have been a big deal. Didn´t Carl Sagan, (he of the golden disc and message for aliens sent into space on Voyager

65

fame) say something about any technology beyond immediate comprehension would likely be perceived as magic? So, whether the locals thought it was magic or just clever we will never know, but by all accounts, his approach to life and the ideas he'd come back with had made him popular guy. However, his biggest claim to fame was that he's the first in what was to become a tradition of 'thinkers' asking the big questions, like *"Where does everything come from?"*, *"What is reality made of?"*, and *"Where do we all fit in with all the stuff that goes on around us?"*By today's standards his answers were all wrong, but that doesn't diminish the fact that he asked the questions. He was important not because he was right, but because it gave all those that followed something to argue against.

Before Thales there was no discussion about these matters that we know of. It may be that this was simply because no one had started the discussion, or that it took a wealthy, good looking, young chap with bright ideas and the cajones to talk about them. Once Thales started asking big questions and came up with his own 'big idea', it stimulated others to push back at him and start thinking of ideas of their own. Thales's big notion was that everything at its deepest level is made from water. He was convinced that liquid (aka water) was the common denominator for everything around us – the sky and clouds were just waiting to form back into water, and even the hardest rock was formed of liquid spewed from the hot depths of a volcano, and even the very human form that we are all made from collapses back into a liquid form after death. As far as he was concerned his was a compelling theory backed up with evidence all around us. Not surprisingly, not everyone agreed. His forthright approach gave people the chance to scoff and then come up with a better suggestion. He started the ball rolling of *'if not this, then what?'*, which all these years later is just as useful an approach as it was back then. He did also propose that magnets and amber have 'souls'; his thinking was that movement equates with life, and life has a soul, therefore because magnets move when faced with another magnet, and amber will move when rubbed, they must have a soul. Later philosophers would refer to simple logic like this as a syllogism but in the sixth century BCE the concept of rationalism and logic didn't exist in the way we understand it now. The inquisitive nature of Thales was how it started, at least in the Hellenistic culture that gave its name to philosophy.

He's also one of my personal favourites (although be prepared, because I do tend to say that about most of these guys) because he demonstrated how **making money** comes about when you ask a better question, not necessarily when you put in extra effort. Again, a concept still as useful now as it was then. From the very beginnings of the discipline Thales demonstrated how it is that all philosophy and thought-leading thinking doesn't have to be about obscure metaphysical ideas. The link he makes from asking better questions about his reality and the ability he might have to profit from it is one that every boss might learn from. Okay, I accept up front that not everyone can be like a charismatic Thales, but every boss in any circumstance can ask themselves a better question with a Thales-like intent to profit from the seemingly mundane and obvious.

His Environment: His seaside home in Ionia is as idyllic today as it must have been back then. It was a prosperous place, where, much like Australia in years to come itbegan life as a colony, not made up of convicts but of Grecians fleeing war – but then like the Australians would do many centuries later, they formed their getaway into a full-blown city-state on the back of sheep driven economy. Their southerly location on the coast made them an obvious trading post, with wool as their main export. Apparently, things went well for them from the outset and by the time Thales was born the relatively new city-state was prospering.

The coastline there is beautiful. Despite climate change it can't have changed very much from his time; the weather is mostly wonderful, and the food from the ocean and the Maeander river that flowed into it is and was plentiful. Unlike today the place wasn't overrun with Ray-Ban-clad tourists piling off a tour bus and ruining the tranquillity. They may be good for the new economy now that sheep aren't such a big deal, but they aren't nearly as tranquil or picturesque. It was one of those places that if you kept fit and well and didn't come down with a bug (no antibiotics back then so if herbal remedies didn't do the trick you were all but dead) you could live a reasonably long and happy life. The same could not be said for back home in Greece; Athens was pulling itself apart with wars both outside and from within, yet here across the water on their patch of fertile land all was well, and apart from the occasional visitor from the capital the Milesians were probably left to their own devices.

By the time he was thirty, Thales was living in a rapidly changing world; after years of decline, the Greek State to which Miletus belonged was being reformed. Their new 'leader' called Solon, was pushing through reforms which among other things made the lending of money for profit illegal. Politics, particularly when money was involved was not all that different back then to the world we live in now; their society was always on the brink of some war somewhere, their finances were always in a mess, and there was regularly unrest among the general populous. All of which meant Solon had to tread a fine line between protecting the privileges of the rich and enriching the lives of the poor. How familiar does that sound? Now part of Turkey on the Anatolian coast, Miletus was in something called Greek Ionia, far enough from Athens not to be immediately impacted by the political upheaval, but still part of the State and so aware to some extent of what was going on. Yet, with all that upheaval going on, Thales was less caught up with opinions on how the State worked than he was with his own thinking about how the world works more generally.

He was a big thinker. Maybe that was unusual for his time, maybe not, who knows? It is much more difficult to know if the few pages of writings that have made it through the centuries tell us that there weren't many big thinkers back then, or if there just aren't many writings that survived through the ages. Either way, Thales was a stand-out thinker because of the theories he proposed and the number of things he studied. He must have started travelling when relatively young because it seems he'd been as far afield as Egypt and had been plotting the stars along the way. Therefore, all we can say about his environment with certainty is that it afforded him the freedom to think, to travel, to learn, and as we shall see, to experiment with his theories - particularly, as I mentioned already when it came to show how to make big money.

His Culture: Not a great deal is known about Thales upbringing, however, he must have had some opportunity afforded to him, as evidenced by his ability to travel as far afield as Egypt and probably its surrounding countries, and that he had access to learning. Whether that was stimulated by an abundance of natural confidence in the young Thales, or perhaps the support of mum and dad we will never know; this was hardly a time when kids went off on a parent-funded gap year, nor were most people in this part of the world particularly well off, but certainly he'd either had enough in his pocket or confidence enough to figure out how he'd survive to step onto a ship and wave goodbye to home.

By Thales' time, the Milesians were settled, but had not long become part of the league of Greek settlements, so were still a young city-state. They were officially Greek but were not actually part of a unified Greece. That must have made for an unusual culture – still Greek but not like the rest of Greece. My guess is that they didn't think of themselves as Greek at all but were part of a long tradition of the colonists from the other side of the Aegean that had founded settlements like Miletus just under a century and a half after the fall of Troy. It's a safe bet to assume that whatever was supposedly imposed upon them by Athens that they did as little as necessary to satisfy their political 'masters' and might even have seen the Greeks as an occupying force rather than a natural source for leadership. All of which must have shaped the thinking of the developing Thales. Add to all this his exposure to another big chunk of the civilised world and it goes some way to perhaps explaining how he turned out to be recognised as the world's first philosopher.

His Skills: Supposedly, at least according to Plato many years later, Thales was 'intense' and apt to be preoccupied with whatever he was doing - without taking as much notice of things around him as was good for him. Apparently, while intently watching the stars he walked right into an open well - fortunately, there was someone there to both laugh at him and help him out. Intense of not, it is evident that he'd learned a great deal on his travels. Whether he was stimulated to ask new and deeper questions about why the world works as it does, or if he borrowed some knowledge from others, we will never know. However, what we do know is that he is credited with being the first person recorded as saying that the things we see, touch, sense and hear don't happen due to the will of the 'gods'. He developed the skill to notice what was going on around him; to see patterns in nature where none had noticed them before, to look up into the skies and link the movements of heavenly bodies with events that happened again and again down here on the ground, and to grasp the concept that there is a huge dynamic and complicated system at play which can be glimpsed but not totally understood.

Thales developed considerable skills in both geometry and astronomy. Being able to predict the movement of celestial bodies was useful for fellow travellers, particularly at sea. So useful in fact that he produced advice for navigators on how to use the stars to chart their journeys - at 39 he became the first person credited with predicting an eclipse. I can only imagine the faces of the people in his home town of Miletus when this tall charismatic character predicted precisely when the sky would go dark when it should still be daylight – and that this dark would pass revealing the day's sunshine once again. It's also likely he could use Babylonian charts of the stars if that's how he predicted the solar eclipse – one can only guess how many other marvels of the night sky he was then able to explain. It's little wonder his opinions were treated with respect.

His Beliefs: When I imagine meeting Thales, I see a man driven by curiosity and a burning desire to answer his own questions.

He was interested in how the world worked and was confident enough to share his unique thinking with the rest of the world. He had courage to speak his mind, the self-confidence to act on his thinking, the creativity to link experiences with potential outcomes, and the initiative to act on them. You see, he developed a personal theory about how the world 'worked' before anyone else in recorded history. Okay, it's easy to laugh at it now knowing what we know, but he didn't have the benefit of a modern curriculum and access to Mr Google. His theory was that everything came from water; his travels at sea had convinced him the world was a sphere because he'd seen for himself how the horizon was curved.

Add to this that it was well known at the time how heating solid objects could turn them to liquid, including volcanic activity spilling out liquid rock to create new land. He surmised that all land came from liquid and that the source of all liquid was water, therefore, everything was fundamentally made of water. Underpinning this was a belief that there must be a rational explanation for everything, - even those things that seems inexplicable. His contemporary, and someone who became known as the second of the Miletus philosophers, a chap called Anaximander, went further than suggesting the world as we know it came from water by adding that human beings were born in the belly of a fish. This wasn't necessarily a pre-Darwinian insight, but does illustrate how different they were allowing their own thinking to be. While the people around them were thanking a pantheon of greater and lesser deities for the gifts of everyday life, they were developing new and startling beliefs to challenge the foundation of their world.

His Identity: I don't think he imagined himself a thought-leader at all - I think Thales saw himself as a scientist, even before people had figured out what a scientist was; he gathered evidence and did his best to test it, much in the manner any scientist might do today.

Being a big imposing and impressive man who wasn't shy about sharing his thinking, I imagine him brimming with confidence and I don't think he was he shy about backing up his rationalisations with hard evidence, even when that evidence was somewhat sketchy - like claiming magnets were alive because they moved on their own in the presence of another magnet. However, his most remarked upon example was the fact he noticed the regular changing of the seasons. So what? He noticed the *seasons changing* – big deal!

You see, while it may be remarkable to us that people didn't just 'know' that the seasons were predictable, nevertheless it was so. Indeed, it I quite possible that other societies which came before the town of Miletus knew all about the seasons - it's a matter of record that for example solstices were know well before then in other cultures. Yet, in Miletus they weren't up to speed with the changes in the weather. Apparently, according to the best minds in Miletus before Thales put them straight, it was a gift from the gods when the sun shone, and the rain fell - and it would be some time before crop forecasts became part of their regular vocabulary.

The fact is, Thales hadn't just noted that there were regular seasons but also that lots of rainfall in spring followed by plenty of sunshine in summer always led to a bumper olive harvest. He also noticed that the big wooden olive presses were always in great demand after a good harvest - but could be picked up for a song at any other time. It speaks volumes about how Thales believed in himself that during a period of rainfall that (when no one was interested in olive presses) he went out and bought up every single one he could lay his hands on. Come summer, when the sun shone again, and the harvest was plentiful the olive farmers needed presses but now, all the presses were owned by one man – so, Thales came to the rescue.

Now, a man only interested in short term gain might have tried to fleece the farmers by charging exorbitant rates for his presses, but Thales was smart enough to know that it'd be more than just a one-time deal. If he'd asked too much, they may have paid him that one time, but they'd never do it again. Therefore, rather than make them buy the presses at a premium he rented them back to them at a reasonable rate instead, making his money back in no time and still retaining his assets. This investment into a possible profit from a rise in value of stock is probably the first recorded trade in 'futures'! In other words - he invested in something that hadn't happened yet, then established a business on the back of it.

There can be little doubt that he was a larger than life character, constantly challenging himself and those around him with questions. However, possibly the most remarkable aspect of this story, and a true glimpse of his identity is that he didn't need the extra cash. In fact, he told people that the only reason he'd done it was to show them how easy it can be to do well and make money if only you begin to see the world differently and ask better questions.

His Purpose: Unlike Philosophers who were to come, Thales doesn't seem to have an obvious purpose to his existence except to learn more and understand what makes the world do what it does, and where possible do something with it.

Thales used his knowledge of weather patterns to make money out of oil presses, he demonstrated how science worked by engaging the town in the solar eclipse prediction, and there's even a story about him using what he knew to cross a river that was too big to span. He did it by diverting it into two smaller rivers then building a bank between the two, allowing a bridge to be built over each of the now smaller parts of the river. While knowledge to Thales was important, what seemed to matter to him most was how to make that knowledge useful.

Thales is very different to some we will hear about - he wasn't shipwrecked and miraculously rescued, there's no record of him being locked away by his parents to prevent him following his own path, or sent overseas against his wishes, or some other trigger in his early life that set him on the course he followed. Nor does he appear to be motivated by any religious or spiritual belief, although he is known to have believed in the immortality of the soul. All we can surmise is that he was an intelligent man, who was not afraid to back his own judgement, or put himself 'out there' to be judged by others - he just seems to have wanted to make the most of the time he had and was intense in his approach to whatever he did. Remember that well he was supposed to have fallen into? It's funny if he did fall in, but it's also a lesson; that if you want to be as learned as Thales, as popular as Thales, and as smart as Thales, then sometimes you've got to be so wrapped in what you do that you too might end up falling down a metaphorical well.

How might he be thought of by his employees, if he was a manager in today's business world?

He's a charismatic risk-taker; someone who appears more casual with his decision making than he is, unseen by anyone but his closest associates he analyses his world in the finest detail and makes his 'left-field' decisions on a sound understanding of reality.

He listens to people regardless of hierarchical rank, sees through corporate politics, considers and measures evidence with detached amusement, and acts as if life were a game already won. His boundless enthusiasm is contagious, as his is desire to question everything – although sometimes this can lead to feeling like they're going in circles. He can become so engrossed in one problem that he comes dangerously close to missing other challenges – fortunately, he is open and honest with his closest team and welcomes their counsel, and together they are successful.

He is liked immensely by the people he leads, although occasionally the team can be frustrated with his propensity to listen without saying very much in return. His team can sometimes be blind-sided by decisions taken without warning or consultation -while more often accurate and correct, this leads to his closest associates doubting his trust in them. Charisma alone may not be enough to sustain a leadership position at the highest level, and a person's considerable talents might be constrained to a lesser role than he might be capable of undertaking. Fortunately, Thales pays an unprecedented attention to detail and is capable of such unique thought combinations that this flaw is overlooked - so much so that his unique approach to harnessing previously unseen potential makes him a stand out leader.

A few coaching questions he might ask: Stepping into the sandals of Thales and being a leader faced with the challenge of changing an employee's behaviour who has up until now been 'stuck', prompts me to think he might ask something like;

i.   *"If everything has a cause then what might be a rational explanation for applying new thinking and action that you haven't done before?"*
ii. *"If you had to explain the coincidences and patterns in your life, where might you start?"*
iii. *"If you were already certain that you would achieve success, even though you don't know yet precisely how, what do you notice that could start you on that journey?"*
iv. *"What could you learn or find out, that may help you decide what to do next?"*

v. *"When you look around you, what can you notice that may be an opportunity that others have not yet seen?"*

vi. *"What do the people you meet with every day know that may help you understand and learn what to do next?"*

vii. *"What knowledge do you possess that you have yet to apply?"*

Chapter 7: #2 All journeys start with a single step

Laozi

His Claim to Fame: This thought-leader did more than provide content for fortune cookies; Laozi is credited with writing the 'Dao de Jing'; a book of aphorisms that seeded a religion called Taoism or Daoism - the difference is only in the translation from Chinese symbols to a Latinised interpretation. The Dao de Jing, or Tao Te Ching (depending on the translation you prefer) might well be Chinese Philosophy distilled down to its essence. It is made up of 81 short poems, each packed with meaning.

Poem number twenty-four is a great example. It starts like this;

"He who stands on tiptoe doesn't stand firm. He who rushes ahead doesn't go far. He who tries to shine dims his own light."

I don't know about you, but I think that's fabulous; in 24 words he's done more to explain why certain politicians are doomed from the outset than CNN or Fox news might achieve in as many hours of continuous broadcasting!

The Dao de Jing is not to be confused with the 'I Ching'. That's another book entirely. If the Dao de Jing distils Chinese Philosophy, then the I Ching is probably *the root* of all that philosophy and was written around half a millennium before Laozi came on the scene. Unlike Laozi's book, the purpose of which was to encourage people to embrace the principles of Dao and live a long, meaningful, and peaceful life, the I Ching is a study of cyclical changes in the universe and people, as such it's used as spooky divination tool - people toss coins (and even bones sometimes) and then divine meanings from where they land on the paper. Don't misunderstand, I'm not knocking it as I've never tried it, but I did want to make sure there wasn't any confusion between the two books. Laozi's claim to fame isn't an oracle, it's a simple and powerful manual on how to live a great life. It's where we hear about 'Qi' and 'Wuwei' - two classic concepts that every leader does well to be aware of - If you've never heard of them before then fear not as all will be revealed.

His Environment: According to legend, Laozi was a government official and administrator in China at the time of massive upheaval and violence. With all this fighting going on there wasn't a need for regular work for the likes of a government administrator, so he lost his job. Apparently, after this he decided to leave China and presumably look for a better life; he got himself an ox and rode it to the far western border of China, from where he departed for that new life but not before writing down his philosophy in what became known as the Dao de Jing. It seems the turmoil of living under one warlord and doing his bidding - only for that would-be king to be killed by another warlord the next week with all the inevitable murder, rape, and pillage that went with it, ...and then with a new set of someone else's orders to follow – was bound to have had a serious effect on Laozi, and it did.

He may well have had his own thoughts anyway about how the world worked and how best to engage with it, even if he hadn't been caught up in some of the worst atrocities in China's history. However, it must at least in part be more likely that the environment had a large part in shaping the man. He was surrounded by the worst type of bosses there can be; one's who use fear to control, and make irrational and unreasonable demands - meting out devilishly harsh punishments when people were unable to comply. The desperation those people must have been feeling was no doubt more acute than a person at work suffering under their own version of a terrible boss (because at least they go home in one piece), but the lack of control a person in that situation feels must be similar.

His Culture: It isn't clear what the behavioural expectations were of someone like Laozi in a culture ravaged by war and petty tyrants. However, back then expectations of behaviour weren't very much different from today being almost always driven 'from the top'. So, if the big boss of a region was small minded, nasty, angry, and often poorly educated piece of work then the bosses down the food-chain (who probably had no idea how to think like a leader) were probably like that too.

Even though he was a contemporary of Confucius he had polar-opposite views on the way a person should behave. It's worth remembering that although Confucius was alive at this time, it wasn't until after his death that the Chinese culture started to be shaped by his teachings. Anyone who'd heard of Confucius while he was alive couldn't have guessed how important the guy's words would one day become. Hence, while Confucius stressed order and ritual, Laozi's behaviour clearly indicated that he did not. Quitting any stability, no matter how temporary to steadily wander through China, sharing his thoughts on 'the Dao' with anyone who'd listen isn't particularly structured. In fact, his approach wasn't structured at all.

Unfortunately, nothing is known about his personal circumstances; we don't know where he came from, who his parents were, or where he studied to become the man he did. Indeed, some experts have speculated that he didn't really exist at all but was either a combination of people, or if he did exist then at the very least his name probably wasn't Laozi. There may be some truth in this as the name Laozi translates as to 'old master', but whatever birth-name he may or may not have been given there is no doubt that the Dao de Jing was written at some time by somebody, and it might as well be attributed to him as anyone.

His Skills: Assuming Laozi was a real person, we know he could string words together in a way that conveyed a deeper meaning than the obvious; the Dao de Jing could give Nostradamus a run for his money in terms of its vagueness and openness to interpretation. It has been suggested that it was written this way to add mysticism to the writing, thereby conveying some far deeper esoteric meaning. Alternatively, it could have been produced in that way to allow people to find their own meaning in it, much like a horoscope can 'speak' to every reader.

My apologies if you are an avid believer in Horoscopes, but please feel free to test out the theory - ask a friend to read you your own horoscope but give them the choice to pick another at random if they wish, so you don't know if it's yours or not. Then listen to how it could or might in some way apply to you (even if you were not the intended recipient).

An approach like that can't have come out of nowhere - he was either already very well read and practiced at obscuring meanings or had been initiated into some other esoteric teachings that he ended up putting into words of his own. It's hard to believe that all simple government officials were equipped with that level of skill. It is not an easy thing to do, to be artfully vague and yet sound as if you are speaking directly the person who's reading your words.

His Beliefs: First and foremost it's worth thinking about what he might have believed about himself, even if he might not have openly said so; there's no doubt he was creative because (how else do you come up with stuff like he did?), that he was dedicated to his own self-improvement, could build strong relationships with others, was compassionate, and had the courage to speak his mind.

He believed that the Dao (or Tao if you prefer) is something that can't easily be explained; to him it is the path to power as well as being the power itself, that the elements of it that we are aware of. It is the things we can see and touch, feel and hear that may be called 'Dao', but these are only elements of 'The Dao' and not its whole.

He said -

"The Dao that can be named is not the eternal Dao; the name that can be named is not the eternal name. The name is the origin of heaven and earth; the named is the mother of all things".

If you imagine him in the 1960's wearing a headband, tie-dyed shirt, old jeans and sandals, saying something like *"It's nature man, yeah we're all part of it...it's in all of us ...it's one thing and everything at the same time...wow..."*

Here's a taste of his beliefs straight from the Dao de Jing[viii]

Dao creates one.
One creates two.
Two creates three.
Three creates the ten thousand creatures.
The ten thousand creatures carry Yin and embrace Yang,
Pouring their Qi together, thus becoming harmonious.

That which people detest:
Being alone, orphaned, lonely, and unlucky –
Yet kings and nobles thus name themselves.
Therefore: creatures
Sometimes lose, yet they gain;
Sometimes gain, yet they lose.

That which people teach, I also teach:
Those who are bullies and hoodlums do not meet their natural death.
I will thus become their elder teacher

I'll wait while you read that again ☺ Seriously, it does take a bit of thinking about, but if the light bulbs fire up in your head like they did in mine as I began to extract some relevant meaning from this, then it's worth it.

To be fair, I'd be taking serious liberties if I tried to unpick publicly what I think Laozi meant by this- a piece known as poem number forty-two. And yet, if I look at it solely from the point of view of a coaching-leader, I can take a stab (I just couldn't help myself). Anyway, he starts off like many of the early philosophers, postulating that something can't come from nothing and hence, in his terminology the Dao came first. In other religions and 'traditions' they say things like 'you can't know the unknowable' which is precisely what I imagine he was trying to say about the Dao - it was 'something', but something so different from our understanding of the world that it defies explanation.

Having established that all the 'stuff' we all experience has its fundamental roots in something real but impossible to articulate, that then facilitates and supports the growth of life as we know it. Who knows, he might even have had insights into how human life evolved - from a single cell that doubled and then the new evolved cell adapted, then they all kept on multiplying and ended up being everything we see around us, who knows?

Once one cell became two, and that two became three and so on and so on - then as if by magic, pow! ...the inevitability is that there were ten thousand creatures. By ten thousand I'm taking it as meaning he meant 'a lot', or 'everything we see today'. Then he gets cute and explains that in all these living things they are neither wholly one thing or another, but always a bit of a mix - a mix of 'yin' and 'yang'. That Yin-Yang symbol we see all over the place is as powerful now as it ever was. If you look at it closely it's two teardrop blobs spun together, one white and one black, and there is always some white and some black in every aspect of it. What makes it so special is that no matter how much black there is, there's also always just a speck of white, and vice versa.

I can picture him teaching his followers a message that in all these 10,000 creatures there will always be some black and some white. His message being that if you think of anything as all bad or all good, you will be wrong.

According to Laozi there is a little good in even the 'baddest' person or thing, and that no matter how 'good' a person or thing may appear that within them (or it) it is inevitable that a tiny amount of bad exists. No matter how it might appear there will always be something of each, it'll always be a mix.

However, accepting that there'll always be a mix wasn't enough for Laozi because the correct balance, that is the balance correct for the context or circumstance was necessary to generate the force called 'Qi' (but more about Qi in a moment).Recognising that there is always a mix is vital: Ask, *"Is an employee 'in it' for themselves or working on behalf of the company?"* - and the answer will always be some elements of both. Ask "Is that person who tells you they love you and would do anything for you being 100% true?" Hm... the answer is that there will always be just a little self-interest, even if it's only a tiny spot in a spiral of something wonderful. Yet, whatever the mix is, if it is properly balanced then this thing called 'Qi' is achieved. Laozi described Qi as 'that vital life force' flowing through everything. If you are anything like me (and if you're not then no judgements please), when I first heard this I thought *"Ah ha! That's where George Lucas got his idea from in Star Wars"* ...hm... well, maybe who knows? One thing's for sure, and that's that he did well **not** to go with *'May the Qi be with you'* - It doesn't quite have the same ring to it as 'the force'!

Be that as it may because though it may just be my innocent interpretation, when I'm coaching the Qi starts to flow - it honestly does. It flows when that balance of polarities, competing priorities, or seemingly opposing forces find the appropriate balance for that person. I love the concept of Qi! I also love something he called Wuwei. He talks about Wuwei a lot and it translates directly in English as 'non-action'. OK, I can almost hear you asking WTF is non-action? Or maybe that was just my response when I heard it for the first time. It certainly is a bit of an odd concept for a culture like ours that is all about seeing a problem and then taking actions to solve them. However, I soon learned that what it doesn't mean is sitting on your hands, contemplating your own navel and giving up. Now, this may be just my own take on Wuwei, but I think it means going inside your head and asking a better question; instead of freaking that there are metaphorical rocks in the road blocking your path, and then stressing out about them, I think Wuwei is all about mindfulness, being in the moment, and ultimately asking yourself a better question. To the onlooker mindfulness, being in the moment, thinking and asking yourself a better question will appear to any onlooker to be non-action. According to Laozi it was this non-action that was necessary for a person to successfully follow the path of power - the Dao.

I don't know about you, but I found the concept of the 'path' difficult to grasp at first too. I started asking questions like, 'how do we figure out which the best path is?', 'what if one path looks right but then leads to a dead end?', 'how can we trust that the path we commit to is the right one?'

I got very confused. However, the best explanation I've heard to sort this out is this - that the actions of rushing about trying to do the 'right' thing may be getting in the way of a natural path to achievement; if you imagine flying over a road and looking down at it, how do you know it's a road? You recognise it for what it is because there are always things lining the road that make the road a road and not just a flat piece of ground. These things that line the road can be recognised from your experience, and you know from that experience how to deal with them. Therefore, if your road to power and success is to be travelled with the fewest obstructions or hold-ups then recognising these things that line the path is essential, and the better you get at noticing what's there the better you are likely to get at progressing along that path. A later Daoist Master said that the 'way' (the Dao) is made up of many smaller ways, and the key to success is to be very good at handling the smaller ways, because once you are good at them all there is nothing to hold up your progress. It's a cool a way of thinking about things now as it was then - very cool.

There are eight key aspects of the Dao de Jing that provide insights into his thinking; Firstly, that the path, the Dao – that difficult to understand or explain 'thing' from which everything springs - the overarching order of the cosmos. He describes it as The Dao 'giving birth' to the 'one' - the origin of all things. The 'one' gives birth to the 'two', the natural balance of 'yin and yang', and then the 'yin-yang' gives birth to the heavens and earth which then give birth to the 10,000 'things' that make up all we see and experience. I think that 10,000 was just a way of saying *'more than a person can count'* rather than specifically 10,000 things. His point being that we mere human beings only pick up glimpses of the whole through what we experience - and we never get to see anything in its completeness. He believes that something or some things, get in the way of our awareness of the Dao and he hopes that the Dao de Jing will help awaken us to it.

Secondly, he recognised that we limit our understanding of nature by the words we apply. This is counter intuitive; as we tend to think words help us gain a clarity of understanding - we imagine that our understanding of a word is so like that of another person as to be indistinguishable - but this is simply untrue. Words (spoken or marked out by actions) are essential for communication but sadly quite poor as a means of achieving understanding. This isn't news; Laozi suggested that whatever words we come up with are restricting because we tightly limit their meaning, while nature itself requires far more than our words can convey if we are ever to understand it. Therefore, he believed we need to disentangle ourselves from pre-existing assumptions about what a thing means and then change our perspective if we are ever to stand a chance of gaining real insight and understanding. Thirdly, that the world and the choices we make in our lives are not binary; they are neither good nor bad per-se, things are not totally righteous or completely evil, and it is not as simple as saying we judge things as either 100% desirable or 100% detestable.

His point is that words are non-natural constructions that people try and impose on nature, and that as such they cannot ever be an accurate representation of any natural phenomena. As we might say today, *"a loaf of stale bread may or may not be attractive depending on how hungry you are"*. In other words, judgements must always be contextualised, and the context in nature is ever-changing.

Laozi's fourth point is about how too much planning always gets in the way of spontaneous action; the instinct that comes naturally and our unacknowledged abilities to process more than we hold consciously are ignored when we pretend that everything can be dealt with by a plan. I'm reasonably sure most, if not all of Laozi's observations resonate with leadership coaches like me, but if not 'all' then certainly this one must. The language he uses like 'Wuwei' may be strange but the concept of trusting our instincts is not – nor is the recognition that sometimes the very best choice of action is to get out of your own way by taking no action at all. My favourite simple example of Wuwei is when drivers dangerously attempt to exit a side road into a fast moving stream of traffic; their desire is to get from where they are to where they want to be as quickly as possible, but when an accident happens (or even if there's just a near-miss and blood pressure rises) the cost of 'trying' outweighs that of simply waiting for a natural break in the traffic. Wuwei in this instance is a conscious choice but waiting for a traffic break is by no means the only example on Wuwei in everyday life. Laozi encouraged us to question each of our actions and consider if there is a need for action at all. He does not ever suggest that we lose our intent or purpose, merely that not everything in life requires effort and action. As a coach I find myself regularly asking client's *"What are the consequences and/or opportunities of waiting?"*

The fifth concept is about the untapped potential of the human mind, and how it may be constricted by the rules we impose on it. My interpretation is that he is asking what might be different if we allowed ourselves to become a mirror reflecting what 'is', rather than trying to impose on nature what we believe 'ought to be'? There's a good deal of attention rightly being given to the subject of mindfulness, living in the moment, or 'being in the room' – thinking about the way in which sense is being made of what's going on around us rather than allowing for our unconscious to fill in the gaps and make stuff up! On the one hand the human mind's potential is outstanding at processing large amounts of information when given the chance (by being fed information), and on the other has amazing potential to imagine what 'could' have been (by using the little we do take in and then filling in the gaps with what our unconscious imagines ought to be there).

His sixth relates to selfishness when engaging in the pursuit of material goods or pleasure activities. Again, it's only my interpretation but I imagine his meaning to be that it is like trying to hear a conversation in a crowded room with music blaring, machines humming, and doors slamming; you know there is a conversation to be heard, but you can't hear it for all the distractions. Therefore, the rhythm of nature is like that conversation - we know it is there but miss out on its benefits because of everything else getting in the way. It's another aspect of mindfulness and when 'in the room - being in the room'.

His final two points are about the necessity for selfless leadership and the return to a life of stability. I'm not sure the literal meaning of 'returning to an animal state' is quite what he had in mind, but his recent experience of brutal warlords destroying property and lives must have weighed heavy on his mind. Leadership today calls for the leader to set aside much of their own needs, and focus instead on the needs of the business, and the people within the business. A leader who's up-front with why success holds personal importance, but who also makes it clear that their own needs can only be met when the needs of the business and the people within it are fulfilled; it is a foundational element of trustworthiness - a necessity for all successful leaders.

His Identity: Laozi had something to say, and like all the philosophers in here was not backward in putting his ideas forward. It is said that the recording of his message didn't happen until he was about to leave China when a border official (who was clearly already a fan) begged him to write down his wisdom so that it may be lost to the people. The five thousand characters and eighty-one chapters of the Dao de Jing are the only record we have that gives insight into his identity, save for the drawings of him.

He is always pictured as a scruffy looking individual, with long straggly hair and a shabby tunic. Perhaps this was his way of communicating that he refused to live by the binary good or bad judgements that everyone else might be applying? He certainly makes that sentiment clear in one of the verses,

"All in the world deem the beautiful to be beautiful; it is ugly. All in the world deem the good to be good; it is bad".

It's as if he is daring people to judge him on their first perceptions, knowing that they will soon learn to re-think their initial impression - and learn from the experience.

His Purpose: There can be little doubt that Laozi wanted to help make the world a better place. His rejection of worldly praise, material goods, position, and benefits are a solid testament to the fact that something other than those things was driving him. The further evidence of the Dao de Jing's content supports his desire to serve the 'greater good',

"The sage does not hoard. Having used what he has for others, his possessions increase; having given what he has to others, he has more and more."

How might he be thought of by his employees, if he was a manager in today's business world?

He's a thoughtful 'hippie', intent on leading by raising personal awareness in all who follow. Without doubt, he is an exemplar of something that's come to be known as 'Spiritual Leadership' - an awareness in the leader that without capturing the needs and desires of the whole person by raiding their own awareness of their personal potential, (at least as much as possible) then that potential is unlikely to be realised.

He is one of those leaders that knows what it's like to have suffered under bosses who are driven by ego; people who have an ego so fragile that they cast around looking for someone to blame even before anything has gone wrong, they do their best to instil fear in those who are supposed to be following them, and who are more interested in pretending to be successful than actually achieving success. Therefore, he does everything possible to be a leader that demonstrates through his actions his distaste for bosses like that. His followers may not know of his history, but it's evident within seconds of meeting him that he is serious about helping the people he works with, be the best they can possibly be.

He makes it clear to everyone and anyone who will listen that business success does not come from making profits for profits sake. The establishing of employee councils wasn't his idea but is embraced by him because he wants everyone at every level to be engaged in the success of the organisation. Few leaders pay serious attention to the 'ripples' their organisations create, and rarely does the immediate 'environmental ripples' and 'people ripples' feature in an organisation's mission statement - and yet, in his organisation they do. This results in everyone impacted by his organisation feeling engaged and perceiving the organisation through a lens that's very different than most.

Coaching questions he might ask: As deep a thinker as he might have been, and as hippyish as he might have looked, I'm sure Laozi would have made a good coaching-leader. He wanted people to think for themselves, so he might well have asked something like:

i. *"If you let go of all your old plans and simply trusted your instincts, what are they telling you is most important for you to focus on?"*

ii. *"If you were to imagine your circumstance as a point on a journey, as if on a road or a path, what might you notice if you were a bird flying high over that path, that it is difficult to see from way down here?"*

iii. *"What words have you not yet used to describe your situation and the barriers to your success, that might help you see things from a new perspective?"*

iv. *"What would have to change about the way you judge yourself, for you to be able to see new opportunities that you're blinded to right now?"*

v. *"If it were not you who were facing your issues, but someone looking on from a vantage point where they can see everything, what might you notice?"*

vi. *"What small things can you do now that might move you on?"*

vii. *"Where is your present path inevitably leading?"*

CHAPTER 8: #3 THE INFINITE AND BOUNDLESS UNIVERSE

ANAXIMANDER OF MILETUS

His Claim to Fame: As a potential coaching-leader this guy may reasonably be thought of as the originator of that overused aphorism *'Blue Sky Thinking'*. Anaximander pioneered the idea of there are no borders to what a person might imagine, and that their dreams are constrained only by the rules or parameters imposed by themselves. Thinking, according to Anaximander can be unbounded if we only allow it to be.

Anaximander's big claim to fame is the principle of *all things*. This is what he called 'the infinite'. This concept might elicit nothing more than a shrug today, but we are talking about the sixth century BCE and as far as we know nobody had said something like that before. Hence, he was big news at the time:

The Ancient Greek word for his version of the infinite is *'apeiron'*, which literally means that which has no limit. He thought the apeiron was infinitely big- so big that not only did it encompass everything humanity could see, even in the night sky, but also what they couldn't see. He imagined it stretching around the cosmos in which we live and extending indefinitely in space and time. If you have a hard time thinking about that concept now, imagine what it might have been like when most people saw even relatively short journeys as an adventure.

Not only did he come up with 'the infinite' idea, but he also disagreed with Thales assertion that all things sprang from water, and instead believed that all things came from something that we cannot name and that is beyond our human understanding. The similarities to Anaximander's *'apeiron'* and Laozi's *'the one'* are either astounding or expected, depending on your point of view. They either both came to a unique but similar conclusion by chance, or both recognised what's going on independently and gave it a different name. We will see a lot of this as we progress because while each person makes their own addition or little twist to things, the fundamentals seem to stay reasonably solid - no matter which side of the world they've originated. The only thing that changes substantially is the way the knowledge is applied - and then the additional beliefs extend from it.

So, Anaximander came up with this name *'apeiron'* and concluded that everything came from it, as if being separated out from a jumble of many things within it. His words are the oldest quote that historians have of an early philosopher. He said;

"Things come to be and are destroyed according to necessity, for they mete out penalty and retribution to another for injustice according to the ordering of time"

In other words, ...'dust to dust' (assuming that dust is where it all starts).Now, it might be something of a stretch to suggest that Anaximander had figured out the 'law of conservation of energy'[ix], but it sure looks like he was close. From a practical viewpoint I read this as meaning that while things may come and go, it will all balance out in the end - it is what it is and will be what it'll be, because it's all essentially made of the same stuff anyway - yet, within that 'stuff' is the potential to create anything. This guy would have made a hell of a life coach!

His Environment: He too was from Miletus and like Thales he enjoyed the prosperity of that thriving community. However, unlike the Thales he's not reported as experiencing the environment of Miletus in quite the same way. Not for him the falling into a well because while being so engrossed in other things or the application of 'new' thinking to show how easy it is for anyone to make their own fortune. In fact, it might have been quite the opposite experience for Anaximander; it's said that he didn't just sit quietly contemplating how the universe moved in cycles, but actively did his best to notice how it was changing in front of his eyes. He was a realist rather than a man of theory - he wanted to explain his thinking to people by what they could see, touch, feel, and experience for themselves.

Believe it or not, he might well be the very first person to have talked about climate change[x] because he was first to suggest the world was heating up, and that the seas were retreating - as the liquid seas turned into moist air and evaporated into the wind. Okay, not quite global warming[xi] as we understand it today, but an awareness of 'activity' the 'weather' and the experience of a changing environment. He saw the cosmic cycle of heat overcoming cold being manifest before his eyes. Sadly, I can only imagine what he'd make of today's polluted and plastic-strewn planet.

Much as we all see today's world through our own unique lens, he saw his through the lens of the wool-trading, olive oil-producing, sun drenched coastline and inland groves, as it's likely did everyone who lived there at the time of Anaximander and Thales. It will have been different to the way in which we all see our own world - they will have had their economic and cultural priorities just like we do, all of which means his musings might have been as easily dismissed by them as irrelevant as today's dire warnings are dismissed by those who simply don't see them through their particular lens.

The point is that he demonstrated by his observations and commentary all that time ago, that things are not 'what they are', but are 'how we see them' - a terrific lesson for leaders today. Bosses tend to assume that the way they see the world is the world as it is, but they are wrong.

A leader knows that their own viewpoint and understanding is but one of many, and that to engage other people they must ask questions to determine other people's understanding of what ought perhaps to be the same thing, but in most cases is perceived as different. Thus, the way each of the philosophers engaged with their environment tells me that the rocks, trees, sea and sand were only the canvass on which each came to paint their version of life in Miletus.

His Culture: In a similar way to Thales, his views were accepted and discussed in the market place and social gathering places of Miletus. He was only slightly younger than the big guy but was still able to make his own mark. Clearly, Anaximander was as much a force of nature as his immediate predecessor.

The constant and dynamic opposition of forces within a unifying environment that Anaximander described as the apeiron was mirrored in the culture he experienced, and most likely became how he saw himself - a man tussling with his circumstances to both make himself clear and make his point relevant and of interest to the people around him.

When a person becomes absorbed, even obsessed with an idea like this, it must affect the way a person sees themselves. This idea of opposition and unity 'happening' on at the same time is an idea we will hear again and again as philosophers to come try and make sense of it in ways that help people. Anaximander may be a name you were unfamiliar with before reading this (I know he was to me before writing it), yet he might well be the first person to have talked about an idea that is still a big deal today.

His Skills: Apart from his engagement with Thales, we don't know where he learned how to think the way he did. There wasn't a creative thinking course that we know of back then - and even if there were, I'm not sure it would have produced the unique point of view that came from this man. There's no doubt that Anaximander had thinking skills, nor that he was a sponge for information always keen to try and use what he learned for something of practical benefit - and that he travelled far and wide to soak in as much as possible. In fact, he's known to have travelled all the way to Sparta. It was in Sparta where he used his knowledge for the practical purpose of 'telling the time' - apparently, he amazed the people of mainland Greece by introducing them to a device that was probably the precursor of a sundial.

He was also an early cartographer, producing a map that depicted both the land and sea - admittedly wildly inaccurate, but at least he was the first to 'have a go'.

Unfortunately, there's no sign of the map anymore, but he is reported as having produced one that was widely talked about at the time. Finding the 'Anaximander map' sounds like a great theme for a new Indiana Jones[xii] movie! (I'm open to offers for writing a screenplay if you happen to know any Hollywood producers).

Seriously, this guy was cool because not only did he achieve all this, but he must have made a real impact back home by demonstrating his knowledge - one item of note is that he probably used what he'd learned on his travels to set up way of measuring when the solstice was to take place. We don't even think about figuring out the longest and shortest days of the year - we just know when they are, but back then they didn't, at least they didn't in Greece until Anaximander told them how to figure it out. We know that in Ancient Egypt this had been known for ages, but it looks like Anaximander was the first to bring this to the Greeks, and like plenty of people after him was credited by some for coming up with it when it was probably just a transfer of knowledge. Still, it's nice to know that the Greeks didn't invent everything!

His Beliefs: For the record, I don't think this was his idea - but it appears he believed all things are 'cyclical'. Thales had made a big deal out of the weather cycles and their effect on olive growing, while Anaximander went beyond that and developed his own very colourful understanding of the cycles within the cosmos. He believed that because of some, as yet unexplained event, a ball of intense fire came to exist - within which the earth was encircled. He described it as being *"like bark surrounding a tree"*. According to him, the flame then burst outwards into rings or circles that were enveloped in clouds of vapour. Then, as these expanded, holes developed in this vapour that now allow us to see the balls of fire that hold the heavenly bodies we now see in the sky.

The first time I heard this I jumped straight to the idea that he'd figured out the 'big-bang' - unfortunately, I'd make a terrible detective! It may sound a bit like he was way ahead of his time and was describing the birth of the universe as many people understand it today, but he wasn't. I'd just jumped to a conclusion based on a couple of familiar sounding descriptions.

The leader in me was reminded that stepping back and taking in the whole before making assumptions is the smart thing to do. The real learning here is that a leader must take the facts first and then see if they lead to a conclusion, not grab at random facts and stick them into a pre-existing conclusion just because they fit. Jumping to conclusions and then running with them without seeing the whole deal is a very 'boss' thing to do.

Forgive me, I don't know if it's me or it's the essence of the way I'm imagining Anaximander's 'thinking' creeping in - either way, it does help shape some great questions. By the way, my first big clue that he wasn't a proto-physicist genius was his explanation for thunder being *"the clouds banging together"*. Yeah right, that'll be it then (not)... so where's the noise when they collide in a clear sky, eh Anaximander? Nope, not a genius, but still an interesting thinker.

A thinker with some great attributes even if some of them might have been pushed to their limits; his enthusiasm for example - it's great to have but get carried away and it's easy to start believing your own opinions as if they're facts. He was clearly creative and persuasive, and even tried to put some detailed flesh onto the bare bones of his ideas. For example, one of the more interesting conclusions he came up with (by adopting the 'ignore pre-existing conclusions' approach) was when he thought about how humans had come to be. He didn't just buy into whatever was the socially accepted creation 'myth' of the locals but was brave enough to ask his own questions. This bravery isn't to be underestimated; it's tough to push against a tide of opinion - even tougher to recognise that there is a tide to push against.

Hopefully, you can see how as a possible leadership-coaching idea this could be easily transposed into any 'origin' question... like, *'How do customers choose what they choose?'* or *'What makes an employee behave a certain way in certain circumstances'*. There are many 'tides' in life that are all too easy to go unrecognised. Anaximander questioned even the seemingly obvious; He noted the fact that baby humans have no way of surviving without grown up humans taking care of them, so it followed that no original or proto-human could have come into the world without first being equipped to survive.

Okay, Anaximander might have been an original thought-leader at asking questions, but he could have done with a bit of help in answering them. The poor guy concluded that the most likely answer to the proto-human conundrum was that the first human must have been born out of the belly of a fish - popping out into the world fully formed. After all, fishes do that don't they?

Quite how he made the leap from needy-baby to fish parents I have no clue. However, I have a sneaky suspicion, with nothing to back it up except it sounds maybe-plausible, that he might have heard some weird stories out of Egypt about a long-forgotten creation myth. Sumerian cuneiform tablets tell of Babylonian creation myths that include 'fish' gods [xiii]preceding humans. Hence, I wonder if something like this might have prompted his thinking - he went to Egypt , definitely spoke to some interesting people who must have shared with him more than just how to make a sundial, and then had this pattern of noticing what's around him and making connections - so... fish gods, creation, real fish, baby fish... and there you go, a new theory.

Who knows from where the humans-come-from-fish theory really originated, but it must have been quite a 'sell' to convince the people of Miletus that their ancestors might have had fins and swam in the ocean because there's also an interesting fishy-link to the story told by the Dogon people of Mali, half a world away on the African continent. They have an oral tradition of encountering *'fish-beings'* who taught the art of civilisation to people[xiv]. So, to cut him some slack, maybe there were a few fishy tales going around at that time - stories that made his musings sound less out of left field than they do today.

His Identity: Although no one can truly know how another sees himself, it's clear that Anaximander wasn't afraid to put out some wild ideas into the world. Maybe it was his inevitable competition with the tall good-looking Thales that pushed him to go just that little bit further. Whatever his motivation, he certainly did 'go large' as the saying goes; for him it wasn't enough to give an explanation of the things the people of Miletus and Sparta could see, hear, touch, or taste, no - his idea of an explanation was to take the whole cosmos and find ways to communicate how it all began, the unbelievable expanse of it, and even that there may be other worlds out there like ours that we can't yet see. All I can say about the way he saw himself with absolute certainty, is that there's no way he allowed himself to sit in the shadow of anyone - he had his own ideas, and they were big, huge, no - infinite!

His Purpose: It is a matter of record that along with Thales he established a school that became known, not unreasonably as the *'Miletus school of philosophy'*. That's not meant to suggest they created any establishment or designated a place within which to dispense their wisdom. It was an idea rather than a building. Yet, it does suggest some ideas of permanence even if no building or site was established. I think Anaximander might have seen Thales as a shield behind which he could quietly get on with digging deeper and deeper into thought.

I believe he saw his purpose as *'finding the best explanation he could for the world in which they lived'*.

I think the popular poems about the gods (the source of most information about the past) might have irritated him. Irritated because of their simple acceptance of what they were told - and the idea that because something had been said in the past it must be true. He wasn't a person who'd accept that some unseen entity blew the wind in his face or set a flame to the sun - because he'd already figured out that something cyclical was going on, something that was to do with his *apeiron* and not some imaginary god.

If he'd lived at another time, I think his purpose would have been the same, he'd probably have become a physicist and worked alongside Hawking and been happy that 'string-theory' might be at the heart of his apeiron.

How might he be thought of by his employees, if he was a manager in today's business world?

"What goes around comes around", and *"there's always a new way of looking at a problem"* - are things his followers are likely to hear again and again. He's not the typical leader that jumps up on a platform and rallies the troops, he's more the quiet man with gravitas to whom everyone turns for direction.

He is the person who questions the status-quo in our organisational context and wants to know not just what we are doing, but also the specific reasons underpinning why we do it. He asks everyone to open their minds to new possibility - by recognising the things they take for granted and then setting them aside. He encourages us to ask questions like, "What if there was another, better, quicker, and easier way?", "How would this look if we all saw it from a different perspective ...and what might we learn?" as opposed to bosses we have had who insist in measuring even the things they know are ineffective and sometimes simply wrong - yet, they worry more about the 'scores' than getting a better result overall.

The thing that makes him stand out as a great leader is that he listens and remembers; he may ask a question at any time and with anyone in the organisation, not just within the management hierarchy. He asks because he is genuinely interested in knowing more and learning how other people see things differently to himself. Better still than just asking the questions, he remembers the answers and he uses them to help generate new ways of helping us all produce better results. Not only that, but he gives credit where it is due - he is less interested in being 'seen' as the leader with all the answers than he is in being the actual leader that people feel happy to follow.

Coaching questions he might ask: If Thales was a big talker, I see Anaximander more as the quieter sage-like figure, who may have said less but made what he said count.

i.   *"If you unpick your recent actions, what was their core intent and what was the bark surrounding them that others could see?"*

ii. *"If your story till now were a canvas, and your thoughts and desires an artist's set, what might your completed painting be?"*

iii. *"What are you accepting at face value, or belief do you acknowledge that did not originate with you that may be hindering your ability to act?"*

iv. *"What are you assuming or attributing from your situation that if you were approaching things with no prior knowledge may not turn out to be true?"*

v.   *"What opposing ideas or forces within you are fighting for supremacy in your current situation?"*

vi. *"What, within your ability to influence is missing from your situation that might balance your personal scales of justice?"*

CHAPTER 9: #4 LIFE IS LIKE A MUDDY POND

SIDDHARTHA GAUTAMA - THE BUDDHA

His Claim to Fame: Thought-leaders come in more than one 'flavour'; there are leaders who've gone unnoticed - when you hear their name for the first time the response is 'never heard of him!', those whose names ring a bit of a bell, those that history could not ignore, and then there are the likes of Siddhartha Gautama, or the Buddha as he came to be known - almost a category on his own.

Apart from the small matter of starting one of the world's most popular religion she was the heir to a small kingdom in the Himalayan foothills, a husband who walked out on his wife, and an absent father. The fact that he was <u>all</u> those things makes him as special as the philosophy he espoused.

Of course, his biggest claim to fame is that people all over the world still follow his teachings, and (as an aside) there are probably more garden ornaments of his head than any other person in history.

His Environment: Apparently, his father and chief of the Shaya clan was given a prophesy that when he had a son his heir would grow up to be either a great sage, or his boy would grow up to be a king who would go on to unite all the tribes of India. It didn't take daddy more than a nanosecond to choose which path he wanted the fruit of his loins to follow - and it wasn't to be a spiritual leader.

Therefore, when twelve years after getting that prophecy little Gautama was born, daddy, not wanting his son to end up as a 'sage' took drastic action. While most parents set house rules for their offspring, the king basically grounded the poor boy for the whole of his youth. He didn't allow him to see real-life and maintained control of his 'understanding' of the world. Dad's plan was to cocoon young Gautama to ensure there was no chance of him downing the route to become a 'Sage' and did it by confining him within the walls of their palace - literally controlling the young lad's exposure to the real world.

Obviously, the king was hoping that one day he would become the even greater king his father wanted him to be. Hence, young Gautama was raised in absolute luxury, wanting for nothing; his days were spent being entertained by dancers and performers. Instead of experiencing life his mind was filled with tales by storytellers. He was educated by Brahmins in all mental aspects of kingship and trained in the physical requirements of a king by learning archery, swordsmanship, wrestling, swimming, and running to build his stamina and performance.

When the boy became a man at the ripe old age of sixteen, it was time to take a bride. He married his cousin (as you do). Her name was Yasodhara. She was also just sweet sixteen - and although they were just a couple of kids, he spent the next thirteen years with her. Then, at twenty-nine they had a son, Rahula, but instead of becoming a doting dad who like his father tried to control the future of his own son, just one week after his birth, Gautama left home, never to return.

Being grounded from birth to sixteen and experiencing only the lavish furnishings and tended gardens of the king's palace meant that when he eventually did get introduced to the real world, so it's little wonder he had a bit of a reaction. He also lived through some mighty strange times- which may or may not be relevant to his rise in popularity. You'll hear how his interpretation of 'reality' affected him and eventually led to millions thinking about the world differently. Yet, apparently, his search for meaning in everyday 'stuff' didn't capture the hearts and minds of the populous from the moment of his own personal revelation and enlightenment. It wasn't like he was zapped with the knowledge of enlightenment and a wave of awareness went out around the world and the 'Buddha' was born. There's a lot more 'lead and lag' - in fact, it's fair to say that something must have happened to grab the attention of the world at large that made his story relevant.

It transpires there was something like that - a pivotal event that would have captured the attention of the whole world. These events(or set of events) were physical and while open to interpretation were real for everyone to experience. You see, the environment went haywire at just the time he was likely spreading word of his personal enlightenment. The world was hit with an environmental catastrophe - not quite a dinosaur-like extinction event but was extreme all the same. It could be that the combination of his message, and the need for people to believe something would help them make their lives better, was a potent brew.

His birth date isn't absolutely fixed by historians. The best guess is that it was probably around 480 CE meaning he was in his mid-fifties when the skies all over the world darkened and the sun just, well, disappeared - and not just for a day or two, but was obscured long enough for a global chill-out and worldwide crop failure. The world must have been in panic because according to new research he lived through the worst year to be alive at any time in human history[xv].There is evidence that during the years 536 and 537 CE the Earth was plunged into darkness when a thick cloud of volcanic ash blocked out sunlight, causing temperatures to plummet. As a result, crops failed and people all over the world starved to death. Apparently, temperatures during the summer of 536 plunged to between 1.5 and 2.5 degrees centigrade. To put that in perspective, the recommended temperature of a household fridge is right within this range - the whole world would have felt like stepping into a salad drawer. Sadly, for Gautama and anyone else alive during the next decade things didn't get much better - it ended up being the coldest of the previous 2,300 years. That's prime-time for a someone with a message of hope and growth out of 'darkness' to get noticed.

His Culture: Behavioural expectations of a prince were like no one else, thanks mainly to the decrees of daddy the king. Remember, he didn't want that prophecy about becoming a sage rather than a mighty ruler to come true. Hence, there were major restrictions imposed on the boy and the young Prince was to all intents and purposes a prisoner. Of course, the young man had little need to venture far from its walls - everything he needed was provided for him within that gilded cage; when the prospect of venturing outside isn't even considered, thoughts of it just don't cross the mind.

It's hard to imagine not wanting to go outside. Who knows, maybe he did sneak out a little bit - or perhaps he went out but only under strict supervision and only saw what he 'was allowed' to see? What we do know is that, at the age of twenty-nine, just after the birth of his son, and for no reason ever recorded, the prince requested his chariot to go out for a ride. Then, as he was driven around the streets of Kapilavastu he saw things he had never seen before - things that changed him immediately and forever:

Firstly, he came upon someone who didn't look like anyone he'd ever seen within the palace walls. This person was bent over and walking with the aid of a stick, his face wrinkled, his head balding and wearing a straggly beard. Unsure what he was witnessing, Gautama asked his driver what this 'thing' was. To his surprise the driver wasn't at all shocked at the sight and replied that it was simply an old man. His helpful driver went on to tell the prince that old age is natural and comes to everyone over time - even the prince himself. He went on to say that although young people try not to think about it, it is inevitable - and that because people don't think about the passing of days it can come as a bit of a surprise, so much so that old people wonder how it came upon them so fast.

The prince was a bit shaken with this new knowledge, and now curious as to what else he might encounter. Now with his interest in all-that's-different piqued, Gautama soon noticed someone else who looked different.

This person was obviously in some distress, so again he asked the driver what was going on. This time the driver answered that this person was sick - and that illness, even sometimes disability, can afflict anyone unlucky enough to contract a disease.

Clearly, I wasn't there but I can imagine the prince asking if this sickness could affect even him - I mean, if I'd been him, I would have asked that question - wouldn't you? I can almost hear his driver telling him soothingly that he'll probably be fine, being looked after by the finest physicians in the land - and because in this kingdom it's mostly just poor people who get sick. It's not so funny, is it - that not much has changed in a millennium and a half? Not just in that part of the world - but pretty much everywhere.

If that wasn't enough to see in one day, the drive continued and the subdued but intensely interested prince then noticed something else he'd never seen before.

This time it was a person who was wrapped in cloth and being carried toward the burning ground. He had no idea what was going on, it was all new to him -although I'm sure at some level it's instinctive to recognise death. So, I'm not so sure he needed the charioteer to tell him that he was witnessing the carrying of a dead person for disposal. But, the driver spelled it out for him anyway.

Unbelievably, the prince not only hadn't thought about where people's bodies go after death - because he didn't even know what death was. Hard to believe, I know - and remember this isn't my story, but one that's been passed down through the generations, so let's give it the benefit of the doubt.

Apparently, he had no idea that one day he, along with everyone else would say goodbye to this world and die. If this was true, then I imagine he must have been beside himself to discover that shuffling off this mortal coil was inevitable. What a bummer to find out that even for a wealthy, young, powerful prince, the grim reaper was going to have an appointment whether the prince liked it or not.

Blimey, he'd only just learned about getting old and being ill, and now he faced the reality that he too would one day be a corpse to be disposed of. It must have been tough to be told that life is a very temporary situation - prince or no prince.

By now this chariot ride must have lost any buzz he'd hoped for. The happy-go-lucky prince-of-all-he-surveyed had just been told that there were things that money and power couldn't buy. That must have been a shock. By now he must have been sure the day couldn't get any worse or weirder, but it did;

On the way back to the palace he saw one more thing that was unusual - an incredibly thin person, dressed from head to toe in bright yellow, and carrying a single bowl as his one and only possession in the world. Pointing to the odd-looking person he asked the driver what the yellow dress and bowl was all about? The driver replied that this was a pious man; an ascetic, a person who had given up all worldly goods to live as simply as a human might possibly live.

This time the prince just looked on in silence. I think he must have been wracking his brain to figure out why someone would willingly live in hunger and have just a bowl and a yellow smock as their only possessions. As this strange sight faded from view, they arrived back at the palace and 'normality' - but for Prince Gautama life would never be the same, and 'normal' was a thing of the past.

Not unreasonably for someone who's whole world-view had been shattered in an afternoon, that night Gautama found it difficult to concentrate and sleep. it really wasn't unreasonable - I mean, he went off for a nice day out and came back with an unexpected dose of reality. Those images must have been hard to forget, because just seven days after becoming a princely dad with a wife, servants, luxury, and not a care in the world, everything changed.

On that eighth morning he woke up early, called for a horse, and exited the palace never to return. According to the story he didn't stop to wake his wife of thirteen years nor disturb his new-born son. He didn't explain himself, justify his actions, or leave a note. He didn't even pack a bag, he just left.

Or at least that's one version of the story. That had to be more than one, didn't there?

So, in another he had a chat with the king and his step-mum about what he was about to do. He apparently spoke to them in passionate terms whilst making some radical physical changes - he was cutting off his long hair, stripping off his princely robes, and donning his own top-to-tail yellow robe - the kind of robe worn by the ascetics. If this is was happened, they must have freaked - specially dad. After all, he'd kept the boy all but under lock and key for sixteen years, married him off and was all set for him to be the next great ruler as foreseen by the prophesy. Then, after just one trip out on a carriage he was chopping off his hair and dressing like a freak.

The king knew all about ascetics. They were people who lived life with as little as they could; they tried not to eat, drank as little as needed to survive, and left all possessions behind except their simple peasant bowl. They were a source of sages - the thing he had tried everything to avoid the prince becoming. He must have been gutted.

Whichever story of his leaving is true, one thing is not in dispute - and that's that he went. He exited the palace and stepped into a new life; a new life that meant renouncing the pantheon of gods he'd grown up with. That change must have been a tough one - he went from believing something without question the day before, to believing something completely different the next day. Yet, the world had not changed. All that had changed was the thinking of the young prince.

This change of thinking had but one goal in mind; to address the problem of earthly suffering in a way that gave people back control of their lives. Instead of living in fear and praying to a god for this and a god for that, he wanted to learn how to control his mind and body so that a good life could be lived without the need for external intervention. He cut off his long hair, exchanged his clothes for the simple robes of an ascetic, and for want of a better word became what we might call a drop-out.

His Skills: Gautama Siddhartha was far better equipped than most wandering drop-outs; he was already well educated and skilled in taking care of himself physically, even if his other needs had always been tended to. Not long after leaving he settled down to work with two teachers. The first taught him how to discipline his mind, then how to concentrate. However, while this helped, it didn't cause him to answer his query, so he wandered as a serious ascetic, eating and drinking as little as possible until he was so thin his ribs suck out like sticks in a bag. In his own words;

"My body slowly became extremely emaciated, my limbs became like the jointed segments of a vine or bamboo stems, my spine stood out like a string of beads, my ribs jutted out like the rafters of an old abandoned building, the gleam of my eyes appeared to be sunk deep in my eye-sockets like the gleam of water deep in a well. My scalp shrivelled and withered like a green bitter gourd, shrivelled and withered in the heat and wind"

After reading this I struggled to take the little fat Buddha statues seriously any more. I'm sure there is a great reason for picturing him as a chubby chap, but I found this imagery far more powerful. Some years later I happened upon a Tibetan silver statue of an ascetic monk in the tradition of Gautama Siddhartha at this time in his life. It sits near my desk now, right beside a more traditional image of the great man and reminds me that great insights sometimes require significant sacrifice - a lesson in, and of itself. I thought you might like to see the statue -

All I can say is that it's a good job he founded a religion and not a diet company. It was all a bit extreme. However, finally, so the story goes, he sat for six days under an olive tree having eventually had enough. The tree was the line he refused to cross; either he found enlightenment, or he'd die trying. You probably guessed that he didn't die, Buddhism in its various guises being a major religion around the world and all that. As the sun rose that day it struck him that he'd known the answer all the time. That must have been a bit of a downer, but he stayed positive and turned his new-found realisation into something the world could understand and use.

His Beliefs: The strength of character he must have had made this possible even though it also accounted for the less glamorous decisiveness of leaving his wife and new born child. His commitment to self-development, his compassion, and his emotional control were abundantly clear, as was his resilience in the face of the opposing opinions of others who didn't share his vision.

Having experienced those 'four sights' (the old guy, ill fellow, corpse, and ascetic chap), Gautama realised something; that *the natural state for a human being is decay followed by death*, - and that cheerful thought was before he starved himself.

Then at the age of thirty-five while sat underneath an old olive tree, while almost starved to death, he had his great realisation.

There should have been a fanfare and fireworks but as is the way with a new thought - it just popped up in the silence left by not thinking at all. His realisation was simple - that peaceful enlightenment is possible for us even with all that inevitable decay and death. His big light bulb moment happened when he realised that they were inevitabilities that everyone had to come to terms with, opting out wasn't an option.

It was obvious to him that if we spend all our time trying to avoid that inevitability there'd be no time left to do anything else. Its simplicity made absolute sense. Looking around him he could see that almost everyone was might miss any chance to live peacefully, happily, and in harmony during the time they have, despite the reality of the human condition. In that moment he transformed from Prince Siddhartha to the enlightened one, the Buddha.

The Buddha's four 'noble truth's' are; firstly, that suffering is universal. Secondly, that desire is the cause of suffering. Thirdly, that suffering may be avoided by eliminating desire, and fourthly, that by following the eight-fold path it is possible for desire to be eliminated. His beliefs were stated simply and were easy to understand. To make the point that everyone can rise to a life of harmony and beauty he used the life of a lotus plant as an analogy; the plant begins life under the waters of the murkiest swamp, but over time finds its way to the light and eventually breaks through the surface. Having made it that far it draws on its own resources to produce a wonderful flower that opens under the sunlight for all to enjoy.

His point was that for a person to rise out of the swamp of life and make it to that life of balance and harmony, the eight-fold path was a must-do journey. Buddhist scholars, monks, and followers will attest to the fact that following the path and applying each of the eight is rarely easy, but that the process of attempting to do is always worthwhile; they are right mindfulness, right action, right intention, right livelihood, right effort, right concentration, right speech, and right understanding.

His Identity: There's no way Gautama can be thought of as a typical wife-deserter and absent father. It is impossible for anyone to imagine what it must have been like for the twenty-nine-year-old prince, to have his world turned upside down, his beliefs shattered, and his values put under personal scrutiny. History suggests that his wife must have had some considerable sympathy for her husband because after overcoming her grief to learn that he had departed to live a holy life, she too give up her riches, dressed in a simple yellow robe and ate only one meal a day, and both she and her son became committed to a religious order. With one fell swoop he left the life of a prince and entered the world of the sage, finally achieving the status that had been predicted by the soothsayer a dozen years before his birth.

His Purpose: It doesn't matter how his life began, he ended it as a supreme influencer and opinion-maker, affecting millions of lives. If ever there was anyone who walked-the-talk it was him. Like the people who've been considered prophets, it was his destiny to become a religious figure himself.

Unlike competitor prophets there's nothing mystical or weirdly metaphysical about him, just a view of life based on hard-won experience. The four noble truths that came from those four sights led directly to an eightfold path, the journey upon which could take anyone from the state of ignorance that he'd once been in and achieve a state of peaceful enlightenment. From the age of thirty-five until his death at eighty, it became his purpose to share this knowledge throughout the world. You must admit, he didn't do a bad job!

How might he be thought of by his employees, if he was a manager in today's business world?

He knows the value of personal values, and the power of a collective belief. He knows that desires cause suffering, so provide an environment where there's no tension between having those desires and meeting them.

First and foremost, he accepts without question that every person under his leadership will have their own values. He sees his job as a business leader, to make it as easy as possible for each person to 'live' their values within the business-belief-system he has asked them to play a part. His 'magic' as a leader is that he doesn't try to shoe-horn everyone into accepting his values - he knows that some people might recoil at the thought of leaving their wife and child to follow a 'higher calling', and that's okay. He doesn't want to convince anyone that their values are wrong and his are right. He does not try and defend his values and as asks his managers to never put any employee into a position where they must defend their own. In practical terms this means that if someone values family time more than advancement and more money, then that's okay. Equally, if another person values the 'choice' afforded by advancement and more money and is desirous of doing whatever it takes to get there, then that's okay too. That is, both are okay with the proviso that the behaviours they exhibit and the actions they take are consistent with the beliefs he and the business espouse. In other words; if he believes that a quality standard must be achieved for customers to be satisfied, then both the person valuing family time, and the other person wanting to get ahead as quickly as possible must adhere to that belief.

Everyone in the organisation knows that it'll never be the company that gets in the way of meeting their desires, but it'll be something they must figure out themselves by matching opportunity to whatever they value most.

They all know that beliefs are merely 'things' accepted as being true without the need for on-going proof or verification, and that his arguments, ideas, and analogies the leader presents are powerful enough to engage them - and to have them accept these business beliefs as if they were true. It's almost a given that once people 'believe', then almost anything is possible.

His employees love the apparent control they have over their own working life - with none of the insinuated 'rules' and 'politics' where people then tend to say one thing and think another. They love the challenge that comes with knowing what 'great' looks like and the camaraderie that comes with working alongside people who believe the same as you do. Everyone you speak to says what a great place it is to work.

Coaching questions he might ask: While it's true that trinket shops all over the world have shelves full of Buddha statuettes of him as that little chubby bald fella just waiting for someone to rub his head for good luck, he has a place as a thought-leader relevant to the workplace as well as his role in founding a religion. The thoughtfulness he brings to being a leader is in direct opposition to the knee-jerk ranting of an ineffective boss.

i.   *"How have you evaluated your intent when measured by the outcomes you are achieving?"*
ii. *"If it is true that removing a boulder from a path requires both effort and leverage, what leverage,*

and effort might be required in your circumstances?"

iii. *"If you were described by someone you respect as having the right understanding to overcome the barriers in your way, to what might they be referring?"*

iv. *"If you were to break a convention you have held to be important so that you might achieve something more important, what might it be?"*

v. *"If you were to take just one small newly considered action that you are certain will take you closer to your 'ultimate-goal', what might that be?"*

vi. *"What new aspects might give you the additional certainty needed to continue on the path you have chosen?"*

vii. *"What specific words have you used in the past that worked to achieve your needs, that could be applied now?"*

viii. *"When you think about the achievement of your goal, what does right-mindedness mean to you?"*

ix. *"When you think back to a time when your concentration was so focused on being successful that nothing stood in your way, what specifically were you thinking about?"*

CHAPTER 10: #5 EVERYTHING IS CONNECTED

XENOPHANES

His Claim to Fame: The key message to take from this guy is that being a leader rather than just a boss doesn't mean you leave all your own strong opinions behind, but it does mean you find better ways to express them.

He told *stories* to get his point made - and he told them so well that he made a massive impact on his society. Xenophanes, (pronounced *Zen-off-an-ees*) isn't a name most people are familiar with, yet it seems that he came up with the famous 'world-view of Aristotle' a few hundred years before the great man was born. If I was him, I'd be looking down now and blaming the alphabet, I mean who's going to bother going all the way through to 'X' when you get such a lot at the letter 'A'! I don't know, maybe that's just my imagination reflecting how lazy I was at school to not ever get to the X's?

What I do know is that few people question that the way Aristotle made us look at the world came from anywhere but Aristotle, yet, the fact is that Xenophanes was saying pretty much the same thing centuries earlier. That being said, the mater isn't clear - did he really have an epiphany that was nicked by Aristotle years later, was it a bit of literary sleight of hand, or perhaps it was just accidental plagiarism? Some scholars think that maybe the fact that it was Aristotle himself who wrote *about* Xenophanes means that the truth regarding who said what might have been bent a little, or at least viewed through a 'tinted' lens so that the thoughts of both were aligned.

I must admit I scratched my head when I read this and wondered why would he do that? I don't imagine someone with Aristotle's temperament admitting to the world that he might not be an original thinker (more about Aristotle's temperament later). It makes much more sense to me that Aristotle was as intrigued as I was to dig into the thinking of a philosopher and poet from so long ago - and was simply pleased that his own thinking had been mirrored - after isn't it nice to know you're not alone?

Apart from living to the ripe old age of 92, something of an achievement back then - not only for avoiding getting any infections (there was of course no penicillin back then), but also avoiding the wrath of people he probably upset - because he was a well-known social commentator. A commentating critic who doled out his opinion with a stinging delivery. An example of this was that Homer's Iliad and Odyssey[xvi] were as popular then as the Old Testament is in Oklahoma[xvii] today. While most people were apt to accept the book as actual-fact not fiction, again much like anti-Darwin evangelists, Xenophanes did not. He was vocal in telling anyone who'd listen that Homer's depictions of gods as being human-like was straight-up wrong. Xenophanes scoffed that anything coordinating and controlling the universe could not be as flawed and fragile as mere humans. His opinions did not go down well.

The nearest analogy I can come up with is to walk into one of those huge TV evangelist sessions and start arguing with the 'fire and brimstone' preacher that his translation of the Bible is inaccurate - and his interpretation is not at all what the writers intended. I sense that would not go down well. Nor did it for Xenophanes when he did something similar.

To make the analogy more accurate you'd have to add to the 'blasphemy' that God doesn't have bad moods, nor does *she* act like a sociopathic child effectively pulling the legs of his pet insects by sending them plagues or threatening floods. Yup, that'd go down like a lead balloon, as was Xenophanes' attack on the works of Homer – they were similarly poorly received.

He was a rational man born into an irrational world - something with which many leaders can empathise. They, like Xenophanes must find ways of communicating so that people 'hear' them. For Xenophanes that way was to wrap his message into stories and metaphors.

His message was that just because we can see, hear, feel, and sense things doesn't mean they're real. He wanted people to think more deeply, even when it wasn't something people wanted to hear. He realised from his experience of sniping at Homer, that the people liked their god stories. They liked the 'fact' that they could rely on their gods to do god-stuff, and that those same gods had mood swings just the same as people. Xenophanes realised that people find it comforting to think they know something, even if they are completely wrong. That's just as true now as it ever was. A boss may think it clever to dismiss the hopes of the workforce as unrealistic and then take no responsibility when crushingly poor morale and crippling performance - whereas a leader knows that while keeping hope and ambition alive with believable stories and metaphors does not guarantee success, it certainly makes it more likely.

His Environment: Xenophanes was born in Colophon in Turkey, now just a set of ruins near the village of

Degirmendere around 40km south of Izmir, and 24km north of Ephesus in Ionia. It's a lovely part of the world. Pictures now topped mountains in the far background, and the coast of sparkling sand and sea of clear blue water. Colophon was a small town surrounded by lush vegetation and was bustling with early commerce, specialising in the breeding of horses - something that set the place apart as a prosperous location with luxurious homes and lifestyles. For the young Xenophanes it must have been a terrific place to grow up.

Unfortunately for him, the stability wasn't to last long. In his teens the place was attacked and overrun by the Persians, forcing him to flee. He made it to Sicily where he spent the next twenty-five years of his life in a wandering existence, before finally settling back on the Ionian peninsular in Elea. His experience can't have been unlike many of the refugees of the modern world; brought up in relative comfort and safety, only to have it cruelly ripped away, and then finding yourself in a strange land without roots, money, the language, and any credibility to settle in a new life and career.

The upheaval he experienced and the inevitable need the young Xenophanes must have had to think on his feet, is likely to have caused him to question everything. Scholars now refer to him as a natural epistemologist (deep thinker to you and me), but I see him as a fabulous example of someone who wasn't prepared to let misfortune shape his reality. It might have taken some time, but he learned that he who asked better questions was better prepared to deal with whatever came their way.

His Culture: The behavioural expectations of a Greek man at that time did not match the way Xenophanes behaved - remember his scoffing of the Homer tales of god's and titans? This was a time when power was wielded by those who took care of god-worship. The politics of the day were as much about the interpretation of various god's 'wills' as it was about real-world events - and god help them (pun intended) if people chose not to believe.

One might look around today and think that not much has changed. Okay, it's not 'gods' now that are interpreted but instead the blunt sword of democracy is wielded in a similar way; some politician gets elected (even by the slimmest majority) and then starts justifying their every action as 'the will of the people'.

In an organisational setting the distinction between a boss and a leader in this regard is that the boss feels confident to question their own decisions and not assume that because they hold a title it makes them automatically a representative of the 'will' of the organisation - whereas, that's precisely how a boss behaves. Just like those ancient Greeks, the boss doesn't react well to having their interpretation questioned -bosses are intensely threatened by someone else's lack of belief. It's as if they think when someone chooses to *not-believe*, their own conviction is somehow diminished.

I'm not only talking about religious beliefs or convictions, although they are an obvious example - but of any belief - like people who believe '*workers* are oppressed can get very agitated when another worker claims to be happy. It's weird how they try desperately to convince that person their happiness is an illusion caused by manipulative management.

Political events in any country, but most obviously in recent years have seen people become almost tribal in accepting the beliefs of one 'side' or another. Often, people will prefer to say nothing than engage in honest conversation about their beliefs - for fear that they are questioned by the opposition. It is the fear of having to justify beliefs and convictions that can be scary.

It must have been like that for Xenophanes too - and I'm betting he learned fast that to be a thought-leader he couldn't alienate people in the way he might have done in his younger days. He certainly wasn't going to influence them by questioning their faith in the gods.

Bosses just don't get that distinction; they become emotional when challenged and are apt to use pejorative language when asking questions themselves - like demanding 'why' someone thinks one way or another. (BTW 'Why' isn't a great way to ask a question as it can be quite negative). It is similarly true for those who 'mock', versus those who 'quote science' in respect of divisive issues like climate change, genetically modified foods, deep long-term storage of nuclear waste. Both sides get caught up in their argument, forgetting that the goal is not to go into battle with the other 'side', but to achieve a new outcome.

The culture of Xenophanes' time made it harder than it needed be to express alternative beliefs and get past argument and into new outcomes. However, let's not fall into the trap two and a half millennia later by thinking we are in a better place. A place where there are more boss's than leader's organisations, causing them to get stuck in argument, rarely achieving the positive change that could otherwise be within their reach.

His Skills: Xenophanes was different. Unlike most of the philosophers I've included, he was a poet first and philosopher second.

Xenophanes was creative in the sense that he found ways to express ideas so that people understood and accepted them, he was empathetic to how people might hear his words and though supremely self-confident in expressing his own beliefs was strategic in landing a more complex message with his audiences. The attention he paid and the light he shone on words was as bright as the clarity he brought to the things he noticed around him; whether that be his observations about the behaviour of the 'gods', the imprints of long-dead animals in rock, or connections between sea, wind, clouds, and rivers. He was eloquent in rationalising the 'apparent' versus the 'true'.

His Beliefs: Perhaps it was because Xenophanes believed in moderation in all things, including alcohol and food that he lived to such an old age. It's worth remembering that this was a time when wealth was celebrated by excess, so being fat and drunk wasn't cause for other people to tut under their breath at your lack of self-control, to elicited admiring glances at your good fortune.

His beliefs were formed out of the polarity between one the one hand his conviction that our senses are flawed, and on the other that we should take notice of what 'is'. For example, he seems to be the first person recorded as collecting fossils and guessing that the world was considerably older and more interesting than most others of his time believed. He could see past the irrational explanations attributing everything to some god or another, and looked for links between things that were connected;

"...the sea is the source of water and wind, for without the great sea there would be no wind nor streams of rivers, nor rain water from on high; but the great sea is the begetter of clouds, winds, and rivers."

He had an open mind and was adamant that when piety becomes dogma, the cause is arrogance - another message that resonates as much in this century as it did in his. In the perhaps clumsy way I'm using the term 'boss', isn't it true that they tend to err toward established corporate dogma, and that even while they claim to have an open-mind they cling stubbornly to a world view that makes no sense?

For example, how many bosses insist they see their workers at their desks for 38 or 40 hours a week, despite numerous studies demonstrating that 'time at the desk' does not equal 'productivity'? The moderate, more pragmatic view of Xenophanes is exemplified by leaders who treat each person as an individual and hence shape their work expectancy to meet reward. An entrepreneur I know of, greatly influenced by the 'Four-hour work week'[xviii] agrees quarterly outputs and weekly reporting for each employee and claims his company's productivity is better than a traditional.

His Identity: I don't think he saw himself as a philosopher per-se, but as a simple poet - a man with a message using clever words to convey it. I sense that he was immensely confident but never arrogant, his confidence being drawn from the internalising of his own rationalisations. That's to say, if confidence is 'knowing that you know', then by thinking deeply about the observations he made and the rationalisations his thinking conferred, he must have ended up with plenty of certainty - that came out to the world in the form of his confident verse.

Such confidence meant he never had the need to defend anything, because he more than most would have accepted that the way in which he perceived the 'apparent' world around him was not just likely to be different to every other person alive, but pretty much guaranteed to be different.

After all, how many other thought-leaders were there in Colophon? Probably none. Therefore, if you read his words there's both an obvious confidence that his thinking is right, and a sense of his own acceptance that such confidence might only apply to himself alone - and everyone else was probably reading his stuff with a '"say what?" or at least a raised eyebrow.

Isn't it the mark of a true leader that she or he has that kind of confidence? It doesn't come from blind arrogance, hubris, or moronic stupidity, but from the deep thinking that has already tested their ideas and set them into the context of contemporary reality. A boss is inevitably too busy concerning his or herself with attempting to be 'right' by those they consider stakeholders - while the leader, like Xenophanes has no need for concern over such matters because they're already confident that what they are saying is right and true.

His Purpose: Of course, I can't know for sure, but I'm as convinced as I can be that Xenophanes was an entertainer at heart - don't ask me why, it's just a feeling. I think it may be because of the light-touch he brings to such a serious issue. Which is not to suggest that I think good leaders are also good entertainers (but it doesn't hurt if they are). What Xenophanes does demonstrate is that touch messages don't have to be delivered in a tough way.

He clearly was a deep thinker but didn't necessarily need to wrap himself in the rationality of philosophical logic to feel validated. He had way more confidence than that. It was enough for him to write a poem about a subject, make it entertaining, and then 'sell it' to his audience with conviction. He knew they'd take away more by 'buying' the message in his story than by ramming his challenging ideas down their collective throat.

In fact, his poems and stories are the only reason he's remembered. They are the only way his philosophy has been unearthed and understood. Even so, it's not clear if he felt *so* strongly about gods not being people that he made it his mission to 'change his world', but if it was, I think he got it right by spreading his word through the media of entertainment. If he was around today, he'd be entertaining with his ideas, just as much a social critic, just as moderate in his approach, but also just as clear that dogma and deity are most definitely not the same thing.

How might he be thought of by his employees, if he was a manager in today's business world?

I think they'd love him. Think about it - here's a guy who challenges the big issues and can see them from other perspectives. He's so clear about the 'desired outcomes' for the business that they cease to become goals in the traditional sense, and instead become something of a collective 'mission'. Each person has agreed with him how they best can serve that mission, and he in turn has agreed how much that contribution can be remunerated fairly - and an open and honest conversation takes place with each person to ensure completely that equanimity is reached.

Missions roll on, people develop at their own pace and making use of the best opportunities, and the relationship between employee and leaders, and between employee groups grows stronger with every collaboration. At the first sign of 'ego' or 'politics' polluting the positive atmosphere, Xenophanes engages with the people concerned, using stories and metaphor to separate their feelings from the situation - helping them to see things from a different perspective. When the people concerned can re-engage, he integrates them seamlessly back into the workforce, but, if because of some external influence beyond his control a person refuses to engage with their missions, they are sent on their way to find a workplace more suited to their needs. He is tough but very fair, and the workforce love him for his consistency; they know where they stand, know what to expect, and know that they are in an organisation devoid of stale 'dogma' of any kind.

Coaching questions he might ask: I imagine his questions would be bounded by the acceptance that every person's reality is their own, and that it is neither true nor untrue, but that whatever is apparent to them might be a cause for action. This is the position of a positive Leader who, unlike a Boss who assumes his own understanding of the world is the only one.

i. *"If all we accept as real is connected, then what is the source of your current desire?"*

ii. *"If your own 'younger-self' sits by you as you are now, what do you say to each other that is both surprising and helpful?"*

iii. *"Should another person fail to share your beliefs, if that no cause for you to fail to believe in them, what actions must you take?"*

iv. *"Thinking of the situation you wish improved; what might you do if the things that are obviously not apparent to others, but you perceive with clarity, are an illusion?"*

v. *"When you held a believe with conviction that you later found to be without foundation, what did you learn that might be useful today?"*

CHAPTER 11: #6 IS CHANGE CONSTANT?

ANAXIMENES OF MILETUS

His Claim to Fame: Okay, a pop quiz - who said -*nothing is constant but change?* Well, whoever else might be credited with it I'm reasonably certain that to his credit this guy, Anaximenes thought it first. Less creditable is that he was one of the original 'flat-earthers'.

Anaximenes takes us back to ancient Greece again, but this time on what now is the Turkish west coast. His teachers were the larger-than-life Thales and Anaximander. If his name is confusing because it's so like Anaximenes, it might help to think of him as 'Menes' and his teacher - the guy that was convinced we were once fish-people as 'Mander'. Mander = fish people, Menes = 'unlimited change'. You see, young Anaximenes had his own theory that differed completely from Thales and 'Menes'. He thought that everything we see, hear, and feel comes from something he called 'the unlimited'.

According to him, the unlimited was mist, vapour, and air- and that the world we know isn't a ball, after all what sense did that make, eh? No, he thought a ball shaped world was wrong. He reckoned the world was flat and floated on a cushion of air. His solid argument being that it was 'obvious'. Hm, well, maybe it felt that way to him - although he wasn't by any means the first flat-earther because even 'Mander' had been certain the earth was flat. It's worth remembering that was just as certain that the first 'men' were born out of the belly of a fish. Clearly, these chaps felt free to think and express themselves. In other cultures, at other times, a person claiming we are all descendants of fish might be locked up- or worse.

Meeting philosophers in Miletus, 'Mander' and 'Menes' must have been like waiting for a bus - there were none for ages then suddenly a line of three appear at once.

'Menes' got to his universal change theory because he could see that everything seemed to be made of water (or at least a liquid) - even rock was 'wet' when it came from a volcano, air was damp with water vapour, clouds were made of rain, and they were surrounded by water - and the thing he notices is that none of these things stayed still. They were all moving, constantly shifting from one from one state to another. This told me that the movement from each state of water was constant and hence his conclusion - dynamic change is constant. The only constant is 'change'.

By the way, as an aside I always thought all these ancient folks assumed the world was flat - how wrong was I? I was gobsmacked to learn that around 2300 years ago a guy called Eratosthenes not only knew the earth was a sphere but was also the first to calculate its circumference. Working out of the library of Alexandria, he used long poles over a fixed distance to perceive the curve of the earth in measurable terms. Clever, eh? Who knew? ...Okay, you probably did - but for anyone out there who paid as little attention at school as me I hope it was interesting.

His Environment: Like both Thales and 'Mander', Anaximenes probably enjoyed the pleasant sea air, rocky shoreline and good farming land in that region of Ionia. There had to be worse places to live at that time in history, (just ask Laozi). However, most prescient about his environment is the fact that he grew up in the company of philosophers. Growing up with Thales and 'Mander' as role models must have raised his own expectations of himself. I'm guessing that's where he got the confidence to put forward his own ideas. Let's not forget, the general population were living by a different, less rational code. They accepted without question that their fate was driven by 'gods'. They credited their successes to one god or another who were 'obviously' looking upon them favourably. Their failures weren't the fault of gods but were their own fault for doing something to displease them. No wonder people aspired to be gods - all the credit and none of the criticism.

However, the lack of any personal attribution for success must have made it challenging for people like Anaximenes to sell his idea 'it's up to us' to be either a success or failure depending on how we interact with this ever-changing 'liquid' world we are all part of. The idea was new. Perhaps it was so new that the power it contained wasn't ready to be recognised just yet. It's more likely that people of the time just scratched their heads and muttered under their breath that these philosophers were a bit bonkers.

His Culture: As a student of philosophy he will have been exposed to a wide range of ideas, engaging in all manner of discussions, and will have been expected to develop his own thoughts and conclusions. From the very practical and pragmatic stance of Thales, to the more creative and imaginative approach of 'Menes', there must have been high expectations of the young 'Mander'.

The term 'school' wasn't intended to suggest groups of young people in classrooms. The Miletus 'school' referred to a group of like-minded people being invited to learn from one another. Clearly, the more senior both in age and thinking would have held some rank, yet all were invited to contribute. Not much is known about how they went about that in Miletus - it could have been sat around in a field, under a tree, or over a mug of fermented grape juice and water.

His Skills: Not much is written about Anaximenes except to say that he was quite practical, and so took to there being a ration explanation for everything like the proverbial duck to water.

He must have been bright to have been invited to study with such men of note. It is not known if he travelled or had any additional skills in his thinking armoury, yet it's unlikely he would have come up with the idea that a flat earth floated on air, and then condenses into water before heating up to become floating air again - constantly moving. I somehow doubt that this would have come about without him having some reasonable education beforehand.

His Beliefs: Anaximenes had his feet firmly on the ground. He had bought-into the belief put forward by his teachers *that all we can see, touch, hear, and experience* had to have a rational explanation.

When noting that sometimes rainbows could be seen in moonlight, he didn't jump to the conclusion that it must be some 'mythical being' making it happen. Whereas others of his age from Miletus might have given credit to a 'god', 'Menes' did not. Or when he was describing the phosphorescent glow given off by an oar-blade breaking the water, he didn't attribute it to the gentle touch of a goddess. Instead, he rationalised that it must be the effect of the sun's rays on compacted air. This is what he is reported to have said about his theory; *"Air differs in essence in accordance with its rarity or density. When it is thinned it becomes fire, while when it is condensed it becomes wind, then cloud, when still more condensed it becomes water, then earth, then stones. Everything else comes from these."*

It may just be a theory, but it certainly also sounds like a solid belief. I'm honestly not sure if this meant he was creative or merely deluded, but it does demonstrate self-confidence, enthusiasm, and optimism, as well as a healthy dose of critical thinking.

His Identity: From everything I've read about Anaximenes I imagine him not only to be a good student of both Thales and Anaximander - able to reconcile the differences in their thinking and come up with his own take on things.

I also think it worth noting that by the time he came along, the Miletus 'school' of philosophy was already established. Just because he lived locally didn't mean he was a shoe-in. There must have been plenty of students competing to be a recognised philosopher 'in their own right'. Yet, only *his* name is remembered, not that of a contemporary. Only he is celebrated as the third in what became known as the *Miletus philosophical tradition*. Like all 'next generations', they strive to be a better version of the one that went before. I can imagine his identity in that way - a sort of Jean-Luke Picard to Thales' Captain Kirk, and Anaximander's Spock.

His Purpose: Anaximenes not only considered air, vapour & water as making up of everything, but also that it makes up the 'soul'. It follows that if life comes from vapour, and that the soul is also formed of vapour, then constant change between air, water and earth must mean that the vapour of the soul must also be moving too. It's likely to have occurred to him that changes to a person might be caused by the interaction of their soul vapour with the world.

I'm only guessing, but if he truly did make this connection then it's also a fair guess that his purpose might have been to share this with the world. He might have hoped that this knowledge might cause people to treat each other differently - and better. The logical conclusion that 'choice' probably causes change in the world is powerful. It would have caused his purpose to be about encouraging people to think more deeply and more rationally.

His challenge was that if people were apt to blame or thank a 'god' for everything that happened to them' then it'd be very difficult to encourage self-direction. After all, what's the point of being a self-starter if some god has already decided what's going to happen to you? I imagine his 'explanations' were to kick-start a feeling of personal control and direction; *'If I have a soul and come from air, then I might influence what kind of soul I develop and what sort of water or earth I become'.* It may sound like a long-shot, but he must have been taken seriously or we wouldn't know about him today - his name lives on.

How might he be thought of by his employees, if he was a manager in today's business world?

I think he's the kind of leader that believes with absolute certainty there's a cause for everything that happens. His naturally reflective style might make him appear a little less inspirational than other leaders, but what he lacks in rah-rah he more than makes up for with logical thinking and the strength to avoid jumping to conclusions.

His own tendency to accept anything as a potential 'cause' for any 'effect' has made him open to the wild and whacky suggestions that sometimes come from the workplace. Unlike the sort of boss who sneers at unusual ideas or dismisses suggestions from people they don't consider qualified to comment, he listens to everyone. As a result, they are more confident in coming forward knowing that they won't be ridiculed no matter how outlandish or unusual their idea. Fortunately, his logical approach means that 'wrong' input is set aside quickly and without fuss or criticism. He makes it clear that without gathering up many possibilities it's more difficult to filter them down to something useful.

His engaging style supports both confidence and team work from the workforce. As the foundation of his belief is that everyone is ultimately responsible for their own outcomes in life, he is not afraid to ask searching questions of his team. He is politely challenging and simultaneously motivating by seeking the personal control each person must improve their own situation - and that of the team around them.

Coaching questions he might ask: His personal mantra of change being constant, resonates with me loud and clear today. So, his questions come from the natural curiosity about what that change might mean in a practical sense.

This translates very well for any contemporary business leader.

i.   *"How might you construct an understanding of your circumstances if you were to replace what you had believed to be its foundation, with something new?"*

ii.   *"If water turns to steam when the energy of heat is applied, what energy must you apply to your circumstances that will help them change?"*

iii. *"What else is constant in your life as well as change?"*

iv.   *"When you look up and see the ever-changing shape of clouds in the sky, how does your lack of certainty about what shape comes next fail to prevent you from enjoying the day?"*

v.   *"When you think about the most surprising changes you've been through in your life, what was it about them that might help you now?"*

vi.   *"Where have you found your certainty about this situation, and assumed it to be true?"*

CHAPTER 12: #7 UNCOMMON, COMMON SENSE

PARMENIDES

His Claim to Fame: He is the 'father of metaphysics', it was he who formulated the 'dark cloud of deductive reasoning' and left us with the evergreen statement -*'Opinion is no substitute for fact'*. Not so evergreen was his contention that the world is a squiggly, bubbly, blob. Yes, it's not a typo - a blob.

Let me explain how he got to 'blob' - just imagine a world where everyone holds a belief about how 'things' work, but you have a different idea. *Okay, I get that I may have described you right now - which is a good reason to be looking back and realising how little has really changed.* Whether then or now, people can allow their assumptions to become real. Then they defend those assumptions *as if they were facts*. How any bosses do you know like that - people who have made their mind up about the way 'their world' must work? Have you noticed how they refuse to entertain anything else, even if it becomes clear to everyone but themselves that they're as mad as a box of frogs?

How he got to a 'blob' - Parmenides was a brave soul who wanted to test and challenge everything. Metaphorically, he stood up when everyone else was sitting down, turned left when all his mates 'knew' that he should be turning right, and was not going to let a silly little thing like everyone else telling him was wrong stop him from asking questions. He didn't do it to be bloody-minded, but because he didn't want to be fooled into accepting something that may not be true. Great leaders are like that - they find a thread and keep pulling at it with questions until it either confirms their suspicions or convinces them to trust what others might believe.

We are still in Greek territory with Parmenides, and he's known as their father of metaphysics because he's probably the first person to seriously enquire into the nature of... nature - and this is where he got the idea of an ever-changing blob from. His thinking is a natural extension from Thales, 'Mander', and 'Menes' - Thales wanted to know how the world fitted together and what it might be made of, as did the other two with their versions of that make up. Parmenides extended that thinking because he accepted that while they had observations about what made up the world, he wanted to know where the things that made it up came from in the first place. He went further than anyone before by asking this, apparently unanswerable question. He asked questions about what controls things it if it isn't the 'gods', and what might it all mean to us mere mortals if the gods weren't real? Anaximenes might have nudged thinking in the direction of the 'power of personal influence', but it was Parmenides who took the bull by the horns and called it out.

You've got to love his thinking. If anyone was way, way ahead of his time it was Parmenides, because his answer to it all was simple -"*all those things you see, feel and hear, they're not real*". He might not have used those exact words, but I'm sure you get the idea.

He wasn't wrapping this in cotton wool, he was telling anyone who'd listen that their senses might not be making sense. He'd say something like, it's all just an illusion, nothing lives or dies, and that 'reality' (if it can be called such a thing) is in fact something that remains motionless and changeless for all eternity. He'd say that it's us who are creating all the movement and all the change, but that the 'thing' we are all in and part of stays as it is.

That all sounds a bit weird, eh? He tried to explain this weirdness by saying that everything we experience is a paradox. He reckoned life is a paradox because the human 'experience' is both tangible to a person in the moment, but at the same time comes out of *nothingness* - and therefore by its very nature is intangible. He was close to articulating the idea that it was *the person* that caused his or her reality to be as *they perceived it*, and not some fixed 'thing' that they were merely observing.

Fast forward to a twenty-first century school science class where it's common knowledge that the *intention* of the experimenter has a tangible effect on the *outcome* of a quantum level experiment. Which is perhaps why the musings of Parmenides don't feel too strange today. However, what is remarkable is that this was an awful long time ago - long before the renaissance and the scientific revolution, from which I had in my ignorance imagined all these new theories had begun.

The truth is, over the past few years while I've been researching for this book, I've come to realise how much I didn't know. Maybe it's just me, but I had no idea these guys had come up with such great thinking so long ago. Just this morning I stopped by our office and spent a little time chatting with the admin team. I started to tell them a few of the stories I'd found about these long-forgotten thinking-hero's and they were as amazed as me that the results of their thinking are as applicable now as they ever were. Julie, (a qualified coach in her own right as well as being the stalwart of head-quarters) insightfully noted that *"these are things that society has forgotten we already knew..."* She is so right.

Anyway, back to Parmenides and his application of almost three millennia old logic to the world around us. The logic aspect is worth noting because he's also remembered as introducing something known as the **'dark cloud of deductive reasoning'.**

Imagine him trying to explain his ideas to every-day people in the market square, all busily going about their business of trading bread, olives and local goodies. It's hardly likely he'd start pointing at a loaf and cry out *"Afto den einai pragmatiko, einai mono i antilipsisas"*- which, according to Google translate means "That's not real, it's just your perception". To make sense of what he was saying he had no choice but to start with basic logic and work from there.

He attempted to be as straightforward with his explanations as he could, and then put forward clear arguments to support his off-beat conclusions. Unfortunately, I'm not sure he did such a great job. Maybe he if he'd started with something catchy like; *'If you could have anything you wanted, would you like to know how to get it?'*... and then incorporate his theories into a pitch for people to accept that if everything is an illusion then they had at least a chance at changing it.

Of course, he would have had to add the rider that he didn't really *know how* to make those changes...yet, but at least he might have held his audiences for a little longer than he did. Having tried to pick my way through some of what he said I'm sort of amazed anyone took notice at all. Goodness knows what might have happened if he'd tried to be clever instead of making it simple, because his simplest explanations still sound cryptic to me.

You decide - If this is simple,....then so am I! How about this one;"*We cannot speak of what is not*". Yup, that would have stopped me in my olive-buying tracks if I heard it in the market square... not. Of course, with the benefit of 20-20 hindsight we can deduce he means - what we see, hear, and feel may appear real but cannot be trusted. He was trying to convey that science, using deductive reasoning is a far better route to understanding the world than simply taking things at face value and jumping to conclusions. As a thought-leader this was breakthrough stuff - and any successful leader today knows that it's naive to jump to conclusions without considering as much as there is possible to consider. Rubbishy bosses jump to conclusions - normally by blaming people for things that aren't really their fault, then compounding their rubbish-ness by holding unfair grudges based on wrong-thinking.

But still, try as he might his approach wasn't catchy. Yet, as cryptic and misunderstood as he might have been by most people of his day, his methodology, that of looking for indirect proof - '*reducto ad absurdum*' is still with us today, (even if it does sound like a spell from Hogwarts[xix]).

The big deal about deductive reasoning stemmed from people before him speaking of 'things' coming into the world out of nothing. To Parmenides that didn't make sense. How could something come from nothing? The foundation of his thinking was that for something to appear it must have started as something else- something that already existed, even if we can't perceive it. The fact that we can't see it was irrelevant as far as he was concerned. See it or not, 'it' had to be there.

What that's left us with is the concept of thinking about things rationally and reasoning, - even if means ignoring what appears 'obvious'.

His Environment: Parmenides was held in high esteem by the people of his home in southern Italy, what was then the Greek colony of Elea. He had much sought-after skills as a legislator. Indeed, so clear and logical was his legislation on their behalf, that the people of the colony ascribed their prosperity and their wealth to him and his work at organising their laws.

This city he called home was founded when he was just five years old by Phocaean Greek refugees; Phocaea being the ancient name for Foca- a city in northern Anatolia in Turkey and was the mother-city of several Greek colonies who fled looking for a new home rather than be subdued by a Persian invasion. They settled on the now Italian coast and built their new environment from scratch. It's likely that the rolling green hills, clear blue skies, and olive trees were as an attractive place to live as they are today. Certainly, the shift in circumstance from being threatened by foreign invaders to living under their own newly constructed rules in safety and relative security, must have buoyed the spirits of those who remembered how it used to be back on the near-edges of the Asian continent.

There's little evidence of what it was like to live there, and Parmenides left only one piece of writing in the form of a poem, nattily entitled 'On Truth' (or sometimes translated as 'on nature'). However, the fact that he felt able to write a long poem reflecting on the things around him, as opposed to writing about anything more urgent suggests the environment was calm and provided the space for a deep thinker like him.

His Culture: Regardless of the expectations of his peers, I imagine that it's probably fair to say Parmenides established his own behaviour expectations. After all, he did write the laws for the city and did formalised what became known as the 'School of Elea'. His rules, his game.

The poem he wrote features a young man on a cosmic journey in search of enlightenment, who learns on this 'spiritual' journey how to ask better questions, snappily referred to as epistemic guidelines of enquiry - personally, I think asking better questions is easier to handle. It's apparent that he knew Thales quite well, and that he might have been somewhat in the shadow of the big-guy. While every story featuring Thales paints him as an extrovert with plenty to say, I get the impression that their culture might not have had space for two Thales's, which will have meant Parmenides must have found his own identity and created his own means of differentiation from the man he paints as being in the limelight.

How amazing must it have been to live in a small community that was home to forward thinking larger-than-life characters like Parmenides. People like him created a culture of breakthrough thinking, using poems to communicate big ideas, and capturing audiences with their readings in the city square. Having said that, it's all too easy to for me to see the world of guys like him through rose-tinted glasses; I can mentally conjure up a wonderful sunny day, green rolling hills, and the crashing waves of the ocean and imagine it as a holiday paradise. However, this was long before the dawn of the local convenience store, shopping online, or weekly trips to the supermarket. The reality for them must have been tough - a battle to simply survive, never mind ponder the minutiae of the universe. All of which does makes me wonder how well people like him were really received by the everyday folk. People who were getting up at the crack of dawn to milk their goat before breakfast, grinding their own oats, and starting a fire from scratch each time they wanted to cook anything. Were these an audience ready to listen? Perhaps not.

So, maybe these deep thinkers were as removed from their reality as our deep thinkers might be today. Perhaps in hundreds or thousands of years the future versions of you and me won't be paying attention to the moronic tweets of power-hungry politicians or fame-greedy reality 'stars' but will be reading something else by someone else entirely. I certainly hope so. Therefore, he must have believed his behaviour to be consistent with some aspect of that culture, or he would not have stood in the market square gathering folk about him and telling his stories of the world as an ever-changing blob. He would not have been encouraging people to rejoice in the fact that as something cannot emerge from nothing nor disappear into nothingness, their life now is only a reflection of part of their existence.

Maybe his deductive reasoning was as appealing in its own way as 'trusting in the gods' - after all, they didn't say that life was eternal, but he did. That must have been a plus for him. What more motivation could an ordinary person have but to know that the efforts they made now would continue to bear fruit for as long as creation itself?

Hm... come to think of it, I'm sure I've seen people who might be considered reincarnations of Parmenides saying something similar at the top of their voice outside of shopping centres. I guess what goes around, comes around.

His Skills: Parmenides must have been something of a charismatic character, good at building relationships -I say that because he managed to gather around him a group of other philosophers who wanted to learn from him.

I sense that he became a go-to guy for deep thinking. I guess he could see things from their perspective, then use his confidence and conviction to get them 'on board' with his ideas. The poem, 'on truth' is both logically presented and is certainly deep - very deep. I take from what I've learned about him that he was one of those *special people* who could entertain new ideas without feeling threatened. What I mean by that is that most of us like familiarity, don't we? New thinking that doesn't fit in any of our existing mental 'boxes' can feel strange. So, what do you do with things that don't make sense? In Parmenides case he quite literally argued that things don't make sense and don't have little mental boxes already. He said that it was in fact quite natural for them to not make sense because senses are an illusion.

If he'd had a little more creativity as well as solid logic, he might have made his point more easily. Instead he asked himself questions like *'what really exists if everything I see, hear, feel, and am aware of is an illusion?'* The answer he came up with in Greek is the word *'Esti'*. A literal meaning for Esti is 'is-ness' or 'being'...or it can mean 'they are'. Saying what really exists is not the things you can see but 'Esti', their 'is-ness', must have been as helpful as a chocolate fireguard. I can't imagine that anyone would have understood it, except maybe his philosophy followers.

I think this struggle with communicating new ideas as a thought-leader is something we still see in contemporary leadership. What makes Parmenides stand out is that he didn't shy away from trying to communicate his ideas.

The thing about leaders who don't give up on engaging their followers is that they do end up getting through. If they're like Parmenides - respected for a specific skill and willing to gamble their credibility by sticking with their message until (at least some) people start to get it, then the positive difference they make is lasting. However, if they are more 'boss' like then the notion of lasting change becomes irrelevant as they engage themselves with trying to superficially 'win' - whatever that might mean. Leaders with a Parmenides-like desire for answers are the opposite of the bosses you simply won't find anywhere near the 'deep end'.

His Beliefs: His was as much a journey of self-development as it was a search for better answers. The passing of a millennia or two hasn't changed human nature - people reject what they can't understand, and they get angry or frustrated when someone tells them 'things' they believe are wrong - even when faced with solid, scientific, and/or well-researched evidence. If you want to test that theory, try selling 'Dawkins' in an evangelical crystal cathedral and see what manner of 'spiritual' welcome greets you. (Not recommended by the way).

Describing the world that people could clearly see, touch and feel as nothing but an "ever changing blob" was hardly likely to gain much traction. Neither would a description of nature as *'the one'* held in a perfect sphere make sense to anyone but fellow mathematicians who might have grasped what he meant. I'm sure he knew what he meant by 'the one', but as for the rest of us - not so much. This was probably because the explanation for his journey was kind of freaky - as in what turns out to be an autobiographical poem his insights were given to him by a 'goddess'. This goddess took him for a chariot ride in the clouds and explained 'it' (his theory of the world) to him. As a believable explanation it didn't land so well. It was unlikely to have helped his credibility with the general population -unless of course he was invoking the god-thing with already committed believers. Sort of, if the gods explained his ideas then they must be true?

The fact that he wrote his poem in the same pace and style as Homer says two things about him; firstly, he was skilled enough to do it, and secondly that it meant something profound to him by making that effort. Now, whether it meant *'this is the best way for me to get my message across'*, or *'this is an epic story like Homer's so pay attention'*, or something else entirely, we will never know. However, my money is on the Homer comparison. I can't see why he'd concoct this story of himself as a young man being taken on a weird chariot ride with a goddess who tells him all this stuff if he didn't want people to get involved with it as they would with any other epic-style poem. It speaks to his beliefs about himself particularly if his lack of 'practical creativity'. If he'd been more in tune with ways to creatively imagine ways to connect the dots in the minds of other people, he could have used a metaphor to explain his point. Trying to explain how something could not come from nothing or be perceived as something it is not - isn't easy, even with the help of a goddess.

His Identity: There was no doubt, at least in my mind that he saw himself as a person whose role in society was to invest his time in the search for wisdom. The fact that others came to join him supports the notion that he was probably good at it. He was comfortable taking the lead in a discussion and asking tough questions that others either simply didn't think to ask or were fearful of the answer. When he posed his deep-thinking questions, he didn't shy away from arguing his point logically until the logic ran out. That was the whole point of rational argument, but can you imagine what it must have been like to talk to this guy?

I picture him as the person who 'needs' to be right - you must know the sort of person I mean?... you know, the one that no matter the subject or the context always puts themselves forward as knowing the answer. Can you imagine… *Me: "Oh, I think it might be a nice day tomorrow"* **Parmenides**: *"It will be as today but only seem different, and therefore not better"* **Me:** *"Whatever you say Mr P, have a good evening"* **Parmenides**: *"My evening is no different from my day, it only appears so because our senses deceive. Esti is all there is"* **Me:** *"Whatever dude, …I'm off down the Taverna"*

His Purpose: As much as I'd like to claim he was on a mission to send the world on a 'downer', I don't really think that's where his mind was at. The *'life is everlasting because it's just a blob'* might not have been the most eloquent description of what would one day possibly contribute to the laws of thermodynamics[xx], or become the law of Conservation of Energy - not as big a stretch as you might think as Parmenides considered our world a closed system and so everything in it must remain constant, even if it takes many forms.

It's clear to me that he saw his purpose as using the power of reason to educate, support people in having more control over their lives, and be the better for it.

How might he be thought of by his employees, if he was a manager in today's business world?

He's the kind of leader people must learn to love. At first meeting it might have felt that he was unnecessarily challenging, but after a while it was obvious that all he wanted to do was to remove unnecessary wrapping around things we might otherwise take for granted as being 'immovable' or 'unchanging'. The people with whom he works closest have learned to adopt his approach and have developed a depth of thinking themselves that helps in every aspect of life.

He's long been forgiven for any clumsiness in the way he asks and answers questions. The fact that he doesn't become frustrated himself when others struggle to understand the ´point´ he's trying to make means that people around him don't feel stressed - after a while they find a way together to express what inevitably is a unique and new viewpoint on an old problem. His way be being naturally encourages teamwork because there's always someone there to chip in creatively with ways to take his ideas forward.

If you asked any of his people to describe him in one or two words, they'd say things like 'intense', 'quirky', 'powerful', 'brilliant'. He's a leader that embraces rationality without the need to be superior about it. The fact that he has a higher purpose than trying to prove himself 'right' makes him a true leader and never just a boss.

Coaching questions he might ask: His conviction that opinion is no substitute for the truth had to shape the questions he'd ask if he'd been a coaching-leader in our time. If everything that is, is - and anything that 'is not' and therefore, outside of human understanding, his questions would be focused on what you know, but might not be as aware of as you could be.

    i.   *"How, being very specific, do you know that what you have assumed is true, is indeed certain?"*

    ii.   *"If you had to write your own set of laws that caused you to be the best that you could be, where might you start?"*

    iii.   *"If you were a detective in your own story, what is worthy of further investigation?"*

    iv.   *"If your life so far has been a path, where do you think it might one day be leading?"*

    v.   *"When you think of a time you allowed 'opinion' to become confused with 'fact' it makes you feel a certain, so how might remembering that feeling helpful to you now?"*

vi.   *"When you think of the time you surprised yourself the most, what did you do that gave you the confidence to do it?"*

CHAPTER 13: #8 IGNORANCE, THE SOURCE OF WISDOM

CONFUCIUS

His Claim to Fame: A heads up here before I start on Confucius; clearly, it's possible to write a whole book on this guy's claims to fame, just like I could have done for the Buddha and a few other big names in philosophy, but that's not the point of this book. Therefore, I'm just picking out some of the juicy bits of his life and times to illustrate what questions he might ask if he was around today as a leader.

Confucius, like a great artist long dead, might be surprised to discover the thought-leading impact he made. Not that he was an artist, just that he his work wasn't properly valued until he was dead. His legacy of thought and sayings have stood the test of time and for more than 1000 years were the foundation of Chinese social norms. Sadly, Confucius didn't live to see the seeds of his thinking take root and blossom into the social norms of the dynasties to follow.

Scholars reckon he made more impact than any other philosopher. I'll leave that up to you to decide if it's true, but certainly we can all agree that in the world of philosophy there are probably as many people who can quote Confucius as anyone else; Descartes catchy *"I think therefore I am"* might win as the single most known phrase, but I bet the ten sayings I'm going to quote here will be as, if not more familiar. Probably my favourite is his apparent twist on the Christian 'golden rule'. Of course, because chronologically he came first his rule was ahead of the Christians although even having grown up as a Church of England Choral-Scholar I didn't know that, and so I'm guessing I'm not alone. Here's what Confucius said;

"Do not do unto others what you do not want done to you"

I'll come back to it again, but for now it's worth recognising at least one distinction between this and the more familiar 'do' unto others as you'd wish done to you may sound subtle, but while the Christian version is a suggestion, Confucius puts it more like a self-serving warning - it sort of says if you want to avoid pain yourself then don't put pain out there in the first place.

There's even more to this than meets the eye, which is the best way to think about the value Confucius added to philosophy; his thinking was deeper than most people gave him credit for, his sayings and aphorisms needed to be studied to be understood, and he was much more than any religious proponent with a dogma to 'sell' - he was much, much more.

His Environment: One of the things I love about Confucius is that he's proof that to make a great impact on the world as a thought-leader you don't have to look like Brad Pitt.

If Thales looked like a Greek god - standing tall and proud with chiselled, handsome features - then poor 'Kong Zi' (Confucius as we know him in the West), was his polar-opposite. He was hunched over, born with a big lump on his forehead, and had bulging eyes. He was most definitely not what you'd call a good-looking man. His unfortunate genetics may have resulted from the fact that his ageing father, desperate to sire a male offspring had sought out a peasant girl barely out of her childhood to bear him a child. At just sixteen she became pregnant by the seventy-odd year old, and to his great delight bore him a son.

While dad might have been pleased, unfortunately the rest of the paternal, rather well-to-do family were not so impressed. This became clear because when dad passed away little Confucius was still a child in arms, but the family disowned both him and his mum. They wanted nothing to do with either mum or child. Sadly, this meant the very young single mum had to make it on her own to both protect and bring up the boy. The strain of this obviously took its toll, and she died while still a young woman, leaving the boy who would one day be known the world over as 'Confucius' to fend for himself.

His Culture: This was a tough time to be fending for yourself in China. It was in a mess - lasting dynasties had come and gone, leaving now smaller territories without formal government, and at the mercy of local warlords seizing power. The world that Confucius was born into must have been the inspiration for some of his most well-known sayings. Goodness knows, the people of that time must have been ready for some inspiration.

Unlike his counterpart over in India, I don't see Confucius sat under a tree waiting for enlightenment to come his way. I'm certain that he too believed in meditation, but he also believed that a man *must stay alive* to mediate for one more day! In his situation - wandering around the war-torn states of ancient China, staying alive wasn't so easy. I can only wonder at how many atrocities he must have witnessed or heard about to have come up *with "Do not unto others what you yourself do not desire"*. No sir, that one didn't pop into his head in a moment of clarity, it sounds more like a plea than the doctrine for life it would later become.

His Skills: Confucius started from the premise that for people to behave in ways that serve themselves and others they needed a shove. That they weren't going to do it on their own was self-evident, but whether he thought people were fundamentally good given the chance, or evil if left to their own devices isn't clear.

Later, those who followed in his footsteps and practiced his philosophy would have very firm views about the fundamental nature of human beings, but for now it was enough that they buy into a set of 'rules for life'.

His skill was to combine the pragmatic with imagination. He firmly believed that once a person understood their 'place' in the big scheme of things, that person can be free to become someone of virtue.

His pragmatic instincts may have come about as a matter of necessity; not being able to land a job in government when you know in your bones that it's what you're best suited to do must have hurt and having to move around the country simply to survive can't have been easy. Yet, he had the grit to do whatever he had to, he kept on preaching the same message even though he didn't appear to be getting anywhere and went to his death without a hint that he'd become one of the greatest names in philosophy.

Wherever he went, people warmed to his message - and once they'd gotten over the bulging eyes, disfigured lumpy back, and generally ugly visage they appeared to warm to him. Therefore, it's self-evident that he must have been

161

good at building rapport, and good at keeping the interest of people listening to his views on the best way to live their life - without peeing them off, overtly challenging their beliefs, or coming on too strong.

He wrote enough for him to be remembered and for his 'rules' to be understood, but unlike some of his Greek counterparts there are no wordy treatises to wade through and interpret. His messages were clear, concise, and simple;

"Know your place, understand your responsibilities, and live the best life possible within those circumstances".

His Beliefs: I've already mentioned twice his plea to 'do not impose on others what you yourself do not desire'. What he is suggesting is that people consciously think about good actions before responding in the moment.

To unwrap his belief about this 'Do to others as you would have them do to you'[xxi] - adopted by Christians as something of a 'Golden Rule'. The difference is subtle but important; the Christian version is action-oriented, suggesting that you think in the moment. Confucius however reflects his pragmatic approach to everything - recognising that we all have the temptation to inflict our opinions on other people but don't like it when they do it to us. Ain't that the truth, eh? Right here is the difference between an effective leader and a rubbish boss - the boss expects people to accept their opinions and do as they say simply because they are the 'boss'. The good leader acts with well-considered intent - they've thought about it and will focus first on a person's *desire* only then will they talk about what to *do* about it. Confucius was the first to clarify one of the foundations of behavioural change - *you can't get someone to change unless you help them find a way to want to change.*

So, he's telling us to recognise and change what would likely happen if we didn't think about it **before** we get involved in any action. Which is why, sadly, in practice the Christian golden rule has little bite, it's suggesting we are motivated toward pleasure - to do the 'right' thing. Confucius knew that a desire to do the right thing isn't universal, and that people respond to emotion. He was smart because he recognised people tread a path that's guided by the avoidance of pain.

There's no way of knowing if he'd realised that people are *motivated* by emotion, and that their true response in the moment is not to move away from pain toward pleasure, but to move away from *more pain to less pain*. I think he'd come to know from his own experience that life is less than fair, not necessarily logical, and far less pleasant than people would like it to be. His life was difficult, and he could see that the lives around him were also fraught with pain; hence, the notion that actions are always a balance between less pain and more pain must have made sense.

He didn't want people to live a totally spontaneous life, reacting with emotion to whatever felt okay in the moment - and 'trying' to do the best they could, if it would simply lead them to more pain along that road. He saw all around him that without 'structure' and 'thinking ahead' the world could quickly turn from something good into a box of snot (my words not his).

Given the balance between pain and more pain, I think all he had to do was to ask a better question, bring it to a person's attention - and they would choose what to do without further discussion. It's probably why his strict adherence to *ways of being* might not have been all that pleasurable, but they probably did lead to less pain.

Don't forget, during his life the world he knew had been plunged into a war that must have seemed never ending. Therefore, the first of his rules for a *'constant relationship'* applied to the Sovereign - no matter how long a person would maintain that role, and without judgement as to their appropriateness in that role.

Confucius kept things simple with straightforward rules:

Firstly, by saying that the Sovereign had a duty to rule their subjects well and take care of them, and in return the subjects had a duty to the Sovereign to obey and respect him. Secondly, at a more personal level he took the same approach to responsibility by saying that the father has a duty to take care of the son, then for the son to obey the father. Next, the husband was to take care of his wife *(don't go there about women's lib because Confucius's words make no sense to us today and it'd be easy to condemn him as a chauvinist pig - but I think we should cut him some slack and agree that he was only reflecting the views of his time, eh?)* He continued that the wife should obey her husband. After that, the elder brother must look after the younger and the sibling must obey his elder - and for brother I think it's reasonable for us to assume it also apples to sisters. Finally, he said for friends to take care of each other, and to listen to each other.

I've paraphrased of course, and don't claim to be a Confucian Scholar but hopefully I've captured the gist of what he believed would make a practical and pragmatic improvement to the lives of the people in China at that time. Clearly, he was right, because after his death his way of thinking was accepted as guiding principles. For a time, his rules were law, and even today are considered full of great wisdom, but it's sad that he went to his grave believing his life's work to have failed.

I imagine Confucius might have died a much happier man if he had known with internal certainty that one day destiny would force his ideas to the forefront of people's minds, simply because the ideas were good, useful, and made a positive difference to the otherwise turbulent lives of the time.

His Identity: Did Confucius see himself as a prophet, or perhaps a world-leader in waiting? I don't think so - neither sound right to me. I think it's much more likely he held himself to the standards of a teacher - one who didn't care what class you came from, or even if you could afford to pay for his wisdom, but simply someone who saw himself as a person with something to share.

He was absolutely a thought-leader, but not an actual leader of people, or a man born into wealth and privilege, but he did do whatever he could to lead by example. He put morality before all else and understood the true power of restraint. He also spoke of meditating to gain clarity - probably the closest approach to the *'mindfulness meditation'* movement that's popular today.

Recently, I caught an episode of the US 'Today Show' with Trevor Noah interviewing ABC News anchor Dan Harris. The relevance to Confucius is that Dan suffered a panic attack in 2004 live on air, something that was watched by millions. Rather than allowing it to sink his career Dan has used the experience to write two books on mindfulness -

his latest for sceptical people who think meditation might only be for those with a less pragmatic approach to life. Confucius said that *the more a man meditates on good thoughts, the better his world and the world at large.* Don't get me wrong, I'm not suggesting Dan Harris is the new Confucius, merely that I think the great man would approve of Dan's approach to facing up to life and share the fact that even a minute of two of meditation in a busy day can do something to make life better - even if it's only a little bit better.

Confucius was apt to say that all good things are difficult to achieve and bad things much easier to get. If that's all you knew about the man it'd be fair to think of him as a miserable so and so. However, I don't see him as a misery at all - and I don't think that's how he saw himself. It's not miserable to seek respectfulness, tolerance, trustworthiness, quick-witted ness, diligence, and generosity in people. He had a name for the achievement of these six attributes. He called it *'Ren'*, and that the achievement of Ren led to naturally living by 4 principles. The principles of loyalty, fidelity, ritual propriety, and reciprocity. Each of them is sincere and honourable - and ultimately positive. It'd be hard to be a miserable or downbeat person when making a point of telling everyone who'd listen that they should *"never be content with doing nothing"* whatever their circumstances.

He sounds like a pretty positive dude to me. I think I would have liked him a lot.

His Purpose: He wanted, apparently more than just about anything for his way of thinking to be adopted by someone

- anyone, so long as they had some power to influence people.

His wandering from region to region might not have been only to find work, but a personal quest to be heard- not simply paid for doing some administrative task for one warlord or another. It must have been as frustrating as heck to have a head full of fantastic ideas that had the potential to make a difficult world a better place.

It must have been as frustrating as heck to have those great ideas and not have anyone listening to them or taking them seriously. It may sound odd to say this now, but I see him as someone ahead of his time. Not a prophet, but a good solid forward thinker - a person who could see how connections between people worked, and how they could be strengthened. I believe he might have eventually concluded his life's purpose was to wake people up to the stark reality of life *as it is*, not as they might like it to be. A student asked Confucius if there was a single word he should live by – he wanted to know if perhaps a word that would always provide him with guidance and truth? Confucius gave it some thought, and then replied with the word ´*Chu*´ - which roughly translates as forbearance, tolerance, or self-control.

He wrote many of his arguments cryptically so that people would have to think more deeply about what he was saying and what he was getting at. Looking back, I don't think he would recognise the imagery and positioning the world afforded him after his death. It's doubtful he'd recognise himself as a thought-leader followed by millions. he certainly wasn't while he was alive.

Ultimately his message was simple *"What you know, you know; what you don't know, you don't know, - and THAT is wisdom"*. Finally, it'd be remiss of me if I didn't include his ten most popular and simple lessons for life. So, here you go:

1. *Everything has beauty but not everyone sees it*
2. *Our greatest glory is not in never falling but rising every time we fall.*
3. *Learning without thought is labour lost; thought without learning is perilous*
4. *When you know a thing, to hold that you know it; and when you do not know a thing, to allow that you do not know it - this is knowledge*
5. *I hear, and I forget. I see, and I remember. I do, and I understand.*
6. *If I am walking with two other men, each of them will serve as my teacher. I will pick out the good points of the one and imitate them, and the bad points of the other to correct them in myself.*
7. *Never contract friendship with a man that is not better than yourself.*
8. *It does not matter how slowly you go if you do not stop.*
9. *When it is obvious the goals cannot be reached, do not adjust the goals, adjust the action steps.*
10. *Wherever you go, go with all your heart.*

How might he be thought of by his employees, if he was a manager in today's business world?

There's no doubt he's dispelled any notion that looks are related to becoming a successful leader! His rules are not something made up to simply keep order and discipline in the organisation, but rather a set of beliefs he lives by. He genuinely does see the best in everyone, but isn't blind to their weaknesses - he simply prefers to focus on their strengths, and how to use them within a structure he believes in.

His team know that success is important, hence his positive outlook isn't an excuse to fail - but know too that if a problem causes them to slip up, their first response must be to get up again as quickly as possible. They know they're expected to apply fresh thinking to every challenge and to learn not only from their own mistakes, but also the mistakes of others. There is a powerful feeling of certainty in a leader who supports a person when they stand up for 'what they know they know', and for being able to ask for support and be honest when they don't know.

He's a leader who steps up and leads by example, constantly seeking out new experiences by learning from the best in others, constantly moving forward towards his goals, and constantly adjusting his direction whenever necessary.

Coaching questions he might ask: There's only one way I can imagine stepping into the great man's robes, and that's to use his life-lessons to shape his questions. If he was Leader these are the kind of things he'd ask.

i. *"What could possibly be good, an opportunity, or a chance for you to evaluate the positive in an otherwise dark situation?*
ii. *"When have others believed you to have failed, but what you were really doing was preparing a different approach to succeed?"*

iii. *"What do you know for certain, and what have you learned about dealing with this kind of situation successfully in your past?"*

iv. *"What have you assumed, jumped to a premature conclusion about, or guessed that might prevent you from making the optimal decision?"*

v. *"What words might elude you now, but when memories and experiences are accessed begin to help you think of what best to say next?"*

vi. *"When you think about this situation, who do you know that would screw this up, and who comes to mind that'd handle themselves well... and what do you want to learn from each?"*

vii. *"If you could choose someone that you know or have known to be your mentor, what's stopping you from asking?"*

viii. *"What are you doing today, - right now, and what comes after right now... that's taking you closer to your goal?"*

ix. *"What have you given up on because you started to believe you'd never get there... and what would you start to do if you knew with absolute certainty that one day it might be achieved, but that by stopping now you rob yourself of that chance?"*

x. *"If you set aside the specifics of this situation and just reflect on 'who' you are; what do you believe about yourself and about the way things ought to be that will cause you to do whatever it takes to be successful?"*

CHAPTER 14: #9 ALL THINGS ARE OPPOSITE

HERACLITUS

His Claim to Fame: He's the first person I could find with the nickname 'The Riddler' - Marvel Comics eat your heart out. Sadly (for him), one of this chap's lasting claims to fame isn't being the original 'Riddler', but some inadvertent smart advice for leaders - that no matter how sure you are, if you are a leader, you'd always be better off taking advice before making a final decision. The Riddler's story can leave no leader in doubt that a 'second opinion' is always a good idea.

As well as his more Marvelesque nickname he was also known as the 'dark philosopher' and was called 'obscure' because of the impenetrable nature of his writings - take this mind-bender for instance; *"If you don't expect the unexpected you find it out, because it is not to be found out, and pathless"*. He probably ought to have been called the king of the double negatives for that little teaser.

Apart from all the nicknames he is now known as the first properly 'quotable' philosopher, probably because of his pithier sayings, many of which have been adapted over the years. Probably my favourite is, *"A man's character is his destiny",* a sentiment that is still found in even the most modern self-help books - and even something similar that made it into the world of Harry Potter[xxii].

The truth is that one or two of his ideas significantly influenced later philosophers. Not that they made a big deal of saying that their insights were derived from a cranky old guy from way back - an old misery who considered most people dimwits. Although his name did stick to one of his big ideas - something that would later be referred to as 'plurality', but he described as *'Flux'*. It means two seemingly opposites are different ends of the same strand, or if you like, two sides of the same coin. He saw night and day as not different states, but the one *thing* in a constant state of flux. Another, that strikes a chord with me as a coach is the notion that *"You can't step into the same river twice"* - meaning that what seems like something you know well, may not be precisely the same as you've known it before.

His Environment: Heraclitus was from Ephesus which at his time was a Greek administered settlement sitting in the estuary of the river Kaystros in Asia Minor. It's now a world heritage site along the Turkey coastline and used to be home to the Temple of Artemis - which by the way was one of the Seven Wonders of the World.

He was part of a wave of new natural scientists - people with the desire to know about the world around them, and who weren't happy with the explanation that it was this or that god was responsible. They were all Greek settlers escaping from trouble back home and presumably delighted to find somewhere to live in peace. What better environment could there be for the young Heraclitus to hear about the guys over in Miletus and think, *I'd like to do that too.*

Okay, I made that up. There was no Instagram picture of Thales proudly standing by his olive presses, or Anaximenes playing with condensation to prove his point about water changing forms. There was no CNN or Fox News (not that they would be covering philosophy mind you even if they were around). So, I'm guessing that he might have heard stories from travellers - and there were plenty of them because Ephesus was the hub of a trade route. If anywhere would hear news about what was going on in the Greek ex-pat world it'd be Ephesus.

His Culture: He was born with a proverbial, if not literal silver-spoon. Mum and dad were local aristocrats and he probably could have done anything he wanted. So, he did - he became a philosopher, wrote down his thoughts, and then stood alone in the market place reading out those thoughts to the passing crowds. Heraclitus would speak about anything and everything -on the cosmos, on politics, on theology. Mum and dad must have been so proud.

Maybe the lonely nature of his chosen profession was to blame, but whatever the cause, Heraclitus was a grouch. He was a misery, and reportedly more than just a little bit rude. If there had been a Christmas, then he'd be leading the 'Bah-Humbug' school of philosophy.

It's possible that what he'd gained in cleverness he'd lost in awareness of people and EQ[xxiii]. He was apt to describe people as children, and that their ideas were merely toys. Nothing patronising about him then, eh? However, Heraclitus was a big deal in his time. Along with Parmenides he's probably the most significant philosopher of the time in ancient Greece and stayed that way until the time of Plato. Their collective ideas about there being 'something' beneath the surface of a superficial reality were the foundation of what became a European worldview.

The expectations of philosophers by this time were that they provided clarity for everyday people. Like Parmenides, Heraclitus was asked to write laws and statutes for the citizens of Ephesus so that they could all live together more easily. Yet, unlike his fellow philosopher in Elea he actively chose not to. I imagine his irritation with ordinary people, and that fact that they could not *'see'* the world as he did was frustrating. Like any non-people person who thinks himself misunderstood, he retreated into a caricature of himself as the dark, mysterious, arrogant, and irascible Grinch that others would do well to steer clear of.

His Skills: Apart from the obvious skill of being able to set aside the 'obvious' and ask deeper questions without the certainty of having an immediate answer, he was something of a cryptic writer. He was skilled in getting people to think about the message by trying to figure out what the heck he was trying to say.

In fact, that might not be as strictly true as it could have been - possibly because when fragments of his thinking were quoted out of context by later philosophers it made him sound obscure, and it was this that attracted the nickname 'the Riddler'. Here's an example; *"All the men that exist in the world are far removed from the truth and just dealings, but they are full of evil foolishness which leads them to covertness and vain glorious ambition"*. Then there were the simpler expressions of his more complex ideas, like *'the way up is the way down'*. You may have to think about that simple sentence for a minute or two to get into the idea of 'polarities'.

Heraclitus might have been a genius and recognised as such if he'd had just a smidge of relationship building skills, but he didn't. He was a true 'thinker' - in that he could not understand why other people didn't instantly agree with his understanding of things. After all, to him the ideas were just common sense. If he'd been a leader of people and not just a thought-leader he'd not have been a very good one. He was at the extreme edge of some otherwise very useful strengths - he wanted his thinking to produce results, which is a good thing, but that was never going to happen without empathy and collaboration.

His Beliefs: He was a man of nicknames, not just the Riddler, the Obscure and Dark Philosopher, but also the 'Weeping-Philosopher' - this was due to his melancholic and negative view of live, the world, and everything. He truly was a miserable so and so.

Quite then how he managed to stir up enough interest to gain a following, particularly when he was prone to refer to anyone and everyone who didn't understand him as 'stupid, is a mystery. Yet, there were people who called themselves the 'Heraclitans or Heraclians' (depending on the translation). Why? I have no idea because he doesn't strike me as being the most charismatic of the philosophers of the time. If people were going to follow someone, you'd think they'd choose someone pleasant. Admittedly, there weren't very many philosophers yet, so perhaps his acolytes were simply short of someone to hang around with, or then again history could be selling him short. I don't think there's any doubt he didn't suffer fools gladly - which means memories of the man might be tainted by bad blood.

Here's how he thought of the world - *"All things come out of the One and the One out of all things. ... I see nothing but 'Becoming'. Be not deceived! It is the fault of your limited outlook and not the fault of the essence of things if you believe that you see firm land anywhere in the ocean of Becoming and Passing. You need names for things, just as if they had a rigid permanence, but the very river in which you bathe a second time is no longer the same one which you entered before."*

Heraclitus referred to the *'source'* of all things as being the divine 'logos'. He wasn't referring to the branding of Coca-Cola, Apple, or Google, but a co-ordinating principle of knowledge and order. The divine logos was the 'one' that he was talking about. His belief was that this was so far removed from the life and understanding of everyday people that they became blind to what was in front of their eyes. In his words, *"As a single, unified thing there exists in us both life and death, waking and sleeping, youth and old age, because the former things having changed are now the latter, and when those latter things change, they become the former."* The 'Riddler' does seem to be an apt nickname because while he might have completely understood what he was talking about, the rest of us are left in the dark. Although this quote*, "The unapparent connection is more powerful than the apparent one"* makes things a little clearer - perhaps, just a little!

His Identity: He might have believed that the world was in constant change, but clearly, he didn't think he personally was part of that change. He seems to have stayed with this persona of a non-people-person throughout his life. At his prime and the height of his popularity (although 'popularity' may be an overstatement, perhaps celebrity is more accurate).He was invited by the King of Persia, who was a genuine big-deal, to visit his palace to discuss his philosophical thoughts. While his contemporaries might have been flattered by the invitation, Heraclitus was not.

He turned the King down with a contemptuous reply that wouldn't have won him any friends. He didn't necessarily think himself better than everyone else... just, that they weren't as smart as him. As for people puffed-up with their own self-importance because they happened to be a king or something - they weren't worthy of his time at all.

So arrogant and sure of himself was he, that in his 60th year he was suffering with an oedema - that's a swelling of the soft tissue due to the accumulation of water just beneath the skin - he did something so incredibly stupid that he effectively killed himself. If he'd asked anyone - anyone at all, he might have made it to his 61st birthday - but he didn't.

He turned down the government of Ephesus who wanted him to help with writing better rules, but at the same time blamed them for his refusal. He might have wanted to help them, but his excuse his excuse for writing 'better' rules is he couldn't because *"they were already bad"*. That didn't make him popular.

After that, he moved away from the main settlement and retreated up in to the mountains, living a hermit-like life, eating only vegetables and plants - not all of which might have been good for him. Then, when he fell ill, rather than coming back to the city and seeking medical help from someone who might know what to do, he insisted on keeping up his 'Riddler' persona. Instead of asking for help and telling them what was wrong, he went to the doctors and posed this question; *"What should you do to create drought out of rainy weather?"*

With no clue what he meant, how could they help him? His response to their supposed 'inadequacy' was to storm off cursing them for being so 'stupid'. Therefore, he chose to apply his own cure - if you recall, it was an oedema he was suffering from. Believing that he could evaporate the water from his own body, he buried himself up to the neck in cow manure - yes, actual honest to goodness, still-warm cow manure - and then waited in the sun for it to heat up, and then for the swelling to go down. Suffice to say, it didn't work. The sun did its job, but instead of curing him it killed the poor, arrogant, miserable, and difficult Heraclitus. I suppose at least he died with the courage of his convictions. #idiot

His Purpose: Whether he realised it or not, he succeeded in synthesising the human experience with the fundamental reality of a natural world. He may have accused people of being asleep to what was really happening around them or became frustrated because they weren't quite as bright as he was, but if his purpose had been to make a difference in the world then he did succeed. Few people, if anyone really trust everything they see and hear, or take for granted that their senses can be trusted completely. All of which started with Heraclitus.

How might he be thought of by his employees, if he was a manager in today's business world?

Okay, let me start by saying that his 'troops' aren't voting for him as leader-of-the-year any time soon. No way am I advocating great leadership as being a miserable son-of-a-biscuit, an arrogant toss-pot, or someone happier to clad themselves in cow poop than be honest enough to be vulnerable. Those attributes are much closer to what I've been proposing is the worst kind of boss.

However, his team have learned from him that being smart isn't the same as being successful. He's taught them that treating everyone else as idiots is at best only a short-term-win and at worst prevents you from gaining collaboration at the time you need it most. He's shown them that even the brightest minds can get things terribly, irretrievably wrong - and that those kinds of mistakes can be the death of you.

Coaching questions he might ask: If any of our would-be coaching-leader philosophers were going to ask less-than-obvious questions it'd be this guy. I'd don't think he'd be intentionally obtuse, but he'd want the person he's asking to think deeply before answering.

i.   *"What are you assuming is true that if questioned more closely, might not be true at all, even if you believed it?"*

ii. *"If your concerns are one side of a coin you can't see, then what is on the other?"*

iii. *"How many times have you claimed to have lost something, yet, you know it is somewhere to be found?"*

iv. *"What are you assuming to be true because it has 'always' been this way even though for other's it has not?"*

v.   *"If you were to awake tomorrow and see something useful that, while being there before hadn't been seen by you until now, what might it be?"*

vi. *"If, for just a moment you accepted you might be being 'stupid', what is it possible you could learn to your benefit?"*

CHAPTER 15: #10 AS ABOVE BELOW

DEMOCRITUS

His Claim to Fame: Here we have another philosopher with a natty nickname - Democritus was known as the 'laughing philosopher' because he emphasised the *value of cheerfulness*.

Judging by what appears on our 'news' we could do with more of that today, and as for the world of business, I can't be the only person to enjoy working for someone with a cheerful disposition more than a misery-guts. Some leaders may feel that they have the weight of the world on their shoulders, but us mere troops don't want to see that. We want a leader we can trust - one with a cheerful demeanour and maybe a smile. A real one.

The less than cheerful Aristotle - part of the next generation of philosophers - wasn't enamoured with the theories of Democritus, but even though he was probably his chief critic he also praised Democritus for the quality of his arguments - which must have included the cheerful way he presented himself. Aristotle recognised that his thinking came from a sound foundation of understanding of natural science, even if he believed he was dead wrong in his conclusions.

Many hundreds of years later, others will claim that what is *'as above is also below*[xxiv]*'*. Democritus didn't say those precise words, but he was the first person we know of to think something very similar. Although it would be exciting to say he did, it's fair to say he did not invent the science of atomic physics, nor was he ahead of the game with

Darwin - I mention this because he was the first person to start talking about a world made up of 'atoms'.

Yes, believe it or not there was a florid faced chubby guy with a beard, chugging on about the atomic structure of the universe two and a half thousand years ago. If you heard mental-fanfares, now would be a good time to stop - because although he used the word 'atom' (factually, it was the Greek 'atomos'),he didn't mean to suggest what is meant by atoms today. He might as well have called it 'adiairetos-pragma'[xxv] because he was simply trying to find a word for an 'indivisible element'.

Even so, he was genuinely well ahead of his time, because he *did* figure out that when you get right down to it the world must be made up of *uncuttable particles*.

The kit he had available didn't allow him to see how tiny stuff is made up - but his imagination started a conversation that we all recognise. Not bad for twenty-five hundred years ago, to figure out that these tiny uncuttable elements are combining and then recombining to form new things. Not bad at all to have sussed that although the world appears to be constantly changing, the uncuttable particles at its source are unchangeable.

His Environment: He was born in Abdera, 17 km east-northeast of the mouth of the Nestos river in what's now Xanthi, Greece. It was a town with a rich mythical history, its foundation being attributed to Heracles, - the great-grandson and half-brother of Perseus whose resume as a god was impressive; not only was he the rather odd offspring of god-couplings, but apparently also the god of strength, heroes, sports, athletes, health, agriculture, fertility, trade. oracles, and the divine protector of mankind. Phew, what wasn't this guy responsible for?

Clearly, if the townsfolk of Abdera believed that their little part of the planet was made special by being founded by such an illustrious character, then they probably thought themselves special too. Democritus would have grown up in a prosperous and desirable place to live; it held a strategic position for Greek safety reasons being in control of both main roads through to the mountains and along the river and having a bustling port position right on the main sea-goods traffic road. Not quite the holiday hotspot Xanthi is today, however the rise and fall of the lucrative tobacco trade it benefited from a hundred years or so ago, replaced now by hordes of fun-loving tourists does demonstrate how quickly things can change in that spot along the coast where different people's and cultures have always come together. for as long as they've washed up on those shores. It may be a case of seeing things through rose-tinted shades to imagine that his inheritance plus the prosperous town and interesting travels, equals a fabulous life.

His Culture: The translation of his name means 'chosen of the people', which means either mum and dad had delusions of grandeur or the culture then was all about naming kids in the hope that they rose to the challenge.

I can't help thinking we could learn a thing of two from that approach; how much more enriching might the world be if we had more Democritus's than Logan's (small hollows) or Oliver's (Olive trees) or my person favourite in this year's top twenty boy's names Jackson (meaning... you guessed it, son of Jack). No offence intended if you happen to be called Jackson (12th most popular), Logan (4th most popular), or Oliver (you came third). Want to know first and second? It was Noah in the number 2 slot, meaning rest or comfort, and at number 1 was Liam, meaning strong-willed warrior and protector. Perhaps it's a commentary on our society that we put strong will at the top of the list followed by comfort, olive trees and small hollows. Personally, I think it has more to do with reality TV than deeper meanings - mores the pity.

Dad had been a major contributor to entertaining the Persian army on their way back home, and as a reward for all the people of Abdera the Persian king left behind a couple of his 'Magi' to help them. It's a good bet that young Democritus had learned plenty from these skilled astronomers, mathematicians, and knowledgeable chaps. It's probably also what prompted him to want to travel to the Middle East, Egypt, and the principle centres of philosophy in Greek territories in search of more. He even spent some time with the Pythagoreans as well as Anaxagoras. He was either unaware that this couldn't last forever - and I don't believe that a man as bright as he obviously was could be immune to the fact that even his ample inheritance wouldn't last forever. Or, he was so caught up in his learning and development and excited by what's he was getting from it that his dwindling finances slipped his mind. Whatever the truth, at some point he was broke. He made it home and was taken in by his brother, but there was a law at the time that said if a person wasted their inheritance and then couldn't support themselves without borrowing money or being helped in some other way, they would be denied the citizens right of a proper burial - and that was a big deal.

How great it would be if we had laws like that today, - just think, without me mentioning names, I bet you can think of at least one well known person who didn't deserve all their loans on the back of the family business after losing all his own dough! There's so much we can learn from the past if only we take the time to look.

However, Democritus's culture was forgiving if the wayward person gave something back to society. Democritus was apparently happy to give lectures for free to anyone who wanted to listen, and to teach the things he had learned and was still learning.

He's reported as spending his time trying to learn more and more about nature; everything from mixing plant extracts, to dissecting animals and reptiles to understand better how they 'tick'. He spent years doing this and earned his way back not the good graces of the people. There are some stories that paint him as being a bit of a 'mad scientist', - like blinding himself with hot glass to see what would happen, but I think that's probably an early version of 'fake news', made up to better 'sell' stories about him after his death.

His Skills: He wrote about more than just atoms; he had plenty to say about ethics, physics, mathematics, cosmology, and even music.

Like plenty of his philosophical colleagues over the ages he was what we'd call today a 'renaissance man' - good at lots of stuff. He was smart, because while Parmenides was certain that nothing *could* change, he managed to square the circle of a fixed quantity universe with the experience *of* change.

Hence, 'atoms' - a one-size-fits-all explanation of an ever-changing but zipped-up world. Parmenides said nothing could come from nothing - logical, if not particularly easy to buy-into when faced with a reality that looks very much like it changes all the time. Yet, Democritus' idea was cool; that there was only atoms and void, within which there are variously shaped 'atoms' - some shaped to be sweet, some to be sour, some to be oily, and so on.

To envision a world made up of uncuttable particles that fool your senses into believing things change was genius. It was a revolutionary concept that must have been a problem to explain when he first came up with it. I mean, have you ever tried explaining something to someone who has no concept of what you're talking about? It's like a teacher trying to explain algebra in words alone - it is just never going to land. Can you imagine Democritus telling his mates about his latest idea?

"Hey, I've had this idea..."
"Another one, eh Democritus?"
"Yeah, but this one's amazing!"
"Go on then, what is it?"
"It's like, you see this flower?"
"Yeah?"
"Well, get this, it's not really a flower!"
"Say what?"
"It just looks like a flower because it's made up of flower atoms!"
"Flower what?!"
"Atoms! They're these tiny things that you can't see, but that make up everything!"
"Flower atoms make up everything?"
"No, don't be silly!"

"Ahem, me be silly...?"
"It's like... flowers are made of flower atoms, and sweet things are made of sweet atoms and sour things made of sour atoms and sharp things made of..."
"Yeah, I get it, sharp atoms."
"You see, you got it straight away! How cool is this idea?!"
"No Democritus, I don't get it... and it's not cool, it's, well... a bit daft."
"What do you mean?"
"How can you say things are made up of what you can't see? That's just crazy! I can see the flower, and if I cut into the flower it's still... a flower! It's not, what did you call it, atoms? It's a flower!"
"One day... one day... people will say I'm a genius."
"Yeah, sure Democritus,...one day, eh!"

Seriously, it can't have been easy, so it's a fair bet he must have been persuasive, or very, very committed. Perhaps his cheerfulness helped his cause, it certainly couldn't have done any harm.

His Beliefs: We know that from a whole-life point of view Democritus didn't believe in a pre-Christian heaven or hell, but if he was wrong and both he and Stephen Hawking are up (or down) there, I bet they are having a great time chatting about string-theory.

It wouldn't have been too much of a surprise to Democritus if there was something after death, even if in life he was adamant that the religious types had got it all wrong - because he believed that the soul is more important than the body, with good reason. He surmised the body is made up of 'atoms'- more accurately 'earth atoms' like the rest of the things we see, hear, and feel, and as such the body is as subject to change as any other natural phenomenon - like a lemon or an olive.

While he believed 'earth-atoms' change, as they appear to wither and die, he thought a 'soul' was made up differently. It was as if it were made of its own unique atom - one that did not and could not change. It, he believed was still made up of atoms but of a different source entirely - like for example fire-atoms, which clearly also don't die off in the same way and may be like those that make up the soul. Therefore, to him the soul was far more important than the body. The body was destined to become frail, shrivel, and then die, but the soul simply moved on. He was a critical thinker who paid attention to the things around him and then added creativity to his own thinking by asking himself better and deeper questions.

As far as we know, he didn't say how the atoms in the soul moved on, or where the soul went in between being in a body. However, he did try to explain his thinking about what made the 'atoms' move and so change what we experience; sadly, it only got as far as that they 'crash into each other', although some sources suggest that he believed it was the fire-atoms that moved independently and were the cause of earth-atoms being forced into movement, and then all that crashing about happens as a result. Whatever the cause, he did believe that its source was because of a universal necessity and purpose.

Even if he didn't explain exactly what that source might be, he was clear that some movement started things off, and ended up with stuff just swirling about. He knew it either had something to do with the weight of different 'earth-atoms' undergoing random pushing about, leading to a random universe - or it was a kind of fatalistic bashing together of atomic billiard balls that might be predictable.

Are we subject to fate or the actions of fire-atoms from our own souls? He didn't know, and all this time later we are none the wiser.

His Identity: I'm guessing it's fair to say that the identity of the young Democritus was probably different to the way he saw himself as an older, even wiser man.

I suppose that's the same for most of us, however, even though his identity might have differed slightly he must have held a strong identity as a person whose role in life was to learn. It's reported that throughout his life he spent his evenings studying and not going out with his mates doing whatever people did for fun back then. Instead, he's painted as the kind of guy who toiled away by candlelight, cutting dead things up and trying to figure out just how the 'world works'.

Anyone who behaves that way must either see himself as on a mission or was 'just that sort of person'. I have a feeling that the latter was true; he didn't rave on about the purpose of his endeavours, he was simply fascinated by what life is and how it comes to be the way it is. Don't forget, he could have used the family fortune to live a cushy life, but he didn't. The law may have reckoned his spending all the inheritance leaving him with zip to live on wasn't cool, but he didn't squander it on ladies of the night and huge quantities of wine, no - he used it to learn, and keep on learning.

The only reason he came home was because he had to, or he would have kept on learning. I think learning was 'who' he was, and the long candlelit nights were just what someone like him did. It wasn't any more complicated than that.

His Purpose: If it's true that learning was what Democritus was all about and consumed his every waking hour, it's hard to distinguish between his identity and his purpose. One may have simply been an extension of the other.

I think his purpose was to learn, and then to share what he learned. He wasn't a Heraclitus-like hermit who thought everyone else an idiot but was keen for people to grasp what was now in his head, even if it was without precedent and hence hard to understand.

That couldn't have been easy. Therefore, he held a purpose that had something to do with adding value to the world by learning and sharing how this world we live in really 'works'.

How might he be thought of by his employees, if he was a manager in today's business world?

He's a leader with a strong team around him. He's recognised that his personal quest to keep on learning is valuable to the business, but only if there's a business for it to be useful. In other words, he's seen the need for people around him to help keep him focused – because he's proved that left to his own devices the money runs out before his curiosity.

His team value him immensely and respect not only his devotion to seek answers beyond 'normal 'thinking, but because he respects them each for the expertise and energy each of them bring to the business. Together, they are a formidable group of people who successfully depend on each other.

The light-touch that he brings to collaboration at every level in the business has been reflected by so many that it is now engrained in their culture – people smile naturally and are relaxed with each other even when facing tough challenges. They know that Democritus will have been 'burning the midnight oil' to come up with ideas, but that he won't be wedded to any particular course of action - his unbending belief in the ever-changing but simultaneously unchanging universe (depending from how far out you view things) means that he is always convinced there's a solution to be found. Or, if it isn't found right now, that one day they will find it.

This interesting, fun, deep-thinking character perhaps isn't the easiest leader to follow – it requires trust and a willingness to collaborate and let go of any personal insecurity – but the rewards of working in a progressive and illuminating environment are fabulous. #BelikeDemocritus

Coaching questions he might ask: It's super interesting that Democritus could embrace the apparent contradiction of saying that all things were 'atoms and void', because by giving the 'void' a name he acknowledged that such a thing as a void exists, and therefore, must be made of something. He had already acknowledged his nod in the direction of those before him who'd insisted that something cannot come from nothing, and yet still was happy to talk about void. I get from this that he's suggesting that 'void' is neither something or nothing but is a different thing altogether. This willingness to bend things a little to accommodate the possibility of it loosening up things enough for the discussion to be useful might affect the questions he'd ask:

i.   *"If the elements of your situation are moving, what are they're moving about in that's causing you to be stuck?"*

ii. *"If you were to identify and separate the various foundational elements of your situation, what would emerge as the one most important on which to focus?"*

iii. *"When you look deeper and deeper into anything, including your situation, what changes and may start to look different?"*

iv. *"When you consider all the alternatives, what might change about the way you're thinking if something else was involved that you didn't yet know about?"*

v.   *What might you have missed, that is at the heart of this issue and that makes it more important for you to consider things more deeply than take any superficial point of view?"*

vi. *When billiard balls crash into each other, the force of one against the other creates a pattern that starts with the first ball, so what was the equivalent of your 'first ball'?*

CHAPTER 16: #11 IS APPEARANCE A DECEPTION?

ZENO OF ELEA

His Claim to Fame: Firstly, I've got to say what a great name; I mean, 'Zeno', wow - I think we should try and have this name make a comeback. It's so cool... "Hello, what's your name?" "Zeno" ...I love it - who's going to forget that name, eh?

Anyway, apart from a great name and being the twenty-five-year-old young lover of Parmenides - this Zeno holds a special place in thinking history; he is known for proposing that not only can common sense *not* be trusted, but that it is full of paradox, and that everything we perceive is probably an illusion. His take on things might be extreme - but what's most important in moving from boss to leader is that he was prepared to question things and apply logic, even when it seems absurd.

It's not the paradoxes that matter but the thinking that they provoke that help make better decisions.

He came up with logical sounding arguments that were patently absurd, but then were difficult to explain *why* they're wrong! Not only did he try and baffle people with his paradoxes, but he also argued that there is something underpinning the organisation of the universe that's a bit weird and paradoxical - and because of that weirdness the universe we imagine to be real, is in fact not real at all. Cue the 'Twilight Zone' intro music.

His Environment: His, ahem, 'mentor' (boyfriend) had founded the philosophical school of Elea and as a student of that school the young Zeno must have been affected to some extent by an environment where he was potential treated differently to others. To be clear, the practice of a respected man like Parmenides having a young male lover was apparently common, hence scandal is unlikely to have played a part in proceedings. However, a close relationship with the head of the school may have added to any pressure on Zeno to come up with his own unique contribution.

In the culture of the time it was reasonable and acceptable to spend time finding ways to support the ideas of your teacher; Parmenides' big thing was that motion is just an illusion and is so far from actual experience as to make it feel ludicrous, therefore, it's a fair bet that Parmenides was ridiculed, at least privately if not in public. So, making the work of his student also subject to rolling eyes and wiggly fingers pointing at heads.

It seems that everything that followed from Zeno might have been meant as a means of 'proving' the ideas of his mentor. He wanted to prove that reality is *unchanging,* and that appearance is a deception. That's a very hard sell;*"...the world of 'sense' with its apparent motion is just an illusion"*. Faced with this challenge may explain why he came up with numerous paradoxes to make the simple point that what might appear 'obvious', is not.

His Culture: The time and culture of Elean society supported the free thinking of young men like Zeno. It sounds to me like the ´California´ of its time – a place where the strange and unconventional are welcomed and accepted.

Rightly or wrongly, I can picture Zeno pondering the world around him and desperately searching for something to make his own. We can only wonder at what first stimulated him with the notion of a paradox. It could be as simple as the fact that his mentor spoke so often of the whole experience of life is a paradox – maybe all he was doing was trying to break this down into bite size chunks to make it easier to digest.

I doubt the clever paradoxes he´s remembered for came to him without first thinking about his mentor´s take on the world. I imagine it more likely that as he started to question the everyday detail happening around him, and that something turned on that light in his mind. Perhaps he saw a bushel of corn or millet fall to the floor and heard only the faint sound of it hitting the stone paved surface, and wondered precisely what caused the sound?

This paradox is that Zeno asks - *why if a single grain of millet cannot be heard when it hits the floor and therefore has no sound, how can it be that any sound is heard when the bushel hits the floor? If one part has no sound, then many parts of no sound should also be silent.*

Of course, that one is easy to answer; he's accused of mistakenly believing that because he can't hear a single part that there's no sound there. To which he might reply that this is his point - that we *assume trust* in our senses in one aspect of a thing and blindly apply it to another, assuming our senses to be correct when they are not.

His Skills: Zeno was captivated by numbers. He was the first of the philosophers to write in prose and not a more poetic approach - preferring clear, straightforward language to make his point. He wrote clearly, using numbers to make his point unequivocally, even if the way he applied numbers might not be so easy to grasp at first glance. For example, his most famous mathematical jiggery-pokery is known as the Dichotomy Paradox - dichotomy meaning the ´cutting in two´. It is also known as the paradox of the 'runner', and although it may at first appear to be obviously wrong - even if you can't quite explain with simple maths how it's wrong –it may be because he´s grappling with the concept of infinity. This may be something that hadn´t been done before, or if it had, wasn´t well known at that time.

Let´s unwrap this; he posited that if it is true that for a runner to reach his goal, he must first run half the distance of the race – that much is obvious, but then he must now run half of the remaining distance, then half of that distance, and so on, halving the distance each time. As the runner must always run half of a remaining distance, leaving the other half still to run, he could never complete the race - according to Zeno there would be no end to the halving of whatever distance remained. It's an infinite set of divisions into tinier and tinier bits, suggesting the runner will never get there. Aargh! It sounds logical all right, but it's stupid - of course the runner will get there. You can stand and watch the race and he will get to the end regardless of Zeno's apparent logic.

Even so, there is a point to this and an explanation as to why the infinity answer is wrong; and that's that the time the runner may complete the race can be figured out in advance, so, if the race is six miles and the runner jogs along at 6 miles an hour, we know he's going to finish in an hour. No logic needed for that, just common sense and simple maths. However, the value Zeno adds philosophically is in this gem of thinking - *if all we see around us can in one sense be thought of as infinite, and yet, our perception of infinite be assigned a value, then it may be possible to unwrap the mysteries of the infinite one day.* Cool, eh (if you can get your head around it)?

One of his other famous paradoxes is that of Achilles and the tortoise. This similarly suggests that because a new point will always be reached, a runner with the speed and stamina of an Achilles could never catch the much slower tortoise if it was sportingly given a head start; the tortoise would reach a point further from the start than Achilles when he started running. He would then run and reach the lace the tortoise was at that moment Achilles started the race. It then follows that by the time Achilles has reached that point the tortoise will have moved again, and again, and again, until the tortoise reached the finish line - logically ahead of Achilles.

Of course, this has been debunked many times with all manner of clever calculations and simple questioning of the assumptions made by him. Again, the hidden assumption in here is that the race is infinite, but it is not. Hence, within the time the race will take, Achilles must overtake the tortoise if he is to finish in that previously established finite time.

When you step into Zeno's shoes it's easy to see how he was using erroneous assumptions in maths to demonstrate how logic can't be relied on. Zeno's point was to make people 'think', forcing them to reconsider everyday 'normality' in a new light, and causing them to find those hidden assumptions – and in effect, question their reality. Clearly, he was creative and good at this - it was a skill he had in abundance. The little tinker, making us all scratch our heads like that.

His Beliefs: Whether he came to the belief that our senses cannot be trusted because of the construction of his examples of paradox - or they came about because of his belief in the deception of appearance, we will never know. All we can say with surety is that he ended up believing the realty behind the *mask of appearance* is unchanging and true, but our interpretations of what we see, feel, and hear are fraught with deceptions.

He posits that all motion and time is just an illusion. One that we have created to make sense of our interaction with 'reality' (whatever that might be) make sense to us. It all sounds very 'matrix[xxvi]-like', which I suppose tells us that ideas come and go.

Of all the people we've looked at so far, Zeno is the most strategically minded and detail-oriented. Whatever he lacked in emotional and relational strengths he tried to make up for in keeping his eye on the prize of logical reasoning.

His Identity: By all accounts, he was a staunch defender of his ideas. He probably felt able to because they were a version of the ideas of Parmenides – and its always easier to defend other people´s ideas than be caused to wade through the inevitable self-doubt that comes when other people question and push-back on our own.

And yet, anyone defending the idea that what you and I deem to be obvious, simply isn't true - must have figuratively speaking had thick skin. I sense that Zeno was such a person. It may be stretch to say that he loved Parmenides, but his behaviour has all the markers of someone who cared deeply not only for the ideas of the man, but the man himself. It's kind of romantic to imagine that the poor guy put up with the world questioning his usefulness as a philosopher because of a deep connection with his mentor, lover, and friend.

He was prepared to challenge people, argue with them, and defend his position to the extent that they would get exasperated with him. Apparently, he drove people nuts! I don't know if he saw himself as mischievous, difficult, or simply happy to be challenging so his point landed. It's hard to say when looking back with scant resources, but I am sure that when a person like him chooses the hard-road rather than the easier option, it tells me that he had integrity, strength of mind and the courage of his convictions. True, he might also have been a pain in the butt - but, as they didn't run him out of town, I'm going to give him the benefit of the doubt and say he was able to make his point and hang onto relationships.

His Purpose: When Zeno was just 24, he wrote a book containing 40 paradoxes. He must have really liked making them up. Like Neo, the hero in the Matrix movie he wanted to shed light on the way he saw the world. He didn't agree with Hericlitus' view that one thing is simply the shadow or opposite of another. He though such observations might be true but were still an illusion hiding something much deeper - something that could become clear if people simply wake up to the fact that it's hiding in plain sight.

He could have chosen a pragmatic route, finding useful examples and hence encouraging people to start looking more deeply at the world around them, questioning their assumptions and discovering new insights - perhaps even 'breakthroughs'. However, instead he seems to have made it his goal to shed light on his belief that we are being fooled by reality, and that something else may be going on entirely. I sense that rather than this making him a go-to guy for useful thinking, it might have made him more like a mad-scientist keep-away-from character unless you want to come away more confused for the encounter rather than less.

Some may say this makes him the father of the new-age thinkers, but that's a mute-point. Yet, it may be true that in a similar way to how new-age thinkers may be considered by some as irrelevant kooks - particularly by scientists and academics today, by the time of Aristotle (when Zeno had long been dead), his work and the paradoxes he created were considered trivial. The fact that we are still talking ºabout them today suggests his purpose might have (at least to some extent) been achieved – and that after all, his work was not at all trivial.

How might he be thought of by his employees, if he was a manager in today's business world?

Everyone likes working for someone who helps them learn. I know it wasn't Zeno who said that "telling someone what to do rather than asking them a 'better' question robs them of an opportunity to learn", but that's how his people see him - the guy more interested in people understanding as opposed to doing just enough to get by.

He has the gift of seeing through veneers of assumption, and then finding ways to shine the light of logic – not just for the sake of it, but to uncover hidden truths about reality. His well-known paradoxes are fun brain-twisters, but he's more pragmatic with this approach as a boss. For example, he´s been known to put people on the spot; when someone responds to a problem with "*...it´s always been fine until now*", he´d ask for an explanation as to how we know for sure things have always been fine, what other explanations there might be for things 'happening' so that they've looked fine until now, and what might have been hidden in plain sight?

The fact that he is willing to ask these questions without knowing the answers in advance, or even having a guess at what might be happening is refreshing. If he asked the same questions but was one of those bosses who thinks he knows it all, then people would hate him. As it is, he´s not - he´s a deep-thinking leader with class.

It might take a while to get used to him, but the effort is worth it. Everyone says so.

Coaching questions he might ask: I'm guess that Zeno would set his questions in the context of life and work-related paradoxes, drawing on his repertoire and building on them.

One of his most well-known is called the 'liar's paradox' and it goes like this - imagine I write on a piece of paper the sentence 'This sentence is false', now what are you going to do with that? If the sentence is true, then it must be a false statement. However, because the sentence claims itself to be false then it must truly be false, in which case it must be true. Ha! Sneaky, eh.

He's conned us into thinking that there must be some value in trying to figure out the infinite flip-flopping between absolute truth and absolute falsehood, when in real life - it doesn't matter. It doesn't matter because there´ll be context around the statement, and context will either make it true of false - not the statement itself.

If this has fried your brain like it did mine when I heard it for the first time, then let's look at how Zeno might have woven his thinking into useful questions;

i. *"If I assume you mean one thing when in truth you mean quite another, and then I agree that we should go forward sharing this 'thing', - am I right to be offended when the you let me down by not doing the 'thing' I'd assumed had been agreed?"*

ii. *"If I look at a jug of water and you look at it too, how do you know I'm noticing the same as you, and how do I know you are seeing that jug just as I am, - hence, this situation you are in is what it is, but is not only what you have perceived it to be, so, what will it mean to you when you find these differences?"*

iii. *"Para in Greek means 'against' and Doxa 'belief', and a paradox is something that causes you to go against your belief, so if there is a paradox in the situation you find yourself, what is it and how might it be useful?"*

iv. *"What have you accepted as ongoing and infinite in your current situation, that in fact may have hard borders, and therefore, not at all what you imagined it to be?"*

v. *"When you consider where you are in your life's journey right now, are you moving or already here? - because if it is true that life happens in instances and not some uncontrolled motion, isn't it then also true that you can decide in advance what your next instance will be?"*

CHAPTER 17: #13 WE ARE THE MEASURE OF ALL THINGS

PROTAGORAS

His Claim to Fame: This guy's contribution to leadership is straightforward - Protagoras realised that what a person chooses to be true for him or herself then becomes their truth.

Bosses don't accept this truth - they want to convince everyone who works for them that 'their' way is best. Their innate lack of personal confidence means they must always ´be right´. That´s not true for leaders. A leader understands they´re fallible and that not only do people develop their own beliefs but sometimes they may be right, when the leader is wrong. Protagoras knew this to be true and embraced it. He recognised that when someone ´knows´ they´ve got it right, no amount of argument will make them change their mind. On the other hand, a typical self-absorbed boss will ´tell´ instead of listening, and worse still, will assume people have been won over, not recognising when lip-service is being paid.

Protagoras is probably the best known 'Sophist' of all time. At the time that wasn't a good thing - even though we've already established that the Greek for wisdom is 'Sophia' (which makes it sound like it should be a good thing), it really isn't. That´s because being a sophist then was akin to calling him an 'Ambulance Chaser' - a bottom-rung lawyer, and about as trustworthy as a rattlesnake ...or maybe a politician!

A sophist was someone who was paid to teach people how to create a winning argument, even when they are clearly in the wrong. They believed that nothing was fixed, be it right or wrong - but subject to argument and persuasion, and if the argument is crafted well enough, even a falsehood could overcome truth.

Typically, they were hired when a person secretly knew they were in the wrong but wanted to 'get away with it'. It´s therefore understandable that Sophists were unpopular. Furthermore, they were not considered 'nice people', as a typical sophist-for-hire wasn´t interested in helping anyone by ensuring that truth wins out, but were conversational mercenaries - pay them and they'd help you, but approach them because you're innocent of a crime, but can't afford their fees and you weren't likely to be welcomed with open arms. Whether this was true or not, it was the way Sophists were thought of by most people.

However, Protagoras wasn´t one of those heartless money-monsters - he makes it onto our list because he was way more than just someone who could put together a winning argument, he came up with the phrase, *"man is the measure of all things"* - and for that he's worth remembering.

Although the thinkers that came before him had probably already realised that the things we experience are not 'absolute', Protagoras was the first to articulate it in a way that could make sense to non-philosophers. He might have phrased his thinking as a question;

"On a bright spring day in Athens, the city is visited by two men; one from the across the sea to the south, and one

203

from far overland in the north. Why is it that the man from the south experiences the city as cold, while the one from the north experiences it as quite warm? Is the temperature not the same for both?"

Within this simple observation, not only did he simplify the idea that we all perceive the same things differently and interpret them according to our memories of 'what is', but he also raised the issue of interpretation being a different sense.

The idea that man has five senses; touch, taste, hearing, sight, and smell were as obvious then as now, but in this case, he was alluding to a different sense: It wasn't touch, because they hadn't touched anything. It wasn't smell, or sight, or hearing, and he certainly wasn't suggesting they were tasting the bright spring day, but some other sense was being interpreted. Some years later, scientists and philosophers would point to sensing heat or cold as the missing human facility, but does that really answer why these two people in his example would have sensed the same hot or cold differently? Like so many important philosophers, his search for answers raises even more important questions. Don't you just love it when that happens?

His Environment: Abdera, as we've already heard, four hundred or more years before BCE turned to CE this was a pleasant place to live - away from immediate war and strife, calm, reasonably well-off, and very pretty. It was even more pleasant for Protagoras because his slightly older Abderian philosophical counterpart Democritus, took him into his own household to teach him philosophy. He was more than a young house guest - he was a student subject to an immersion experience in the philosophical world of Democritus.

Therefore, the young Protagoras was surrounded by philosophical discussion all the time. He wouldn't have been limited to studying from the second or third-hand accounts of what the philosopher Democritus might or might not have said - he was constantly hearing it first-hand. His environment would not just have been filled with philosophy, his whole world would be filled with it. I can only imagine what they might have talked about over breakfast, or how they came together in the evening to interpret their day, it must have been fascinating – and perhaps a little intense.

His Culture: Like his mentor, he belonged to a culture that allowed for free thinking and free speech. It's not clear if his observations made an immediate impact on the people of the town, or even those visitors that might have enjoyed listening to Protagoras talk about his thoughts on the world - after all, they must have been open to all manner of crazy talk so, who knows if the importance of his contribution hit home straight away?

However, it did make a huge impact some years later. Plato wrote about the fact that the observation *'man is the measure of all things'* can be interpreted to mean that nothing can ever be called 'true' or 'real' - because what is true and real to me may not be true or real to you - at least, not in the same way.

It's called 'absolutism' and has been a foundational platform for science for as long as science as we know it has been around. It's fabulous in one way, because it removes any need for arrogant persuasion - as forcing someone to accept other than that which they perceive themselves is fruitless - reflections of philosophers that have gone before in their thought-leadership approaches. Yet, on the other hand (and forgive me for saying so), but it is a bit of a downer for things like religion. I'm sure if Protagoras has been born a thousand years later, we wouldn't be hearing about absolutism - he would have been tortured as a heretic. It just goes to show how context and contemporary beliefs affect the progression of human understanding — kind of makes me wonder what our beliefs about life today are suppressing — and how many bosses treat the breakthrough thinking of their subordinates as heretical? Hm... something to think about.

His Skills: Apparently, before being taken under the wing of Democritus, Protagoras made his living as a porter; carrying goods from one place to another for people, a sort of white-van man without the van.

The story goes that Democritus spotted young Protagoras carrying a bundle of wood. He noticed that the bundle had been tied together with twine in such a way that only a mathematical genius could have figured out how to do it. He immediately accosted the startled porter and announced he was a prodigy - destined for greater things than wood transport. He told him that from now on he would live with him and learn to be a wise man and lover of wisdom - a philosopher.

It's not known if this offer was instantly accepted, or if Democritus was rejected as a lunatic - I guess it depends on how well known he was - and if Protagoras knew of him beforehand. Who knows? However, if the story is true his meeting with Democritus and subsequent training didn't come out of nowhere. Somehow, he had acquired the skill to tie fabulously good knots and bundle wood in ways that were mathematically significant.

However, he acquired it, the skill got him noticed, because it was this skill that kick started his real career. Yet weirdly, maths wasn't his big 'thing'. In fact, he didn't think that geometry and the study of maths for maths sake was fruitful at all - which is directly at odds with his mentor Democritus. Like most people of his time he saw mathematics as more of an art form than a science - after all, geometry and the maths that went with it had the purpose of understanding the natural world around them - and that felt quite arty. It's a pretty cool way of thinking about numbers. Perhaps if my old maths teacher had pitched maths to me as an art-form, I may have paid more attention in maths class. Another missed opportunity!

So, even with maths not being a big deal to Protagoras he still is quoted as saying *"...art without practice, and practice without art, are nothing"*, which rather than meaning practice like doing things over and over, probably meant the practice of doing maths. This openness to the blending of art and science is something that still benefits today's thought-leaders in business - notice how the very best leaders are open to hearing the feelings and taking note of the nuances from their senior people, unlike typical bosses who are not open to anything other than cold hard facts - even if opportunities are missed because of it.

His Beliefs: Following on from that statement about art, it says something about what Protagoras believed if we reword it as; *'art without the practice of maths, and the* *practice of maths without any application of art, are nothing'.* This says to me that the man was connecting the science of understanding with the experience of life, and therefore believed the two to be intertwined.

He believed that it's not possible to unwrap the true essence of one without the other. This mixing of experience and understanding shows up in his belief about the teaching of virtue: His thoughts about virtue had the strength of his self-confidence and conviction in abundance - which probably helped him to be persuasive and pragmatic, with the courage to craft arguments in the face of fierce opposition.

To put this in context, it's important to note that the teaching of virtue was a big deal in the 5th Century BCE. Strangely, it was a Brexit or Mexico-USA wall debate of sorts - with slides as entrenched in their fixed beliefs as NRA gun lobbyists, pro-lifers, or their direct opponents. Remember, Sophists were universally distrusted because of their mercenary approach to teaching the skills of holding an argument. When the person you're paying doesn't care if what you want to win is moral or ethical, or even legal then what grounds does anyone have to trust that person? Such was the thinking and antagonism toward Sophists.

Protagoras, on the other hand wasn't like many of those who had followed in the sophist footsteps. For him, the achievement of improvements in all aspects of life needed to be evident if virtue was to manifest itself. In other words, virtue isn't something that can be taught in isolation because it's so closely entwined with all aspects of a person's life. I think he might have been the first proper life-coach in the history books - he helped people focus on all aspects of their life and actions to seek improvement. He questioned everything, and so must have also questioned those who came to him for help as his success could only be achieved when those he helped were ultimately successful themselves. The though-leading usefulness in business is obvious - great leaders know that their success sits within the field of successes created by their team.

His Identity: He had an interest in something they called Orthoepeia, which referred to the proper use of words. Today, we might call his approach - get ready for another long word... phenomenological - the ways in which we describe phenomena so that other people know what we intend. More specifically, it means the interpretation and communication of a phenomena so that whatever is experienced by someone in the real world is recreated in the mind of the listener. For example, a boss might say *"this is urgent, get it done"* and assume everyone knows what they mean – and yet, how many times has something ´urgent´ meant it needs to be done ahead of anything else, or it needs to be done because my own boss has asked for it, or it needs to be done simply because I say so? By assuming other people understand precisely what is meant(because you know what you mean) is the trait of a boss not a leader. Hence, this´d be a useful focus for so many bosses - an attempt to communicate meaning in a way that ensures their team members don´t have to guess what´s meant or be forced to speculate as to the ´real´ meaning behind what´s been said.

For Protagoras, this fits very well with his interest in the subjectivity of ...well, everything. He cleverly switched the idea of subjectivity from being an intellectual concept into a practical 'tool' - question 'language' and you question subjective meaning. It's clever because he recognised that not only do people experience things differently, but they also express what they've experienced differently - and yet assume not only that whatever they've experienced must be the same for everyone, but also the words other people use mean precisely what you take them to mean too. None of which could possibly be true - and in the case of the Athens example the truth is that the experience of the two chaps on a spring day were different. If they'd spoken to each other about the spring day, the words they'd used to describe it quite possibly would also mean something different to each of them. The same day, different words, describing the same thing but from a different perspective.

Confusing, isn't it? Both the experience and the words used to express it can be confusing – either the same words can be used to express a different experience, or perhaps the same words used to express a different experience, or even the assumption that different words mean different experiences but not those that were really experienced - argh!

Therefore, I think he saw himself less like one of the hated say-whatever-you-need-to-to-win lawyer like sophists, but a teacher of awareness. I think he wanted people to recognise that there was more going on between them than they were paying attention to, and that any satisfaction they felt by 'knowing' what was true for everybody is a myth, an illusion, and ultimately a lie.

He was particularly scathing about the way in which people gave up their choices in favour of imagining what the 'gods' might want. He said, *"Concerning the gods, I have no means of knowing whether they exist or not, nor of what sort they may be, because of the obscurity of the subject, and the brevity of human life"*. So, he wasn't an agnostic as some people claimed, and he didn't say they were all made up, but he was clear that he simply didn't know.

I can all most hear him asking people if there were other 'things' they didn't know to which they paid equal attention, and then gave up as much of their life choices to somehow appease or satisfy someone else? If Protagoras came back today as a 'business consultant' I think his focus would be on his belief that clarity of communication and meaning may be at the heart of many organisational problems.

His Purpose: If all this is true, and I'm happy to step into those shoes of his because I think his purpose is obvious – it might have been less to educate the masses, and more to educate himself.

I think he was smart enough to realise that in life you have to be in a position to help others, even if, at the time that might look like putting yourself ahead of others. He might have said, *'put your own mask on first'* - meaning that when it comes to understanding what the heck is going on around you - like on board a plane, before trying to help anyone else you make sure you're able to whatever needs to be done for the benefit of those less able. His approach to helping people by asking them to examine all aspects of their life and try to understand what is real to them and what is imagined, either because of convention or lack of previous interrogation is indicative of someone who was probably making sure he put his own mask on – by interrogating the meaning of whatever was being said, and making sure he was on a solid ground of mutual understanding.

How might he be thought of by his employees, if he was a manager in today's business world?

You know where you stand with Protagoras. Not only is he consistently clear with his communication – always finding the right questions to check on mutual understanding without appearing to be patronising or micro-managing, but he's also the kind of guy you can be honest with.

If you have a hunch about something, but can't quite find the words to articulate those feelings in a way that makes 'business sense', he is patient and interested. He knows that your feelings must have come from somewhere and might therefore be valuable – and he won't squander the opportunity to find out if they are.

This openness and willingness to explore ideas with his subordinates makes him a leader people are happy to follow, even if sometimes he can be exasperating. By that, I mean there is a downside to being so willing to engage and listen -sometimes his people just want him to make decisions quickly, and it may be that he hasn't quite got the balance right between this need and the need for clarity of communication. His team like him and have learned to ask him tough questions too – and have more than enough experience to 'manage' both his and their expectations.

He accepts the reality that some people have 'bought into' ways to behave based on an ultimately flawed belief based on misunderstandings about what 'higher management' expect from employees. These beliefs he treats much like the way he might have treated the ancient Greek beliefs in the 'will of the gods' - he accepts that such beliefs are merely a mechanism to find certainty in uncertain situations. Therefore, he steps in to provide a different kind of certainty - one that is based on clarity and direction from himself as a leader on top of the situation.

Coaching questions he might ask: I sense that he would have been quite skilled in people interaction, after all, they paid him to teach so he must have been reasonably sociable. I'm convinced that his leadership style would be to ask searching questions.

i. *"How often elsewhere, do you use damaging or negative ways to describe your current situation, that when you think about it now causes you to pause?"*

ii. *"If it's true that when something is unable to be known it's best treated as if it does not exist, then how might you apply this to help you?"*

iii. *"If you were not just in the shoes of the person with whom you'd prefer to achieve a better outcome, but were also to think using their mental filter, speak using their words, and hear those things you expect are likely to be emotionally important to that person, - what might you learn that's of help?"*

iv. *"In your current situation, how would you express what you've been feeling if you had to use words you've never used before?"*

v. *"What are you doing that has nothing to do with your current worrisome situation, but may be causing you distress?"*

vi.   *"When was the last time you surprised yourself in a way that could be useful to emulate in your current situation?"*

vii.   *"When you think of the last significant interaction you had that caused you pain or distress, what might have caused you to evaluate it differently if you were forced to consider it again, looking for a better interpretation?"*

CHAPTER 18: #14 MORE TO SAY THAN MATHS

PYTHAGORAS

His Claim to Fame: Okay, what´s the first thing you think of when you hear the name Pythagoras? A triangle, right? I can't believe you haven't heard of this guy, but please don't assume that his claim to fame is limited to what you learned in school. Pythagoras ´the man´ had many more talents than he's being given credit for by school-teachers.

Of course, we all know him for his theorem regarding triangles, but during his time he was known for much more than that. We are talking about a guy with such a powerful personality that not only did he start his own 'cult' called the Pythagoreans - can't think where he came up with that, but he also made them live in absolute silence. Yes, silence! The only person allowed to talk was him, and here's his reasoning that went something like this; "...*a man's words are careless, unplanned, and usually were a misrepresentation of the truth, so as we are always in doubt as to what to say, better to remain silent.*"

Or of course, it could simply have been a ploy to maintain control. I did wonder whether it would work at home, but one look from my wife told me I was no Pythagoras.

Unlike my household, his cult was full of rules; not only did he have a natural aptitude for numbers and reach 'mythical figure' and cult-leader status, but he insisted that his followers engage themselves as deeply and as intensely as he did. They had to follow a rule that their learning was lifelong, and that they must attempt to understand and unwrap the mathematical mysteries of everything, or not bother at all. It really was an all or nothing existence.

Clearly, Pythagoras must have had high levels of both IQ[xxvii] and EQ to have attracted around 300 followers to join him at a place called Croton in southern Italy - the location might have been lovely, but the rules of admittance - not quite so much.

While today he's thought of less like a real man and more like a name attached to a theory, back then he must have been a force to be reckoned with. Not only did he light the blue flame of interest in mathematics that fired imaginations of millions, and still does, but (and this was a big surprise to me) he's also credited with coming up the title 'philosopher'. A term coined to suggest a lover of wisdom, which probably summed him up perfectly.

His approach to life, and probably why people followed him into this commune of sorts, is summed up in his own words when while attending the Olympic games in 518 BCE. He was asked "Why be a philosopher?" He replied; *"Life... may well be compared with these public games, for in the vast crowd assembles here are some attracted by the acquisition of gain, others are led on by the hopes and ambitions of fame and glory, but among them are a few who have come to observe and to understand all that passes here. It is the same with life; some are influenced by the love of wealth, while others are blindly led on by the mad fever for power and domination, but the finest type of man gives himself up to discovering the secrets of nature, - this is the man I call a philosopher, for although no man is completely wise in all respects, he can love wisdom as the key to nature's secrets."*

He had something there, didn't he? It's like nothing has changed in past three millennia; some people do spend all their energy chasing wealth and are still unhappy, some chase power be it at work, in their society, or even just in the home. Yet, there are still a few that look beyond that - and I think in that respect he was talking to you. Yes, you the person who's spending their time thinking and learning and asking better questions about the nature of life. I've no doubt that in the eyes of Pythagoras you have joined the ranks of philosophers. #GoPhilosophers

His Environment: The Pythagorean commune in Croton, situated right at the foot of Italy was not only a community of people committed to the pursuit of mathematics, but also of music and astronomy. It was a proper full-on cult - all living in silence of course -and following whatever new rules their 'leader' decided was a good idea. In this instance he was acting more like one of those bossy bosses I've been alluding to, more interested in controlling than leading. Yet, just like today in organisations where people openly acknowledge their leader is a bossy controlling boss but stick with him (or her) because *'better the devil you know'*. When you call it out it's a dumb strategy but still happens all the same.

There were 300 people who were so entranced with Pythagoras that they were happy to live away from the rest of society in what can only be described as extreme conditions; in addition to the silence and the complete commitment thing, they were forced to become vegetarians - not for any religious or health reasons, but because of an unusual belief their cult-leader held about what happened to a person's 'soul' after they die.

Their whole environment was centred on a commitment to the idea that the 'square' and the 'cube' of a number and geometry were the keys to unlocking the mysteries of the universe. Those who were 'good Pythagorean students' were invited into the cult-leader's inner-circle and adopted the title 'mathematicians', while those outside this inner group not only didn't get to learn the more intricate details of Pythagorean knowledge, they didn't even get to see the 'leader' in person. Apparently, they were only allowed to hear lectures from the great man that were given from behind a veil, and that these were comprised of cryptic sayings with hidden meanings.

Then there were some very odd things the outer membership, known as the 'listeners' were prohibited from doing, like not to step over a crossbar - which might have been intended in a more metaphoric sense - meaning to not over-step one's position, or something like that. Another thing they were not allowed to do, and there's an explanation for this one, so it could be literal - was to not eat beans, because beans contain embryo's inside them like humans. Whether literally true of not, it's clear that this cult did have some strict rules and extremely controlling aspects to it.

Extreme it may have been, but it might also have been empowering to a good proportion of the members. You see, at that time not all people were equal. Ex-slaves who'd earned their freedom were not the same as 'citizens', they had none of the rights afforded a person of the state - they just weren't owned by anyone. As for feeding, clothing, and housing themselves, well that depended on how effective each was at getting paid work - something that probably was a tough to do then as it is now.

Even citizens were graded according to their birth-right and position in society, with the doors to the better professions firmly closed on anyone perceived as below that station. As for women, sadly, they were not considered equals - they were confined to menial tasks or expected to tend the home for a husband and be a mother to his children. This may be why so many of them were attracted to a different set of rules, because for the Pythagoreans none of this was true. Pythagoras wanted all types of people to join his cult; men of any rank or position and women of any status, were all invited to be equal to any other member. Hence, the draconian rules and inner-circle thing might have been a small price to pay for the certainty of food, shelter, and equality among the group.

However, let´s just rewind for a moment and focus on the early life that might have shaped him - because before all this, the young Pythagoras had grown up on the small island of Samos in the eastern Aegean. It´s just off the coast of Turkey and separated from Asia minor by a mile-wide stretch of water. It was, and still is one of the more populated of the islands in that region and was named by the Phoenicians of earlier antiquity - indicating that it was in use as a trading port way back then.

The mild climate, semi-mountainous terrain, 74% sunshine, and fresh spring water made it a luxurious place to settle. It looks like an idyllic spot, better known now for relaxing vacations and small yachting harbours. For such a small island to have been the birthplace not only of one world-altering philosopher but two is incredible (but more about Epicurus later). Curiously, it was also the birthplace of another influential person by the name of Aristarchus. We shan't be looking at him because he was an astronomer rather than a philosopher, but he is worth a mention because he is the first person known to propose that the earth revolves around the sun.

Hm... I thought I'd had a good all-round education but could have sworn I'd learned that it was Copernicus who'd had that claim to fame? However, it appears I was wrong, and Aristarchus has that honour - at least he does in the Greek tradition. There is a suggestion it was remarked on even earlier, and that an Indian by the name of Yajnavlka had the same idea another around three hundred years before Aristarchus. We know, because it is alluded to in a sacred Hindu text.

It may be that the idea had been around even before that, but it's fascinating that such a tiny island as this, surrounded by clear blue seas with balmy sunny weather, just getting on with the everyday activity of trade with passers-by, ended up spawning not just one great thinker, but three - in the shape of Pythagoras, Epicurus, and Aristarchus.

His Culture: In his youth Pythagoras had learned all about mathematics while travelling through Egypt and had learned to think about numbers as much more than a means of addition or subtraction. He'd learned instead that they offered an opportunity to test, experiment with, and explore nature - and he didn't have to confine himself to scratching out lines on scraps of pottery to work things out. Rather than theorise about the numbers of squares that might go into a triangle, he would draw right angles, make them into squares on the ground and physically count them.

Numbers represented the way 'things' could be manipulated, and as such were almost magical to them. They were trying to understand a world that was yet to be understood, and the formula's and laws of mathematics were yet to be written. Which is why the studying of maths, music, and astrology were undertaken together - for Pythagoras and his followers there was no difference between them, as maths connects them all.

This was a time, when people who took the time to look were learning by observation and being stunned by the result. For instance, Pythagoras was watching a blacksmith at work, and was surprised, not by what the smithy was doing but by what he was hearing. When the smithy was hammering away on a large anvil the sound was deep and resonant, but when he moved to an anvil half its sized sound was different... a higher note. In fact, he recognised that when the two anvils were exactly double the size of each other the notes were the same, but an octave higher.

The eight notes that separated the two sounds were not just musical, but later came to be the basis for the construction of a table of chemical elements - in 1865 the scientist and researcher John Newlands recognised that chemical elements are arranged according to atomic weight, and that those with similar properties occur at every 8th element, just like those in a music scale. It was a truly a remarkable thing to notice for the first time, and Pythagoras is credited with being the one to figure it out.

The culture of observation and awareness of the natural world and human interaction with it was much more apparent than now. Let's face it, we have people who don't know that KFC comes from a bird with wings, or that coffee does indeed grow on trees. We have bosses that follow 'rules' as if they were unbendable despite whatever risks and drawbacks may be entailed, and all too few leaders like Pythagoras who are prepared to use the observational skills of themselves and their team members to assess and analyse the reality they're facing - and do it with an open mind.

His Skills: There's little wonder that we still remember him today, and why he had people happy to leave their old lives behind and follow him into silent cult-hood. He really did see past the obvious and recognise the numbers beneath every aspect of 'reality'. He is quoted as saying:

"Number is the ruler of all forms".

He was way ahead of his time. There's no doubt that Pythagoras was the at the cutting edge of understanding numbers, so, to his followers he must have also come across as being at the cutting edge of ruling all forms.

Hence, it's little wonder that they saw him as an almost 'divine' 'leader'. By all accounts the man wasn't shy, so he too might have bought into the idea of himself as the communicator of 'god-given' information. Information so powerful and new that it could have felt like they'd uncovered the foundational structures of the universe. It was a big idea and he was a larger than life character - when you think about it like that, it just had to end in a cult, didn't it?

Fast forward to now and his ideas may no longer feel like a 'big deal' - we now view these breakthroughs as nothing more than a lesson for children. However, that should in no way diminish the impact they would have had back then, and the skill Pythagoras had attributed to him and that he attributed to himself. He was a smart guy, if not quite as 'god-like' as he might have believed himself to be - even so, he must have had considerable knowledge in the field of astronomy, and he should have credit for that because it helped him realise that there's more to reality than meets the eye.

His teacher had been Anaximander (he of the 'we all come from the belly of a fish') fame. The thing is, while he is credited with things that have stood the test of time, it's also quite possible that he came up with other smart stuff for which good old Plato later took the credit. I'm not saying Plato was an idea stealer - not at all, just that he may have adapted some ideas that first saw the light of day from Pythagoras. For example, the notion that people remember things from a previous existence, that mathematics underpins the whole natural world, and that everything we see, hear, touch, feel, taste, and sense has a mathematical structure. Those all originally came from Pythagoras.

His Beliefs: It's hard to think of Pythagoras as a religious leader - with the strength to motivate, influence and persuade people to follow him, but he was, and hence must have believed himself to be capable of that kind of leadership. Unlike most of the philosophers in here he was both a thought-leader and a leader of people. From our viewpoint it might look like he was better at the former rather than latter but that may not be true. There's no evidence that his rather strict cult regime was anything but a great success. He obviously believed what he was doing was right, and the 300 people in his commune weren't forced to be there - aka a success.

His self-confidence must have been out of the park – at least that's probably how he saw himself. Others outside of his commune might have described him differently as larger than life characters are always 'Marmite'- you're either in or out! Where that confidence came from isn't clear but it is likely he'd been influenced by an older religion called Orphism. This religion had flourished in Croton before Pythagoras settled his cult there and their beliefs must have sat well with Pythagoras's contention that mathematics was at the heart of all things - not because that's what the Orphics necessarily believed, but because their belief that *'the world itself is nothing but the body of [the] god'* was a fit.

Reflecting on this much older point of view could have been the source of his confidence. If 'all' was a part of one thing, then that one thing could be divided into repeating mathematical patterns than came together to form that one 'thing'.

He firmly believed that mathematics, music, and astronomy all had the same source, and could all be aligned. He believed that this was sacred information entrusted to him so that he might share it with the world. I think the modern term might be that he had something of a god-complex himself because of his cult-style leadership. Like the Orphics, he was certain that while the make-up of the world around us and our corporeal bodies was an earthbound manifestation, but our souls were of a different, and a celestial construction.

If all we see is a result of numerical equations, then the soul is the numerical source.

He believed the soul to be at the heart of everything, on a circular course though the cosmos and apparently wandering from one life form to another, before returning and starting over again. It's clear that he believed in the transmigration of souls through animals - that souls left humans and moved on to animals as part of their 'journey' through creation.

The story goes that he heard someone beating a dog and the cries the dog made sounded just like a friend of his who'd recently passed away. It was the cries of this dog that made him realise that animals needed to be treated as respectfully as other humans, and it's why he insisted on vegetarianism in his commune.

I'm just glad it was his theory about squares and triangles that made it through to the twenty first century, but it's a shame this idea has lagged so far behind. Perhaps the big shift we now see in Veganism (and I must own up to being mainly veggie myself) is a sign that a version of his thinking is catching up. Perhaps Pythagoras ought to be the philosophical standard bearer for the new veggie/vegan movement?

His Identity: He often said that it was just a fact that all people were born with too much potential to be evil. Let's just pause for a moment and consider that idea – we all have too much potential to be intrinsically evil. Contemporary writer Tim Gallwey came up with a brilliant way of looking at the performance of people (in business, sport, or whatever) – He said that their performance is directly equal to their potential minus the interference that gets in the way. I happily admit to using this all the time when coaching, and my shorthand for it is $P=(p-i)$, so if you see that anywhere you now know what it means. I think Pythagoras would have loved that little equation because when holding the belief that everyone has the potential to be ´good´, then the only thing a person need think about is removing the barriers that get in the way of being as good as they have the potential to be. Pythagoras knew that the only way people could remove those barriers was by living a good life.

If he did indeed believe in the Orphic-like circular wandering soul, then it's logical that he would be focused on doing whatever he could to help people's souls make the most of their time on this part of the journey. Perhaps he imagined a life dedicated to learning, asking better questions about what seems 'normal' and removing those barriers was the way to create mini-miracles before our eyes. I certainly think he may have seen himself as someone who embraced the concept of 'universal rules' – unquestionable truths that governed everything; the things we can see, the things we know about but can't see, and especially the things that must go on but of which we have no idea.

His fundamental conviction was that observation and awareness is essential, but that reason will always trump our senses. He was a rationalist with a strong set of spiritual beliefs, (and maybe a god-complex)which might have led him to adopt the status of being someone essential to the wellbeing of others. It seems reasonable to think that he imagined himself to be someone without whom people would fail to ensure their souls made the most of their ´journey´. As I said #GodComplex

This combination probably turned his genius into something more than just a wee-bit scary. If so, it's no wonder he retreated into his inner-circle and ruled (the world of his own creation) with such strict doctrines. Despite being as clever as he no doubt was, I doubt he would have survived under the scrutiny of a wider public. It´s a good job for him that Twitter wasn't around in those days. Hence, he was able to bend the people in his little world to his will. Like all cult-leaders he established his own 'greater-good' and coerced his followers to buy-into ´him´, with the promise of it leading to a better life than whatever they'd had. He convinced them that by serving the needs of their celestial soul they would be rewarded after death. Furthermore, he convinced them that 'true life' happens after the soul departs this body. It wasn´t a Jim Jones[xxviii] style death cult but the similarities in the way people within were controlled is obvious. Pythagoras may have been brilliant, but it seems he had a dark side that might have been swept under the historical carpet.

There may be a good reason for that - because, not only must he have been quite a character, but his rhetoric about life-after-death is very familiar, isn't it? Remember, this all happened in the sixth century BCE, a full eight hundred years or so before the Christian religion got started in earnest, and it was happening without any connection between this idea and similar ideas about destiny being driven by character and conduct in the mortal world. Let´s recap - similar ideas to Christianity but without the ´do good while you´re alive´ bit and put forward by a brilliant scientist with a dark side. So, was he ahead of his time? Had he tapped into some eternal truth? Or, was he simply using similarities between his mathematical theories and an existing religion to get three hundred people to drink the 'Kool aid'[xxix] of his beliefs? By the way - there is no indication that the commune ended badly... or perhaps because they were all silent, no one heard about it!

His Purpose: As he accepted unconditionally that *number is the ruler of all forms*, and that *a cycle of reincarnation exists* for all things - I think his purpose was to lead by example - even when that example might be considered by us as ´dark´.

Having said that, I also think he was as mad as a box of frogs even if he clearly didn't think so. The restrictive lifestyle he insisted on for himself and all his followers must have been the nearest he could get to creating something that helped them all focus on those things he believed really mattered. It was logical but way out there in terms of being extreme.

I don't think there can be any doubt that he was a force of nature, a huge personality, and a compelling character. As William Shakespeare put it, *"Thou makes me waver in my faith to hold opinion with Pythagoras"*.

How might he be thought of by his employees, if he was a manager in today's business world?

He´s the charismatic, paternalistic, powerful entrepreneur with complete confidence in himself and the way his business needs to be run. His people know that they are required to always act in ways he will approve. His team know there´s a dark side to him but also know that if they stay focused on the goals at hand, then his dark side can sometimes be used as a convenient means to an end.

There is no room for conversation or questioning of his fundamental rules or ideas – what he says is law. However, within the confines of those ´rules´ he encourages his people to be as creative and intuitive as they need to be to remove barriers in the way of living a good life and running a good business.

In practice, he´s been successful …for a while. When the ideas were fresh and new, and opportunities were there to make them into a competitive advantage, the business thrived. His cult-like status as an outstanding leader (albeit having some less than desirable personal characteristics) was an asset during those heady days of success. Unfortunately, those successes haven´t lasted forever. Competitors have learned from us about moving barriers to success and have been doing it themselves and have caught on to our recipe for success. However, they have the flexibility to pick and choose from contemporary successful ideas whereas our leader won´t listen to anything outside of the narrow confines of our way of doing things.

If we don´t change, and if we don´t make new choices by keeping those aspects of his leadership that work but let go of those things that don´t, then our organisation will eventually fail – a charismatic and brilliant leader is just not enough.

Coaching questions he might ask: Of course, his insistence on numbers being at the heart of everything must come into his questions, but not just that - his cult-leader status might also have led him to dig just that bit deeper than most people might feel able. While this cult-leader thing shouldn't be confused with being the kind of Leader we're looking for, he does demonstrate the power of personality when combined with shared beliefs.

i. *"Does the fuel for your fire-for-life grow or diminish with the approach you're now adopting?"*

ii. *"How do you repair a sequence that breaks down without understanding the elements that have combined to make it so?*

iii. *"If all life is a cycle, then where and what do you want yours to go after your present situation is resolved?"*

iv. *"If you are going to find your true resonance with life, what aspects of yourself must you come to terms with?"*

v. *"When things don't add up, if you blame the numbers rather than where those numbers came from, what is likely to be the result for you?"*

vi. *"When trying to find your way through a maze, does it matter more how you got lost in there or how you find your way out?"*

CHAPTER 19: #15 WHAT'S LIFE LIKE VIEWED FROM A DUMPSTER?

SOCRATES

His Claim to Fame: Socrates must be the biggest name in philosophy there is, and his fame has its roots in two words; *'righteous living'*.

Even people who haven't the first clue about philosophy have heard of Socrates. He's the first of the 'Big Three' in Ancient Greek philosophy and thanks to Hollywood there's a certain imagine that comes to mind when he's mentioned. However, Socrates was not the white-robed wise-old-boy from the movies, but more like the *'wide-eyed on-a-different-planet'* homeless guy who stank like a dead cat and if alive today would make a point of sitting next to you on the bus to ask you questions. Yet, unlike any homeless stereotyping Socrates asked questions that were significantly a cut above the mundane - even for people who had a home to call their own. In fact, his biggest claim to fame was a preoccupation with asking better and better questions.

This stinky, long haired, unkempt, and frankly ugly bloke with bulgy-eyes—was someone who would accost people in the street asking them odd questions out of the blue. Like, what is courage, or piety, or virtue? He asked, because he claimed not to know, and was considered a pest by the good ordinary folk of his time because most of the time they didn't know either. Fast forward to today and they'd be astounded to learn that he's one of the names recognised by almost everyone on the planet who's heard of philosophy.

There's an important distinction to draw here; up and until Socrates all the important names in philosophy have been well-off. They had plenty of time to cogitate about how the world is the way it is - hence theories about it being made of water, air, or something else entirely, ...like something called atoms? None of which was important to Socrates. The metaphysical didn't bother him at all - Socrates' response to it was something like; *"Bla bla bla! Who cares what the world is made up of - it'll still be here tomorrow whatever you decide it is and wherever you decide it comes from!"*

Okay, those are my words not his, but they do capture his approach. You see, he was much more interested in how people 'lived' than what it was that *allowed* them to live. His search for answers was all about the best way to live life and the choices people can make, as opposed to the others who tried to explain things no one had a choice about anyway. Which may be why people got to know about the smelly guy with frog-like eyes, worn out shoes, shabby clothes and no material goods other than he was wearing - because he spent his time speaking to whoever would listen, talking about things they weren't used to hearing.

He liked to ask questions even when being questioned himself. People got to know about Socrates and so the ancient Greek equivalent of youngsters in hoodies with nothing better to do would round on him and ask questions they thought would be difficult, or impossible to answer. For example, he was asked if virtue can be taught? He repliedthat there was no way he could he say when he didn't even know what virtue is – so, how could he know if anyone could teach it? He went on to ask if the questioner could help him out by asking, "what *is* virtue anyway?"

The questioner and his pals then go on to say what they think virtue is, and by even trying to answer, they fell into Socrates trap. By using more and more ever deepening questions Socrates leaves them in no doubt that in truth, they don't have a clue what they're talking about. Essentially, he used logical questioning to tie them in knots.

Sneaky, eh? Yet, to those 'in the know', he was said to be the wisest man in the land. Why did they think he was the wisest of them all? Well, it was because they were told he was, that's why - and probably because he did come up with some very good, deep thinking stuff - like this;

"To fear death gentlemen, is no other than to think oneself wise when one is not. To think one knows what one does not know. No one knows if death may not be the greatest of all blessings for man. Yet, men fear it as if they knew that it is the greatest of all evils; and surely it is the most blameworthy ignorance to claim that one knows what one does not know."

Before I get lynched by anyone that's studied the classics, I'm bound to point out that Socrates didn't leave any writings behind for us to study. All his 'words' were penned by his student Plato, or playwrights like Aristophanes and Xenophon who wrote Socrates into their plays and by doing so put words into his mouth - in what are known as the 'Socratic Dialogues'.

Plays like the 'Clouds' were popular, where he was portrayed as a completed buffoon - spinning around shouting "I'm walking on air". It was a stunt that apparently had the audience in fits of laughter - I guess you had to have been there to appreciate how funny it was at the time.

Anyway, either Plato thought Socrates was brilliant or he simply needed to present somebody as the brightest guy on the planet and decided Socrates was a good fit. For our purposes it doesn't matter; if they are his precise words then all well and good, or if they're a stylised version created by Plato then that's fine too. It really doesn't matter - the fact that he studied under Socrates is enough to suggest we get a glimpse of the real man.

It adds to the 'myth' surrounding Socrates that in the early days of philosophy his approach acted as a watershed in the emerging field of contemporary philosophy. In that, before him most of the early philosophers were only interested in trying to explain the experiences around them - they questioned how things came to be, and what made everything do what it does.

Metaphysics, or thinking about the big-picture is the search for explanations about the stuff of the universe. However, as has been made clear Socrates wasn't interested in big-thinking theories. No, not at all - his interest was more pragmatic. He wanted to better understand why people think and act like they do, and how they know they know what they think they know. His approach to philosophy was for it to be useful, for it to make a difference in the way people behave, and for it to be a genuine ´new way of thinking´. He might have raised a scruffy eyebrow to find that now this study into knowledge and thinking is in academic circles grandly called 'epistemology'. Somehow, I sense he was less inclined to be academic and much more interested in getting to grips with the thorny problem of what might still be described as the ridiculous behaviour of everyday folk.

His huge claim to fame is *'Socratic questioning'*. Clearly, it was called that long after he was doing it and if he´d been asked to give it a name he probably wouldn´t have given it his own name but would more likely have called it something more useful such as ´logical questioning´ or ´´questions to force people to learn from what they already know´ - basically, it's the asking of a question that stimulates 'insight'.

Sometimes, that insight is recollection, or making mental connections, re-contextualising something, or learning something new - not by acquiring information from elsewhere but by applying what you already know in a different context or situation. Socrates knew that everyone has more knowledge than they are necessarily aware of - that we all compartmentalise knowledge and sometimes struggle to notice the application of what we know in a new or different context.

Socrates wanted to question everything - eventually that insatiable appetite for asking more and better questions ended up killing him. Back then, just like today there are times and places where the strong emotions and beliefs of others makes questioning a dangerous thing to do.

His Environment: Socrates is seen as creating his own space in the universe - as a man who'd earned the right to say and do things based on his experiences.

Before that, it's worth having a stab and what got him to that point. The fact is there's not that much information about his early life; but it does appear that mum and dad weren't particularly well off, nor were they destitute. Dad was a mason and probably wanted his son to follow in his footsteps. There are some indications that young Socrates did have a reasonable education, but I'm guessing the real turning point in his life came when he was in his late thirties when his world was thrown into chaos. The calm and sophistication of Athens was shattered by the Peloponnesian war. Like most of the men folk of Athens he was drafted into the army and suffered the humiliating defeat by Sparta. One of his relatives turned out to be a collaborator and was installed by the victors as one of the 'Thirty-Tyrants' put in charge of the country - not one of Greece's finest hours - nor the kind of family legacy Socrates would have hoped for.

There's evidence that he'd been a teacher and philosopher before the war, but I'd be amazed if the down-at-heel, intense and little bit scary Socrates hadn't happened and come about as a result of the experience of war. His notoriety as the down at heel vagrant came about when he was a 'vet'. He had seen first-hand the results of life lived without examination, and now knew for sure it was something to be avoided.

His Culture: No matter how 'odd' the man might have been, he lived in a culture that allowed him to have many admirers. Many more so after his execution, probably because in the cold light of day after tempers had cooled and Athens was less jittery about trouble makers, the verdict and subsequent execution must have been something of an embarrassment. The great thinker did not deserve to die a condemned man - and they knew it.

To be fair to them, it must have been a time fraught with danger and mistrust - the war had only been over for about four years and people were jittery about rocking the boat of their new-found peace. I guess there had been enough savagery for one lifetime, so getting rid of a dirty old philosopher who seemed intent on making waves might have been an attractive choice, albeit very sad. These Athenians were people who considered themselves a cut above the savage uncultured societies to their east and north and anywhere past their own outposts - so, I can imagine them being less than proud of the mob turning against a clever philosopher just because he didn't conform to their narrow view of the world. It was one of those times when 'he who shouts loudest gets heard'.

Sadly, there are plenty of contemporary examples that our own history may result in being thought of with equal shame - this time not because a philosopher dared to question the 'gods', but because scientists stood up for basic facts like evolution, the age of the planet, climate change, the fact that investing less than $50 billion stands a chance of solving world hunger for a year while military spending in one country alone tops $700 billion - all in the face of ignorant angry-mobs shouting the down. Fortunately, it tends to happen in the media now rather than the courts - and scientists are not sentenced to death like poor old Socrates.

As an aside, I was driving from Washington DC to Cleveland recently and couldn't believe my eyes when faced with massive billboards urging people to dismiss scientific evidence as lies. I can imagine the old man Socrates at the time he took the Hemlock was thinking something like that crossing my mind, as I shook my head in disbelief at the anti-science signage. He must have felt that his whole life of trying to ask better questions had been one big waste of time.

His Skills: I've said already that Socrates didn't write anything down - you'd think being a mason he would have at least chiselled something in stone, but he didn't.

However, most of Plato's writings about the great man were scribbled not long after Socrates death. Plato was just 28 when he wrote some of his best work on Socrates, and for what it's worth I agree with many experts that this must have meant much that Plato supposed came out of Socrates mouth was as close as he could get to word perfect.

The character he presents through all his writing doesn't change, so I think it's fair to say that the skills the written Socrates displays are probably as close as we're going to get to the ones he displayed in real life. Obviously, the biggest is his ability to formulate better and better questions to illicit better and better responses.

Did he succeed in always asking better questions? That's a moot point if the question he asked himself about what was best, to pay a fine and admit he was wrong or poison himself and say a final goodbye, ended in his death. However, it does evidence his consistency. When the Delphic Oracle suggested that Socrates was the wisest man in the world, it probably had something to do with the consistency with which he caused people to search within themselves to find answers they did not realise were there all along.

His Beliefs: Whatever the Oracle had said, I don't believe Socrates himself ever genuinely believed he was a wise man.

Therefore, the popular promotion of his wisdom did not come from any self-publicity, intentional or otherwise. He was no Empedocles wandering around in ridiculous bronze sandals and an eye-catching big purple belt - who might as well have had a sign reading *'follow me - I'm a wise man'*. No, that was not the way of Socrates.

Socrates asked questions in the search for wisdom within others. This was his own wisdom - one that he was supposed to, according to the Oracle, already possess - although quite how she knew is anyone's guess. The wizened old woman on recreational drugs, living in isolation and earning only from whatever offerings were left in return for her predictions of the future had stated unequivocally that Socrates was the wisest person in all the land. Who then was going to argue with the Oracle? If she said it, it must either be true, or at least becoming true. Therefore, whether he agreed with it or not, Socrates was a wise man. Period.

His Identity*: "When a swan is about to die, it sings. It sings more beautifully than it ever has before, for it belongs to the god Apollo and has the gift of prophecy. So, the swan knows it will die and sings with joy because it is finally about to re-join its divine master."*

Socrates met death with hope not concern. These words come from Plato's dramatisation of his final moments before death. It was Socrates 'Swansong' and celebrates his death before finally downing hemlock and popping his clogs.

His life and identity may be much like the acts in a play; first the youngster following in daddy's footsteps learning to be a stonemason. After that came a period of learning followed by the best way of embedding that learning - becoming a teacher himself. Then off to war and the horrors that must have faced every soldier in that army of blacksmiths, carpenters, tailors, potters, and philosophers like him.

Like the conscripts of any army today when facing an army made up of one profession only, soldiers the experience must have been brutal. The brutality of those experiences must have changed his identity - and maybe is why he started to live like he did. He certainly wasn't the last 'vet' to find it difficult to reintegrate into peaceful society after a gruesome war experience.

Next, he had the identity of the 'Wisest Man' thrust upon him by the Oracle - an identity he neither sought nor agreed with, but one that became the driving force behind the adoption of his questioning style. Then, finally the identity of someone whose life had been so closely examined that he took the decision to end it rather than bend to the temporary will of a tyrannical State. There's no doubt in my mind that the man had the courage of his convictions.

Most of us get to define our identity once if we are lucky enough to be able to think about it enough, but he must have had several through his interesting, if not traumatic life.

His Purpose: As I imagine him sitting across the table from me as I'm writing this, I can see him raising a bushy eyebrow, daring me to assign some grand purpose to his life.

I won't, not because I'm hallucinating but because I don't think he *did* have a grand purpose. His was a life lived in search of meaning, much like any of us who desire nothing more than to make the best use of the time we have on this planet and in this body. Even though it´s often attributed to him, the fact is that he never said, "*the unexamined life is not worth living*", but his star pupil Plato put these words into his mouth, and hence it speaks volumes about the man and his purpose in life.

His actions tell us that he was never afraid to ask searching questions, never afraid to use questions to make a point, and never afraid to force someone into admitting that they knew their answers all along by simply asking better, more insightful questions. If he had any overarching purpose, that was it. Apart from the whole personal hygiene thing, he´s my kind of thought-leader.

How might he be thought of by his employees, if he was a manager in today's business world?

He doesn´t look like a typical business leader. He doesn´t sound much like a typical business leader, and he often doesn´t act like a typical business leader - and yet, he gets things done and remarkably, he does it in a way that generates unity and commonality of purpose within the ranks of employees at every level.

One of the ways he achieves this unity is by rejecting outright anything that isn´t relevant to them all and focusing on anything that is pertinent and real. While his contemporaries might work within strict hierarchies, he chooses to interact with people as and when the need arises. He is just as likely to be spending time with a customer service agent asking questions that inform their current approach to service standards, as he might spend time with the chief accountant asking questions about which reports are still useful and which are not. It's not that he is disorganised, it's that he won't hold meetings for the sake of a meeting when his time might be better spend asking tough questions with people 'in the know' somewhere within the workings of the business.

His goal as business leader is to facilitate clarity in the organisation and stimulate self-development and learning in every employee at every level within the business. The net result is that every employee feels they're engaged in achieving business goals that both are clear and make sense to them.

Coaching questions he might ask: The great thing about Socrates is that we don't have to imagine the kind of questions he would ask because there's evidence of how and when he asked questions for real. In the context of helping someone as their Coaching-Leader, they may have gone something like this;

 i. *"What do you know to be true that you have avoided facing, which is causing you to respond in this way?"*

 ii. *"What if the things you are struggling with, turned out to be the greatest gift you've ever received?"*

 iii. *"By starting with a foundation of those things you've become certain of, what new construction*

iv. *might you create that takes you in a better direction?"*

iv. *"Do you consider your own development worth the pain of learning something new and taking uncomfortable action if that's what's required?"*

v. *"If your life is a haystack, where and what is the needle you are searching for?"*

vi. *"Instead of asking yourself what you don't know, how about starting by defining those things that you are, if not certain, at least aware of?"*

vii. *"Is this the worst you will ever experience; if not or if so, how have you or will you use what you know to do better than merely survive?"*

viii. *"What do you believe about this situation that is preventing you from asking yourself a better question?"*

ix. *"What logical conclusion could you draw from your own circumstances that might explain why you have more control than you have previously accepted?"*

CHAPTER 20: #16 AN IMMORTAL AMONG MEN?

EMPEDOCLES

His Claim to Fame: If Tony Robbins[xxx] had been around at this time, he may well have been Empedocles. Larger than life, inspirational, imposing, and once seen never forgotten. His big message and contribution to thought-leadership was the theory of 'four elements'- that all matter comes from earth, air, fire, and water – probably the earliest theory of particle physics. He captured the imagination of his followers by engaging people in the concept of a cosmic cycle of eternal change. Moreover, he proposed that the there is an eternal battle between love and strife - and that those who followed him could learn how to influence their own position in that eternal battle. Why him? Because he was a divine-being himself with direct access to the immortals. One of his stated beliefs was that people believe only in their own experience – so, he took on the personal of a mystical, magical personality that gave them an experience that was real.

His most obvious claim to fame at the time (Empedocles not Robbins), was that he's 'the' larger than life philosopher of his time. He'd arrive in a town 'on tour', and make himself stand out by wearing bronze sandals, a big purple belt on his robe, a wreath on his head and, although it doesn't actually say this in the text I'd be amazed if he hadn't had some kind of sign saying 'follow me' or 'this way for salvation'. He honestly sounds like an early version of the archetype 'charismatic bloke' that pops up from time to time in history – a person who genuinely believes he's an immortal among mere normal men. However, his approach was sound because by being larger than life - giving them a mystical experience they could not argue with because it was their own, he knew those people would become his followers. Then, just like all the self-proclaimed gurus of our own time who manage to fill auditoriums with eager hopefuls waiting to be told how to turn their lives around, Empedocles seems to have nicked most of his material from the real thinkers from the previous century. He then took centre stage, re-packaged as his own. Not that there's anything intrinsically wrong with that, particularly if a new or contemporary spin for its time is put on solid thinking of the past.

However, I'm a bit dubious about this guy as his 'spin' was more about him than about helping anyone find a way to use the wisdom he was now spouting as his own. His shtick was that a goddess had whisked him up into the sky and bestowed all this wonderful information to him so that he could spread it to others. Yeah, okay that happened. Okay, maybe it did – but, if he'd really had a revelation to benefit all of humankind I think his message would have been more about those benefits than being a platform for his own ego stroking.

His Environment: Hailing from Akragas, known now as Arigento, a thriving city situated on the southern coast of Sicily, a couple of hours drive from the current capital of Sicily, Palermo on the North coast.

I wonder if his outlandish confidence and self-belief might be a foretelling of a group of people that might come to mind when thinking of Sicily? I'm not suggesting he was the Great-Great-Great etc. Granddaddy of the first Mafia Boss – but, who knows? It's not as far-fetched as it might sound because the place was named after the son of Zeus himself– they had a strong powerful image of themselves from the get-go. It was a thriving conurbation of at least 200,000 people during Empedocles lifetime - huge compared to most of the Greek city-states meaning that getting noticed was more challenging than in smaller locations. It was probably the wealthiest and most famous city-state of them all until everything came to an abrupt halt when it was overrun by a Carthaginian army after a prolonged siege.

However, as far as Empedocles was concerned, during his time it must have seemed like the wealth and riches available to its citizens would go on forever. It didn't, and nor did he although he clearly expected it to!

His Culture: Empedocles was a pre-Socratic philosopher, able to study at leisure because of being funded by wealthy and indulgent parents. If during his studying he had to choose between leaving a legacy or being relevant, he chose relevance. His big idea was metaphysical (how the world works) but his approach was to turn that idea into something of the moment - not quite in the service of epistemology (the theory of learning) but more in the service of the man himself.

Isn't it fascinating that so many early philosophers included Egypt on their travel itinerary? Clearly, something that was happening, or had happened in Egypt was important in helping shape how they viewed the world. We know that the Egyptian civilisation sprung up quickly and was probably influenced by the Sumerian civilisation that came before it. The point being that whatever 'scientific' thinking had been going on since the beginning of human civilisation was probably gathered together in

Egypt - hence, it was a budding philosopher's 'must visit' on any travel itinerary.

Empedocles must have been there because one of the most recent discoveries of his writings was in Egypt - preserved on a roll of papyrus. It was a poem – probably because the culture of the time was prone to favour the more poetic and lyrical over straight facts and information. Hence, the writings attributed to him are all in the form of poem fragments.

Empedocles' introduction to philosophy was as a follower of Pythagoras. It's not known how long he followed the ways of the cult-leader or how much time he spent in the commune, but we do know that he broke the rules by eating meat and so either left or was thrown out.

Being who he was, Empedocles turned this possible 'sow's ear' into a veritable 'silk-purse' by donning his ridiculous garb and claiming to be a divine being. His excuse for failing in the commune was that he was now paying penance for breaking the meat-eating rule - he argued that his own experience meant anyone willing to follow him could save themselves the 'pain' he'd suffered. He was suggesting his own god-like countenance could save them from otherwise being misled by temptation elsewhere. It sounds like a contemporary message to me that's obviously been around for a long time - aimed at anyone in search of an improved life.

If it hadn't been for the fact that his own life ended in such ridiculous circumstances, I'd be inclined to label him the first real snake-oil salesman. However, unlike the sneaky snake-oil purveyors who know they're a sham, I think he might have bought into his own delusion. It was to be his downfall - quite literarily he fell down the opening of a volcano with the intent to survive as a hero. He didn't. Oops. #epicfail

His Skills: There's no doubt that the man was multi-talented. If realty TV had been around then, I'm sure he would have been signed up for a series of something eye-catching and ended up as a presenter on some wild and whacky TV or internet show.

His unique fashion sense wasn't the only thing about him that was 'special'. Not only did he dress himself in pseudo-royal garb, he came into town acting as if he were somebody people should take seriously. His confidence must have been impressive, as was his commitment to his role. He must have had the 'X-factor' an entertainer needs to captivate an audience. Having said that, he did make sure he had help - his entourage were not fellow philosophers but a group of youngish boys, all charged with the single job of following him around and treating him as if he were royalty. His approach must have been something like - if he looks like royalty, sounds like royalty, and is treated as royalty then he must be a dude to take seriously. The psychology of 'meeting expectations' clearly wasn't lost on him - it might not have been understood in a formal sense, but he certainly knew how to milk it for his own benefit. It's just a shame that like so many like him before and after, he started to believe his own hype. Once that happens, it's all downhill from there.

However, Empedocles didn't go around smiling and offering a royal wave, instead adopted a grave expression intended to communicate the seriousness with which he took his role in life. Let's face it, there's every chance the guy was a whacko, or at the very least, an eccentric. Yet, he did have real skills - not only was he a philosopher with a big metaphysical idea, but also had been a politician back home in Akragas. He was also a poet and (apparently) a physician - although I'm not sure how seriously he took his bedside manner. Physician appears on his posthumous resume, but I'm guessing that might have been before he donned the purple robes and bronze shoes.

Although his writings have only been preserved in fragments, rather than as a complete body of work, he did have some scientific theories of his own. I think Empedocles was much more than the bronze-shod, purple-robed, olive-crowned people-pleaser he allowed himself to become. I think his ego might have got the better of him and prevented him from being remembered for his contribution rather than his eccentricity.

His Beliefs: His beliefs were as enigmatic as the man himself. Try this for example; *"God is a circle whose centre is everywhere, and its circumference nowhere".* Or, how about this; *"No mortals thing has a beginning, nor does it end in death and obliteration; there is only a mixing and then separating of what was mixed, but by mortal men these processes are named 'beginnings."*

This one is much clearer; *"There are forces in nature called Love and Hate. The force if love cause elements to be attracted to each other and to be built up into some particular form or person, and the force of hate causes the decomposition of things."*Just one more; *'Each man believes only his experience."*

These allow a glimpse of a complex character; someone who at the same time has great courage, but craved the good opinions of others, who is incredibly persuasive and not shy when it comes to self-confidence. However, as he was the first person to propose that there are four essential elements of fire, air, earth, and water – even though this was an extension of the work of plenty of the earlier philosophers we've already covered – he was still a bona fide philosopher in his own right. For the sake of accuracy, I should say he was the first *Greek* person to suggest these elements because they are alluded to in ancient Chinese teachings – yet, there's no suggestion that he knew about it nor that any hint of it influenced him.

Empedocles believed that these elements were/are eternal forces that are equally balanced in the universe - and his special 'take' on things was that this balance was affected by the influence of love and strife – something that people had some means of influencing. He believed that while everything else in the known-world came and went, these essential forces always remained. He believed this because at a metaphysical level, everything is created from them.

There's more than a hint of Laozi about Empedocles when he says; *"A twofold tale I shall tell: at one time it grew to be one alone out of many, at another again it grew apart to be many out of one... these things never cease their continual exchange, now through Love all coming together into one, now again each carried apart by the hatred of Strife... thus far they exist changeless in their cycle."*

He believed that this elegant balance extends to human life and death – which will have been a revelation to the people to whom he preached on his marches through Greece. Prior to hearing him they will have believed that every aspect of life was controlled by the gods. After listening to him their beliefs might have been shaken. If so, it's no wonder they flocked to him like he was a god on earth, because to them that's how he must have seemed. He was now a real-life alternative to hypothetical beings that no one had seen – and his message was simple – believe in *him* and your personal balance between love and strife will improve. He gave them something they could influence while all the gods did was demand sacrifice.

He also had some unusual views as to how 'life on earth' began, and how both human beings and a I also came to be. I warn you, this bit is weird; it's like he'd watched a whole season of Stephen King films in one sitting while smoking something. Okay, I know there were no such movies or any evidence of marijuana, but I hope you get my gist when I tell you that he thought there was a time when separate limbs wandered around on their own. He said;

"Here sprang up many faces without necks, arms wandered without shoulders, unattached, and eyes strayed alone, in need of foreheads... Many creatures were born with faces and breasts on both sides, man-faced ox-progeny, while others again sprang forth as of-headed offspring of man, creatures compounded partly of male, partly of the nature of female, and fitted with shadowy parts."

I did say it was strange. Scholars have taken this as his explanation for the creation of animals - that he was more 'normal' in his thinking about humans, suggesting they came *'from the earth'*. However, in the interests of balance I must point out that a friend interested in all things "extraordinary' told me he thought Empedocles might have been referring to the possible Sumerian legend of the 'Anunaki' –meaning *those who came from the skies*. This theory[xxxi] suggests that at a very early time in human history, beings that were not human experimented with DNA manipulation as they sought to create creatures able to assist them with manual labour. This theory posits that after many unfortunate failed experiments it eventually resulted in the production of the first 'Adamu' - a being created from a blending of the DNA of these non-human beings with that of a semi-intelligent ape - from which proto-humans began. Explained in the Sumerian legends as being created by the Anunaki from clay - possibly because of the use of earthenware containers in the supposed process. Essentially, when Empedocles said humans came from the earth (or clay), he was mirroring the way the Sumerians described the creation of the Adamu.

Trust me, I didn't make that up, it's a real theory - but, as to whether Empedocles had come across it in his travels, we will never know. We do know that the theory comes from an interpretation of Sumerian clay tile records, and that the Sumerian culture predates his by a couple of thousand years - so anything is possible.

His Identity: Whether he meant it literally or not, it's a matter of record that Empedocles did call himself a god. Something had gone to his head.

The bronze shoes and purple robes may have been a mite theatrical, but he did appear to genuinely believe he was some version of a god on earth. It's a shame for him that there weren't people in white coats there to strap him into a straight-jacket because he could have lived a few years longer if there were. You see, his demonstration of god-like powers was to leap into that live volcano I mentioned earlier - his goal being to use his *powers* to survive. He did, and he didn't. A crispy end to a colourful character. Oops.

His Purpose: Was his purpose to share his delusion, to convince his audience that they were all on a physical journey made possible by their soul shifting from its own god-like innocence when it comes into the world - only to fall from grace as humans shed the blood of other creatures and themselves? Maybe.

Did he want to convince people that such abominations against nature? Maybe.

Was his aim to ensure people knew that without balance this time would be followed by a period of purification – one during which they had the choice to either embrace love or set aside strife, or both, in the hope of reaching that elevated god-like status once more. Phew!

I don't know about you, but it sounds like it might be an interpretation of some heavy-duty religious doctrine -but with a light at the end of the tunnel. Personally, I think his purpose may have started out as pure, but probably got a little lost along the way – I put it down to the purple robes and bronze shoes myself.

How might he be thought of by his employees, if he was a manager in today's business world?

He's larger than life, colourful, and absolutely committed to his beliefs. But, it's a good job for him that he's built a team around him with the courage and perseverance to ask as many questions of him as he asks of others – without them there's every chance he could have unintentionally derailed his own successes.

He's managed to keep a tight team of highly skilled executives around him because of his insistence of the achievement of balance in everything they do. There's something about him that's different – other leaders may talk about the importance of achieving a work-life balance, but unlike most of them, he really means it. He knows that everyone will always find an emotional balance between those things they care about most and those things that cause them most concern – and that the higher the negativity of concerns, the higher the balancing negativity of the things most cared about.

His team know that he is right and are willing to accept the occasional eccentricity because of his commitment to this ideal. In practical terms it looks like this:

Employee X is hired because she has great potential but in her previous role elsewhere was unable to be as good as she could be - the pressure she felt was intense - to arrive by 8.30 am sharp, work without personal time except for two 15-minute breaks and a 45-minute lunch and deliver then collect 2 young children to and from school. This negative emotion was then unconsciously balanced in her commitment to the delivery of her work role. She didn't intend for her work to suffer, nor were there any reasons in the way she was managed, her training, and experience preparing her for that role. On paper she should have performed excellently, but in practice her performance was barely acceptable. She was unhappy, her previous employers were less than delighted, hence both were somewhat relieved when she took the decision to move on.

The same Employee X joined us and was immediately exposed to our leader's fundamental belief in the balance between love and strife – life and work. She was asked to commit herself to the production of the highest levels of quality outputs that were within her potential to deliver, and to do whatever was necessary for her to love her work. In return she was asked by her manager about those things that might cause her strife in those areas of her life that were important to her. After speaking of her love for her children and desire to ensure their safety and wellbeing the manager agreed a flexible schedule with her that facilitated both work and home life. Employee X has been here for 4 years now and is one of our most valued contributors - and according to her, she's never been so happy.

The best thing about him is atmosphere he's created at work, and the worst, that he does occasionally need his ego massaged and his wackier ideas reining in, but overall, he's a great guy to have at the helm. It's easy to see when he's going off track – luckily, we have a strong team on who he relies, just to keep us all, including him on the straight and narrow.

Coaching questions he might ask: As he was all about the *transmigration of the soul*, (achieving balance to you and me) - I sense that his questions would be more thoughtful and more challenging than the more pragmatic approaches we've seen so far.

Although this might seem like a stretch for leadership, it's not. One of the fastest growing approaches to modern leadership is 'Servant Leadership' - something that's already embedded in many of the biggest and most prominent organisations around the world. Fast on the tails of Servant Leadership is 'Spiritual Leadership', which doesn't have anything to do with religion or spiritualism - but does take a similar approach to Empedocles in assuming that every person in the workforce is seeking their 'best balance'- and that by helping them achieve their balance, the organisation will get the best out of their workforce.

i. *"If you would answer 'no!' to the question 'do you believe in your position strong enough to jump into the fires of a volcano knowing against all advice that you'd survive?', then what does that tell you that up until now hasn't crossed your mind?"*

ii. *"If there were to be one thing you might regret in a few years resulting from your own inaction now, is it strong enough to nudge you into doing what's truly right for you?"*

iii. *"If you hold out your hands, placing those things causing you strife in one hand and those things stimulating you to love in the other, in which direction do you wish to move right now?"*

iv. *"Imagining yourself re-achieving the god-like clarity you may once have been born with may require you to let something go, what might that be for you?"*

v. *"What do you love more than the thing that's causing you strife that's worth fighting for?"*

vi. *"When you put your hand out, reaching in your mind toward those things you truly desire, what*

256

are you feeling through the pores of your hand that are intended to force you toward a better decision?"

CHAPTER 21: #17 LEADERSHIP KARMA

MOZI

His Claim to Fame: He was living at about the same time as Socrates-but that's not his claim to fame. Mozi is best known for being the source of aphorisms and nuggets of insight that are as fresh today as they ever were.

I'd like to think he was the source of one of my favourites - *'What goes around comes around'*, but that might be a stretch because, okay, he might not have said it exactly like that - but what he did say was, *"When everyone regards the States and Cities of others as he regards his own, no one will attack the other's State or seize their cities"*. In his context, to all intents and purposes this was intended to mean (in my head anyway), what goes around, comes around – do not go attacking other people or it'll come back and bite you.

Could there have ever been a truer word spoken about leadership? Leaders know there is a 'leadership karma' that just 'is'- whereas a boss rarely grasps the concept that whatever they do will have an effect that one day will go full circle and affect them too – often when they least expect it.

When a boss sees problems in terms of what is(in their opinion) right or wrong – blaming the people they consider responsible, and not what is the 'right thing to do' to bring people along with them irrespective of who made a mistake, then in failing to regard the issues as their own they fail to heed Mozi's message - and will be criticised for it. Leaders do heed his advice. They take on responsibility (treating issues as their own) and by doing so align with others to solve problems, and so do not end up as a target for criticism. Bosses tend to be 'ego focused' - they must be seen to be blameless and 'right', while leaders are 'outcome driven' - paying attention only to the effectiveness of the actions taken.

Mozi was brilliant at giving the leaders of his time some harsh lessons about ego versus outcome. This lesson is as apt now as it was then;

"Now, to discard those who agree with the 'right' but employ those who agree with one's self - is not the way to be a great ruler."

Ouch! How many bosses need to hear that message if they are ever to become leaders, eh?

What about bosses who think they 'know it all' but in truth don't understand what's going on, nor how to do the job they're insisting isn't being done as well as it should be. They're the boss not only unable to do what they're asking other people to do 'better', but also intent on confusing the issue with unnecessary unfocused input – they most definitely need to heed the words of Mozi;

"When one cannot accomplish a single task from beginning to end there is no use of attempting many things. And when one is ignorant of a commonplace that is pointed out, there is no use of pursuing wide knowledge."

How about this one for those 'politically inclined' bosses who care more about how they're perceived by their own bosses than they do about becoming a leader;

"His wisdom will not be far-reaching whose purpose is not firm. His action will not be effective whose promises are

not kept."- wow, take that Mr ´the-goalposts-have-changed-again´ boss.

Mozi had great insight into the realities of life. He translated this awareness into stories that people could relate to. For example, in this one he suggests avoiding personal tragedy is no more or no less important than avoiding collective difficulty;

"Now, if carrying her child and drawing water from a well, a woman dropped the child into the well, she would of course endeavour to get it out. But famine and dearth is (sic) a much greater calamity than the dropping of a child. Should there not be also endeavour (to prevent it)? People are gentle and kind when the year is good, but selfish and vicious when it is bad."

The message that prevention is better than cure is one best not forgotten by leaders in today´s business world. Bosses who´ve taken their eye off this ball may be 'gentle and kind' when the numbers are coming in, but then 'selfish and vicious' when the going gets tough. Leaders know that when times are good, they need to understand just why they are good - and ask better questions about not only how those levels can be maintained but also if they could be bettered.

A boss may metaphorically put their feet upon their desk and lean back in their executive chair when profits are rolling in, but Mozi´s message to them is that on days like these they ought to be searching for the reasons why they´re being successful and how they can replicate that success. The good leader knows that days like these can go away way too fast and that their role is to do whatever it takes to make them last. Underpinning Mozi´s message of looking past the immediate in favour of the bigger picture means that a leader seeks to understand the entirety of their brief - they need to know if each member of their team is performing at their very best when the going is good - that way, if things turn bad, they're able to act without being selfish or vicious.

His Environment: Like other Chinese philosophers from this general period, he too came to experience the turmoil of the 'Warring-States' period of Chinese history. A tough time to be looking for work, a tough time to be anything but a soldier, in fact a tough time to survive, never mind become a philosopher who's remembered thousands of years later.

Mozi was born in what's now the Shandong Province of China to parents who weren't particularly well off. His earliest training wasn't as an administrator (which is what he became) but as a carpenter- and a good one too by all accounts. Apparently, he made things like ladders and even model birds with working parts. It seems he managed to elevate himself from this craft position into one of more power and influence, but it isn't known how he achieved that shift - all we can deduce is that a) it was possible because he was a pragmatist, and b) that he had the capability to do it because we was also a realist with regard to his own skills and attributes.

For every good idea he had and every insightful observation there was always something in his teachings that reflected his contemporary environment. I'm guessing continuous war where people didn't know from one week to the next who was going to be the war-lord in charge, has that effect on people. Therefore, some of the things he said may come across as a bit control-freakish - perhaps more reminiscent of the communist Stasi than a guy preaching universal love — like for instance insisting both good and bad opinions that differ from the leader need to be reported or unrest will result.

However, I think this is just a conditioned response to his environment, and the result of not knowing from one week to the next what opinions were going to be acceptable, and what new war-lord-boss has killed the old war-lord-boss. So, I'm inclined to set aside that less appealing side of him and treat it more like a pragmatic reflection of the times rather than a hint at his natural temperament.

As for his approach to rules (in the context of leadership), these too were conditioned by his environment. He was clear that rules were necessary, and while he disagreed vehemently with Confucius, he wasn't anti the idea that there must be rules and discipline for order to ensue. He said;

"The disorder in the (human) world could be compared with that among birds and beasts. The lack of regulations governing the relationships between ruler and subject, between superior and subordinate, and between elder and younger; and the absence of rules governing the relationships between father and son and between older and younger brothers, resulted in disorder in the world."

As a pacifist embroiled in a warlike society who believed in equality (undifferentiated love) - I think he walked a fine line. On the one hand he didn't want to be dismissed as an irrelevant 'dreamer' and on the other, he didn't want to give the impression he agreed or supported a warlike or confrontational approach. Instead, he used rules and conditions to establish parameters acceptable to people who'd never lived without some form of external control.

A couple of thousand years later not much has changed – there's still far too many unnecessary rules in organisations that remain unchallenged for fear of offending vindictive bosses. It's a great pity that some bosses of today forget the way they may have felt about ineffective or inappropriate rules before they climbed the greasy management pole.

It is, and ever was the case that people follow the direction set by those at the top of their hierarchy. When those people forget where they came from, and then sow the seeds of disorder - disorder is what they'll get. Yet, if they lead like they'd like to be led then things will go more smoothly. As Mozi said;

"If all the people in the district follow the example of their head, how then can the district be? Now, how is it that the head of the district was so successful in governing the district? It was just because he could unify the purposes of the whole district that the district was so orderly."

His Culture: This was China at war with itself - a place where people's priority was survival, and once that was achieved, they searched for meaning, and found it in the teachings of great 'masters' of philosophy. Any expectations about the meaning of life Mozi might have developed as a youngster were no doubt shaped by Confucius. There's no doubt, because historical records state that Mozi was a student of the Confucius. Hence, when he started his own school to teach administrators it couldn't have been much of a surprise to anyone that teaching, and philosophising might be his vocation.

However, the 'undifferentiated love' approach to life he proposed didn't go down well, in fact it went down like a bag of spanners in duck pond. It just didn't sit well with a culture where people had become accustomed to scarcity. They couldn't grasp why Mozi suggested they set aside scarcity and pretend that everyone was entitled to the same treatment. How could it be right for him to suggest that a child could have as much affection for a stranger as their parents. Yet, it was his way of expressing a form of equality and personal control.

This made some people angry, but far from Mozi being cowed it gave him an opportunity to explain their reaction – he wasn't subtle about it and described their response as one of human selfishness. That they wanted to control the feelings of someone else, at the expense of the other person. I sense that this might not have gone down well at first, but he persevered- he was able to explain that having love, good feelings and positive intent toward one person does not mean there'd be less for another. His point was that undifferentiated love is inexhaustible and still valuable, whereas material things are often valued because of their short supply.

Hence, *all* people can have all the undifferentiated love they can handle, but no person should have more material goods than he or she needs to live a reasonable life. I think this translates so well into boss versus leader–for example, how effective is someone in charge when they have favourites?

It doesn't suggest being a good Leader means paying LESS attention to those people you happen to know best, but to pay MORE attention to those you don't know well, until you reach that point where everyone is known as well as the next person. Mozi summed it up by saying;

"To work under the appreciation of the people is to obtain their confidence." He wasn't wrong, was he?

There's a couple of things that might have jarred with the culture of his time that require more explanation. Firstly, he made a big deal about the fuss people made at funerals and how they'd waste time and precious resources on someone already dead. He saw this as an example of human selfishness because whoever was wasting things on the funeral could have been using those same resources to help someone else.

It was a fair point I suppose - but might have added to his doctrine eventually drifting away because although logical it didn't pay enough attention the emotion attached to a funeral and the illogical hopes that something goes on after death.

Secondly, he had a beef about music - much for the same reason as the waste in a funeral, but this was about the time and effort people put into learning, playing, and then listening to music. Don't forget, they were in a time of perpetual war and Mozi was trying to influence people to have a better life. It sounds (forgive the pun) most unreasonable now to try and ban music - but seeing it from his point of view back then it may not have been a bad shout, and yet most definitely a step too far. What he missed again was the emotional connection people have to music - much as a bad boss takes no account of a team member's emotional attachment to an activity when it superficially appears to detract from the bigger objective, but at a deeper level may be supportive.

Mozi's doctrine didn't last and Confucius's did. The difference? Maybe because the more structured approach of Confucius was easier to handle - and probably because Mozi's embraced emotion as well as process and rules.

His Skills: He was known as Master Mo - a skilled administrator who ran a school for would-be administrators in what is now a place called Hunan.

Interestingly, he was more skilled than his erstwhile master Confucius in the art of influence - while the old chap wouldn't live to see his doctrine become popular in his own lifetime, Mozi on the other hand did see his own approach to life adopted widely. That must have felt good.

He also lived long enough to experience his approach being rapidly overtaken by Confucianism after his old master's death. That must have been a bit of a blow.

Even so, it didn't stop him thinking and recording his thoughts. He produced a book with the original title - 'The Mozi'. Apparently, when it was first released it had over eighty chapters. Sadly, there are now only 53 that have been translated and that make any sense - it's from one of those translations that I've drawn some of his quotes.

Without doubt he was a skilful communicator - not only did he use anecdotes and metaphors he also drew on well-known stories from Chinese history to draw out his message and land it with great skill. Here's one example;

"They made a code of five tortures and called it law. This is to say, those who know how to apply punishments can govern the people with them. And those who do not know, make five tortures out of them. Can it be that the punishments are at fault? Only, when their application is not to the point do they become five tortures. And, also, "Shu Ling", among the books of the ancient kings, says: "The same mouth can produce friendship or produce war." This is to say that he who can use the mouth well will produce friendship, and he who cannot will stir up the enemies and the besieging barbarians. Can it be that the mouth is at fault? The fault really lies in its use which stirs up the enemies and the besieging barbarians."

If he'd gone straight to preaching, he might have said something like "It's not rules that are at fault but the poor application of them by poor leaders who then blame their employees when that poor application fails to deliver better results." That would have gone down like a lead balloon.

It's what he meant, but he was gentler and yet straightforward at the same time in the way he said it. He has mastered the ego versus outcome conundrum – when something might be factually correct but will fail to achieve the objective is said (even when part of you desperately wants to say it).

I love the quote; *"The same mouth can produce friendship or produce war"* - perhaps that could be adopted as a leadership motto, who knows?

His Beliefs: Firstly, it's worth pointing out that he must have had some serious belief in himself - to step away from the teaching of Confucius and rebel must have taken some nerve.

Even though Confucianism hadn't taken off to the extent it one day would it still must have been a big deal to argue that rather than people 'knowing their place' in society, they should instead treat each other with 'undifferentiated love'.

The anglicised Chinese word for this concept is *'Jian'ai'* and is often translated as 'universal love'. However, that might make Mozi sound like some new-age woo-woo space-cadet hippie - and he was not. What he was trying to say was that he believed all the mess we experience in the world isn't the result of some cosmic plan designed to give us a hard time - but is instead the direct result of human selfishness. If we all treated each other with ´undifferentiated love´ then things would get better instantly, and he was resilient about this in the face of the teachings of Confucius who had blamed problems in society on a lack of social order rather than individual shortcomings. He was convinced that his pragmatic viewpoint made sense, and as such he had no time for Daoism and it's metaphysical 'find the road' by contemplating-the-world-around-you thinking. That was all too far removed from the realities of living in the here and now for his taste.

It's quite remarkable that thousands of miles away Socrates was experiencing the same reflection of big-picture thinking in favour of something way more practical. Mozi would try and convince anyone who would listen that with some simple rules to live by, human selfishness could be minimised. He´d say that at the heart of such a shift would be the adoption of a default position in respect of one person with another - that of undifferentiated love. All I can say is that it must have been a tough sell – it's difficult enough to try and convey what he meant today, but at the time he must have sounded more than a little 'off the wall'. What he meant was that simply because one person is a stranger, and another is a friend there should be no reason why you make your *love* (good wishes and positive intent) available to one and not the other.

He accepted that being someone's friend makes it easier to trust, but that was not his argument - he wanted the adoption of this as a default setting so that everyone's behaviour would change. He passionately believed this would take humanity back to a more primitively simplicity that'd be good for everybody.

He had a three-fold test to help guide anyone living this principle of undifferentiated love with respect to personal interactions–

I.   is your decision to do whatever you're about to do, taken on a sound basis?

II.   is your understanding of the situation verifiable?

III.   is your pattern of action applicable is this situation in particular?

Then before actually doing anything he would ask a 4-fold 'standard' set of questions to ensure whatever you are going to do ends up benefitting society more generally -

1.   will it lead to the enrichment someone less well off than yourself?

2.   will it result in an increase in the population?

3. will it lead to the removal of some danger?
4. will it act to regulate some form of disorder?

I doubt it was his intention for anyone to say yes to all four. However, it was good sound practical stuff - his first 3-fold test made people reflect, then the 4-fold standard forced them to think about consequences. If whatever they were thinking of doing didn't lead to something useful, then it begged the question - why do it? I don't know about you, but I felt like sending this to my MP with a request he circulate it in Parliament - then I stopped hallucinating that it'd make the blindest bit of difference. Hey-ho.

His Identity: Mozi was both an altruist and a pacifist -he moved from town to town searching for work much like his past master. However, his approach to the life of a nomad differed substantially to Confucius -he would do his best to help people along the way without asking for anything in return.

I'm sure there were as many suspicious people in his time as there are now that would have questioned his motives, but it seems he was successful in winning them over - and he was welcomed wherever he went. However, it'd be a mistake to think that he was a gentle soul with no bite. Nope, it seems that Mozi was a fiery character - vocal about the consequences of people having more than they needed, and (in much the same way that Plato would talk about the need for a ruling class to be divorced from owning property as it leads to corruption), he believed that human selfishness is fuelled by having more than a person needs.

He believed strongly that society must be regulated so that no individual could amass more than another, no matter how high up the pecking order they might be. Now, call me old fashioned, but I think it might be this aspect of his teachings that made the powers-that-be ditch him in favour of a philosopher who was happy for each to have his place in society - basically meaning that those at the top could have whatever they wanted, and keep whatever they had.

Imagine if they'd been a bit more forward thinking – and instead of one of the biggest nations in the world growing up with Confucian ideals of rules and the right of acquisition of goods and power depending on position in society - imagine if they had adopted Mozi's ideals instead. Not communism necessarily, but simply that people only use what they need and leave the rest for others who need it too.

His Purpose: The core theme in everything is talks about is the adoption of a positive mental state. Who knew that it was Mozi who came up with PMS? It was something he clearly believed everyone could master if they wanted to.

He might have been naïve about the 'everyone should only have as much as they need' stuff, but then years later Carl Marx and others would say much the same thing - and have millions believe them, so who am I to say he was wrong. It's just that in his time no one of importance and power was prepared to listen and take it on. It's a shame because his positive state of mind went much further than limiting people to only what they need - Mozi said;

"The greatest men know of no defeat. The next greatest turn failure into success"

271

He didn't mean they never lose, just that even when losing they do not accept personal defeat and that it's never over till it's over. He wanted people take decisions 'in the moment' as to what was the best action to take - using his model of 3-fold test and 4-fold standards.

He realised that people would not remember vast lectures when faced with an emotional decision, so he used stories, anecdotes, and metaphors as vehicles that they might remember and act on. One of my favourites is that he wrote about ghosts and ancestors. At first, I wondered why something so out of line with the rest of his teachings would have found its way in, but then the penny dropped. One line makes it clear to me;

"If all the people in the world believed that the spirits are able to reward virtue and punish vice, how could the world be in chaos?"

He didn't quite go as far as suggesting there's a devil on one shoulder and an angel on the other, but it's pretty much the same concept. He wanted people to take what they already believed - which was that their ancestors exert influence in this world - and turn it into something useful that would affect real decisions in the moment they were taken.

Have you noticed that great leaders reflect on their decisions and ask themselves how that decision might land from every position, not just the obvious one that's in front of them - whereas a boss tends not to be 'found in the deep end', suggesting a much shallower approach to decision making –that often leads to regret, reversal, and ultimately recriminations. #askabetterquestion

How might he be thought of by his employees, if he was a manager in today's business world?

People have scoffed at his approach. They've accused him of having high ideals that just won't work in the harsh world of business, but we are still here, and we love the way he leads. Okay, none of us are here just for the money - it's not that kind of organisation.

We have very high standards when it comes to the way we use resources, and we do our best to live our values. I admit that sometimes or competitors try to take advantage if there are potential shortages of resources, but similarly the cost to them of worrying about 'what if we run out of this or that' is something we don't incur. It's a fair place to work - we are all encouraged to think about the way our actions might affect other people, the organisation, and even our society. We all work hard because we rely on each other, and those who carry more responsibility are rewarded accordingly. We all get an equal shot at promotions and either succeed or not based on how we perform. It's an enlightened place to be.

Coaching questions he might ask: Mozi left us with ten major tenets, each of which can contribute to a coaching question Mozi might ask.

They were broadly about;

1. exacting the virtuous from any situation – in other words, looking for the 'good'
2. ensuring you identify with whoever is your superior or you won't have any chance of influence
3. offering up undifferentiated love

4. unreservedly condemning those who take the offensive and seek confrontation
5. being economic in the application of resources and only using what is necessary
6. taking the simplest choice despite 'tradition' and avoiding unnecessary waste
7. engaging with what you interpret as the will of heaven - otherwise known as the three-fold test
8. asking yourself what your ancestors might say if they were a ghost on your 'shoulder'
9. staying on task and not being deflected by unnecessary diversions
10. and finally, refusing to believe that any outcome is pre-determined - no matter how obvious, concrete, or how convincing other people try to be – ultimately, it's never over until it's over.

i. *"How do you really know what you think you know?"*

ii. *"If the person you admired most in the world was an apparition sitting on your shoulder, what might that ghost say you must think about next?"*

iii. *"If you are holding onto anger or frustration, even if. It is not directly related to this situation, how is it affecting your decision making now?"*

iv. *"Should someone be hurt by whatever you do next, what justification do you have for damaging another human being?"*

v. *"What have you assumed will be the ultimate outcome of your situation, that may end up not being true?"*

vi. *"What presumptions have you made about the need for you to take action as opposed to sitting and waiting for someone else to meet your needs before you all move on?"*

vii.   *"What would have to happen for you to set aside any thoughts of confrontation and instead concentrate on how you want to eventually feel?"*

viii.   *"What would you have to do and say for you, others involved, and those unrelated to the situation to look at what you've done and consider it a righteous approach?"*

CHAPTER 22: #18 THINGS ARE NOT WHAT THEY SEEM

PLATO

His Claim to Fame: Clearly, his biggest claim to fame must be that everyone on the planet who's even heard of philosophy will also have heard the name 'Plato'.

However, here's something I'll bet you didn't know -Plato was his nickname and not a real name at all. If you already knew that then kudos, as for me I don't mind admitting I didn't know. In fact, the name Plato is derived from 'Plautus' meaning broad or wide - which on the face of it sounds a bit of an odd name for a philosopher, doesn't it?

It seems the young Plato was no shrinking violet but was a rather flashy wrestler - who knew? His broad shoulders - oiled up for wrestling occasions was probably the reason for the nickname. The fact is his real name was Aristocles. That wouldn't have been confusing at all would it? Aristocles being taught by Socrates who then taught Aristotle. It´s hard enough to remember all these names anyway with more of them being practically the same - thank goodness he had a nickname.

Yet, while it's true that he's one of the most famous names in philosophy, he's still a bit of an enigma. He wrote so much about other people, that his own thoughts are difficult to distinguish from those he put into the mouths of others. It's never clear if these are the thoughts of Plato himself or if he's simply recounting the precise thinking of other people he included in his plays. I can't say I've read them all, but from what I've seen I'd like to think it's a bit of a mix between what he remembers and what he wished he'd said himself. For example, it´s clear that much of what he has Socrates saying he agrees with - then he cheekily adds his own take on things to either clarify or extend the thought just that bit further. However, be it his own thinking or something he'd learned elsewhere, he is the first person to put into words a thought that is as relevant to leaders now as it ever was - and that´s this;

"How do we know that we know?"

This fundamental question is something that distinguishes a boss from a leader -a boss assumes that he or she *knows*, simply because they think they know, whereas a leader listens to alternatives just in case they´re wrong. Good leaders know there's far less chance things end up as a problem to deal with if they've opened their ears to the best possible alternatives. They know it is safer to assume we don't know 'yet', whatever the situation rather than leap to their first conclusion. Business managers learning to become coaching leaders discover a foundational ´understanding´ - leaders ask better questions and bosses try to run everything themselves.

It´s all about memory - a good coaching leader knows that everything is a memory of sorts. It´s either a memory of the past, a thought about the future (that has now become a memory of possibility), or a memory of the present (how a person makes sense of what's going on around them). The way Plato put it was that while a person experiences colours and then names them, that same person can never know if their interpretation of what they´re seeing is the same as someone else calling out the same colours. Are they experiencing the same colour, or do they see something different and simply give it the same name?

Therefore, Plato said something along the lines of;

"No person can say that anything is true 'absolutely' but everything is relative".

We can agree that 'this is blue' relative to both of us, but we cannot say with certainty that our perception of blue is the 'true blue'. It can be true for me, but because you don't necessarily see it the way I do, it may be false for you.

He may have used a more practical way to describe this difference by simply noting that different people have differing tolerances to experiences; one person may think it cold enough to wear a coat whereas another may be content to go out with a single layer of clothing. The actual temperature is the same for both, so is the 'truth' that it is warm or cold? One person may have a tolerance for pain that goes way beyond another, therefore can something be said to be painful or not dependant on any one person's reaction to it?

A boss assumes their perceptions are applicable to everyone. A leader knows theirs are not.

Plato wasn't trying to tie people in knots with this. There's a very practical reason to talk about what is truth and what is not that's just as pertinent in our supposedly sophisticated world as it was in Ancient Greece. Politics is as mired in arguments about 'truth' now as it ever was - debacles such as the election of someone who damages the interests of the majority, but who might have been voted into office because the 'truth' was he or she was the least-worse option. To Plato that would be utter nonsense.

Similarly, the extraction of a country from well-established treaties because the 'truth' to various subsets of society is that that treaty is 'bad', would be treated by him with equal derision. His take on politics was that nobody could know for certain what is 'good' or 'bad', 'right' or 'wrong' - but they could know in that moment if something was helpful or not in achieving something positive for their society. I feel his frustration - if people would stop trying to prove themselves 'right' and instead ask themselves a better question on behalf of society, then the world would be a much better place. Unfortunately, they didn't back then, and I'm afraid our contemporary politicians are just as guilty.

He wouldn't have come out as 'Plato' to make that point, but might have written a sell-out play and put the words into the mouths of dead people (trusted for their wisdom and insights), so that the argument moved from binary decisions of 'this truth or that', to a much deeper question of *do we actually know what the real truth is?*

Plato used characters to make the case that things are complicated – and that the best course to take to avoid falling down a proverbial deep-water-well might not be obvious. Sadly, we don't have a modern-day Plato to help bring things into perspective - sure, we have a plethora of Hollywood writers who do their best to shine a light on what might really be going on beneath the bluff and bluster of media-spin, but we are so drowning in 'media' that the diamonds get lost in the lorry loads of crappy gravel they churn out. This has an unfortunate effect on many modern leaders – they´re being conditioned to take things at face value and not dig deeper and ask bigger and better questions. We really do need a modern Plato. I think Plato influenced people by using what he knew they already knew(often about Socrates and the folk-law that had grown up around him), to verbalise thinly veiled attacks on the state and the way it was managed. It's good to recognise that asking better questions is nothing new, which is why I think Plato is probably THE most important of all philosophers for 2 reasons, firstly, of the famous 'threesome' (Socrates, Plato and Aristotle), Plato is the only one of them to have known both the others. He was a student of Socrates and a teacher of Aristotle. Secondly, he was a consummate a clever writer. He captured the essence of his teacher Socrates by writing down his teachings and gave us insights into many other early philosophers by also recording their stories and ideas. Apart from this, he also left us with his own thinking – thinking that is so profound it has been claimed that *all* philosophy that followed are simply footnotes to the work of Plato.

Believe it or not, he may even have inspired writers of 'Sci-Fi'. One of my favourite insights from Plato was the seeding of the idea that human experience is a hologram of sorts. Seriously, I'm not inventing this - he really did think that our life's experience was just an imperfect reflection of another dimension entirely.

Now, it's true that the words used to express Plato's idea aren't presented as a pitch for a movie deal and are rarely discussed by any but those interested in philosophy. Yet, if you express his ideas using contemporary language most people will nod their heads in recognition of the idea.

Why? I think it's because of two things - firstly, that they might have heard the idea before in the context of a bit of Sci-Fi, and secondly, because it resonates as being maybe, possibly, perhaps an idea that could be true. Having either of these thoughts doesn't mean a person agrees it's true - just that it's not totally crazy.

Here's what he did: Plato tried to figure out how distinguish things that are different - but can then categorise them under the same broad heading. He wanted to understand *how* it is that people know things are the same and different at the same time. The academic term is 'taxonomy', which means the defining of terms under headings of broad similarity, then developing sub-headings to categorise more groups within a group. That's what it is, but doesn't explain how it's possible to make those distinctions. Plato wanted to know what's going on that allows us humans to do that?

We see a dog and know that it is a dog. The dog may be big or small, one colour or a mix, be calm or angry, have long hair or short, and yet we know they are all dogs without having to have it pointed out. He wanted to explain how we do that so, he came up with a theory. He called it 'the world of forms' or the 'theory of forms'.

Now, I must be honest, the first time I heard this I had no idea what he was talking about. Not a clue.

So, when I read him talking about a world apart from our own where there are perfect representations of dogs, or clouds, or trees, in fact perfect forms of everything, I found myself wondering what was going on? However, after a bit more thought I changed the words to make it make sense for me. I translated it like this;

(My words not Plato) *"Imagine we are all inside a computer game. All that we see, hear, feel, and experience comes from the projection of a 'source code'. This code has been written so that there is an archetype for everything a person will experience within the game. As the game progresses it becomes ever more complex and adaptations of each archetype will develop, but the initial source code of the 'perfect' item will always be reflected so that people can recognise what it is they are experiencing."*

I'm not suggesting definitively that Plato was the inspiration for those Sci-fi films that adopted this premise, or that he had advance knowledge of advanced scientific research – but, it's hard to ignore some of the thinking of groups like 'Quantum Gravity Research'[xxxii] that does suggest (whether by accident or design) the things we accept as 'normal' might reflect something else entirely. Spooky, eh?

His Environment: Plato hailed from Athens, and long before stepping into the limelight as a playwright and philosopher was a pretty useful wrestler by all accounts - because wrestling was something in which all fit young Athenian men were expected to take part.

I started this book with a quote from Sir Winston Churchill, and I think that he and Plato had more in common than Sir Winston than thinking he might have said the same thing first if he'd had the opportunity. Churchill was 65 years old when he became Prime Minister. Until then, he'd been a politician and a soldier, but if his public service had ended there, few of us would remember him – and he certainly wouldn't be remembered as one of the history's greatest statesmen. He is quoted as saying that everything in his life that went before had been preparing him for when he took the reins of the country in that time of war. The popular images of Plato are him pictured as an old man because that too is when he came into his own. Most people's perception of him is as a frail looking chap in a toga.

However, like Churchill he had a life before that, so let go of that imagery and instead think of a young, fit Athenian with bulging muscles, a six-pack, and a bright enquiringly mind eager to learn - because that's going to be more like the environmental expectations of a young chap destined to do well in ancient Athenian environment. To be fair, that's where the comparison between him and Sir Winston go their separate ways. Therefore, I don't think there's any suggestion he began life intending to end up a philosopher. He would have studied philosophy as part of his general education while getting on with life and other 'stuff', but it wasn't until he started learning from Socrates that his interest became serious.

I think it's sad we don't incorporation philosophy into real-world activity these days, sadly, it's something that has been forgotten in today's world. Quite why setting aside a 'love of wisdom' in favour of a fixed curriculum is a good idea I'm not sure – particularly when it's one that leaves vast numbers of young people ill-equipped to deal with the challenges of life. Why this is considered a good approach to education is beyond me. Forgive me standing on a soap box, but I can only wonder how much better our world might be if young people studied the wisdom of the past.

It's a fact that none of the great thinkers in this book or those who followed them, were forced to take test after test after test simply to prove to a bureaucratic system that 'their policy' of teaching was successful. Having spent the last couple of years getting inside their heads (not the bureaucrats - the philosophers), I'm as sure as I can be that if any of them were asked about such teaching and testing regimes, they might well have scoffed - they may have even asked if the tests are for the benefit of students or the bureaucratic teaching regimes?

Good leaders recognise this same approach in business – they don´t ignore business imperatives in favour of

knows this and seeks out the strengths of each team member to help maximise them. The boss on the other hand tends to apply 'across the board measures' that assume all his team have equal skills. He or she then puts all their attention on whatever is 'missing' for each person rather than recognising that their strengths are far more important. It's bonkers that in organisations headed up by hugely talented people, this still goes on. What's worse is that the bosses within that organisation do not even see the problem, as far as they're concerned their systems are working and 'what's the problem?' Scary, eh?

You've probably noticed the stark contrast between the approach of maximising strengths and that of bridging supposed education 'gaps' then testing students with the aim of all reaching a fixed level. I think Plato would have been polite, but I bet he would have written a play where Socrates tore the educationalists apart! Can you imagine him ripping into them because of the stifling of extraordinary talent by shoehorning them into a fixed and arbitrary standard? I can almost hear the worlds Plato would have given him as he angrily accused them of ignoring the strengths of young people, - simply because they don't conform to the inevitably dated so-called standards of excellence imposed on all schools. I think it would've driven him nuts that they blindly assumed themselves to be 'right' at the expense of hundreds of thousands of young people, - and I'm only talking about the UK, never mind the rest of the world following a similar flawed plan. You and I can only guess how many business organisations are suffering the same fate, missing opportunities and wasting a ton of money in the process.

Plato might have done whatever he could to change their minds. One of his arguments would probably have been that they wouldn't need to stay at school any longer. Individual potentials could be reached because they could do it in the same time it takes to participate in all those tests as they're now forced to take. Testing and more testing, done simply to justify the politics of education. The more I think about it as he might have seen it, the crazier it seems. Plato would not have been impressed.

His Culture: As mum and dad came from local aristocracy there's no doubt about him having plenty of opportunity for education and travel, at least it did until war intervened and a period of heavily restricted opportunities for Athenians.

Even so, he had a rounded education and once he'd met Socrates became devoted to a lifelong study of nature, ethics, and living a virtuous life. Apparently, the first words he heard from the Delphic oracle were *"Know thyself"*. These were the words that inspired Plato to become a philosopher. However, the pivotal event in his life was meeting Socrates when still a young man, just after coming back from a short stint fighting in that rather nasty and unrelenting war the Spartans. I wish we knew more about how he met Socrates, but it is likely that word of the scruffy philosopher who by that time was probably also a war veteran and who had a lot to say for himself, had spread to young Plato and his athletic mates. What is indisputable is that there must have been something about what Socrates was saying or the way he was living that appealed to the young man enough for him quit wresting with people and start wresting with ideas. In his writing, he made Socrates the central character in many of his dialogues and ended up speaking through him when he thought that people would take to heart what they heard from his Socrates 'character' more than they might from the philosophising playwright. It's a matter of conjecture as to how much Socrates is Plato, but as he was a proper student of Socrates (not some made up connection by Greek wishful thinkers as in many other philosophy student-teacher relationships) it may be that the words he attributes to Socrates are a good indication of what the man was really like.

Plato didn't limit his learning to be a student of Socrates, he travelled to southern Italy aiming to figure out what Pythagoras and his followers were up to, and although he did spend time there it wasn't at the expense of forgetting the other pivotal philosophers who along with the Pythagoreans had shaped the way Plato's generation were viewing the world. Pythagoras was only one strand of many that included the likes of Parmenides and Heraclitus. His doctrine of total flux appealed to Plato (even if it didn't make sense totally even then) as a fabulous means to advance this idea of 'everything being relative' and 'nothing being absolutely true' into a dynamic abstraction that goes like this; if everything around us is indeed not still as we imagine it, but as Heraclitus maintained is a constant flux of movement, then not only is our individual perception of things probably different from each other but also that perception must be constantly changing without our being consciously aware of it. How fabulous is it that studies into quantum 'reality' tell us unequivocally that things do indeed appear to change depending on the person observing them? How amazing is it, that so far in advance of biology unearthing the human 'ascending reticular activating system' of mental pattern matching that he had nailed the idea that we all see the world differently? I for one think the big guy was fabulous, amazing, and plenty of other superlatives along those lines. There's so much of what he said that's as applicable to Bosses transitioning to Leaders as people escaping from the self-imposed 'prison' of their limited perception of reality.

After his extended 'gap' tour of Greek outposts he returned to Athens and set up the Academia in honour of a Greek hero, - from where we get the word Academy. The sign over the entrance read "Let no man enter who has not studied Geometry" because Plato had come to realise that at the heart of this metaphysical thinking was something solid that could be expressed as numbers and geometric shapes. He was like Pythagoras but without the need for a cult, vegetarianism, silence, and weird inner-circles. The Academy was a place of learning, a place where men's or women could attend, and none of the conventions previously attributed to learning. His own student was Aristotle, who faithfully attended the

Academy until developing his own ideas that differed somewhat from his teacher's, and so moved on to start his own school. He wasn't an only child but had two brothers, neither of whom appeared to have much interest in following their brother into philosophy. However, he does use their characters in his plays as foils for whoever is arguing a good point. Nice to keep it in the family, I guess.

He could count among his ancestors on his mums side, the great law giver and Greek statesman Solon. On dad's side he could count Athenian and Messenian kings. It's probable that he was the eldest of five children- the two brothers I've already mentioned, plus another half-brother and a sister. Dad died when he was young, and then mum married her own uncle to keep the family together.

I have no idea if this was as weird then as it sounds now, but perhaps because a tough home life, young Plato left home, his wrestling, and his studies to fight in that war between Athens and Sparta at the tender age of just 15. So, for every 15 year old you know more concerned with playing computer games and filming stupid pranks to get 'likes' on YouTube, than stepping up to do the right thing – then tell them to be more like Plato. They won't have a clue what you mean, but it'll probably make you smile (it does me).

Anyway, if you're imagining he went off to fight in something akin to the Hollywood Sparta movies then you've nailed it - Athens lost badly, and the rather civilised Greek monarchy was then replaced by a less generous Spartan Oligarchy and the Thirty Tyrants rule. That wasn't good news for anyone except the Spartan Oligarchy.

For Plato however, all was not lost - because two of his relatives, Charmides and Critias were prominent figures in this new government. The 'Thirty Tyrants' rule was an unpleasant interlude in Greek history, but a lesson in being a good leader if you look closely. There are always situations where leaders shine despite their senior hierarchy being unsupportive of what they know is right. When this happens, the rubbish boss throws their hands in the air - bleating that it's not their fault, while carrying out terrible instructions. Whereas the leader asks better questions and then does what is required, including ensuring the hierarchy understand the truth and implications of their instructions. They retain their integrity, and the dignity of their team.

His Skills: Without doubt it was Plato's writing ability more than anything that secured his long-lived popularity. Some of his pithy quotes are as fresh today as they ever were;

"Love is a serious mental disease"

"The measure of a man is what he does with power"

"We can easily forgive a child who is afraid of the dark, the real tragedy of life is when men are afraid of the light"

"Wise men talk because they have something to say; fools, because they have to say something"

"The price good men pay for indifference to public affairs is to be ruled by evil men"

"Never discourage anyone... who continually makes progress, no matter how slow"

"Courage is knowing what not to fear"

"Necessity is the mother of invention"

There are plenty of one-liners like this that people have been repeating either in some version or precisely for over

2300 years. His understanding of 'knowledge' was way ahead of his time, and he could articulate that knowledge by using the voices of past philosophers, particularly Socrates, to share this specialised thinking.

At the simplest level his take on 'knowledge' was that far from it being a bunch of stuff that is 'out there' to be either learned or ignored, it was a connected web with which everyone was already stuck to - like a fly waiting for the spider whether we like it or not.

His argument went like this; *'do you know anything about anything?'* The answer must be that of course, everyone knows a little bit of something. 'Ah, ha! He might say - to know you know something, and knowing it, now means you know two things about this rather than the one. Furthermore, there's a third thing you know - that's how you know you know, and if you dig further you'll know a little more connected to a little more. Eventually, this means if you follow the threads you can know everything you need to know'.

Okay, here's an example in practice: The boss asks *"Do you know how to do this task?"* The employee replies *"Well, I've only done it once and that was with supervision"*. *"I'll send you on a course then"* say's the boss.

However, the leader asks the same question and gets the same reply, but follows up with, *"If you had to explain it to me, where would you start?"* The employee would reply and then the leader would say something like, *"and what would you do next?"* If the employee got stuck, the leader might ask *"Where were you when you were shown how to do this bit, and who were you with, and what do you remember?"*

Bit by bit the employee will recall what to do. Finally, the leader will set the employee up with some support if they need help along the way, but essentially let them get on with it. The leader knew that because the employee had some experience and could recall something, there was a string to be pulled at that would help them learn – if they were skilfully questioned, lead to all the information necessary being unwrapped and the confusion unravelled.

Now, these are my words not Plato's, but I hope you get the gist of the foundational skill he was demonstrating - to demonstrate in simple language a complex concept in a way that makes sense. He acknowledged that sometimes the 'knowledge' was to know how to find out more, who to ask, or where to go to discover that next bit of knowledge.

His thinking was that 'out there somewhere' was the perfect construct of everything - that was just waiting to be uncovered. And that the more connections we make, the nearer we get to it. As to if that 'perfection' exists, or instead is merely a mental concept, or is simply an exercise to make the point isn't clear. However, he did talk a good deal about the concept of a realm of 'forms', by which he meant this extreme example of everything at its best. I'm no expert on Plato, but stepping into the shoes of someone who wrote as prolifically as he did, created plays like he did, and had an imagination to rival anyone in his day or now, I tend to think his 'world of forms' wasn't an imaginary place but just an explanatory idea. It may be a rubbish thing to call his idea – a realm or theory of forms (marketing was definitely not his forte) but the concept he was describing was interesting.

However, I think his biggest skill was as a story-teller. Not just because he could write interesting plays, each with a deeper meaning than is apparent at first, but also because he could take complex ideas and turn them into something that anyone could grasp. His audiences 'got' him, because he kept things understandable, and where there was a complex idea to communicate he wrapped it in conversation and also often in comedy.

I think the best example is his 'Allegory of the Cave' – although there was nothing funny about that. It was a thought experiment that is as powerful now as it ever was. He asked people to imagine that they had been born into a system where their lot in life was to be chained to the floor of a cave facing a wall. Behind them was both a roaring fire, and behind that the bright entrance to the cave, illuminated by the daylight outside. However, because the chained people were facing the wall, they never got to see the fire or the daylight outside. Instead, all they could see were the comings and goings of people, animals, insects, and the rest of the world's creation as shadows thrown onto the wall of the cave.

Plato asked us to imagine how likely it would be that these people would accept these shadows as representing what truly exists. They would recognise what things were by shapes and movements they'd come to know, yet, no matter how many times they saw what they assumed was a real person, a real dog, cow, or whatever else, it would never be a true representation of the genuine article – merely a shadow from the fire.

This, he maintained is analogous to the life we all lead - that the things we see and experience are not the real thing, but are just shadows of the perfection that exists in the 'world of forms'. The magic in this allegory is that it suggests anyone can unchain themselves from the floor of the cave and begin to see things as they really are, and not just how we have allowed ourselves to accept is the way the world is. Freedom comes from awareness, and awareness from the asking of better questions. I can only wonder how many men and women are prisoners, locked into a mental cave made all too real by a boss who has yet to learn to be a leader - because the leader works tirelessly to unchain the team from self-imposed constraints preventing them from being their best, while the boss uses the power of position to keep them in the dark about what potential they truly have.

His Beliefs: Let's start with this; *"No evil can possibly happen to a good man in this world or the next, of that I am certain. Evil is only ignorance, learning is only remembering."* His conviction was that if a person was dedicated to being 'good' then in their mind and experience nothing evil can happen to them.

A story goes that one of his followers asked him what a man must do to be a good leader, and his response was along the lines of *"to work tirelessly in the cause of being good"*. I imagine the questioner thought it had to be more difficult than that because he asked, then what next? Plato replied, *"Do not slacken in that regard"*. In other words, his deeply held conviction that the efforts of a person to be the best they can in the cause of goodness was at the heart of all wasn't only a personal development doctrine but applied also to leadership and governance.

In the transition from boss to leader these words ought to be a mantra; leadership is not a reward for long service to a device to weaken the collective power of a workforce, but a an opportunity to do some real good in this world, - and that doesn't happen without continuous and consistent effort, focus and belief.

Plato believed in the souls' immortality. His learning and development with Socrates had taken for granted that all people were born with a soul. They presupposed that the soul and body were separate - not necessarily that the soul was something outside of the body, although they do refer to it as being like a waft of smoke that could blow away at the point of death, and that even if the soul is without any specific form, it might rely on the body for its existence.

He clearly hadn't figured out to his own satisfaction what a 'soul' was, other than it being 'other-worldly'. One unique suggestion was that the soul is like the specific sound of a uniquely tuned instrument. A unique sound that disappears and can no longer be heard on this plane when the body-instrument ceases to be.

Plato's take on this is that if Socrates was correct - in that 'learning is remembering things we knew even before we were born', then it implies the soul must have existed before the body. Therefore, not only is it separate, but it can also exist on its own. Plato takes this belief and adds in his theory of forms by suggesting that what the soul knows before coming into human existence is knowledge of how everything 'is' when 'beautiful and balanced'.

This is really quite cool because all the doubting voices - asking how anyone could know if what Plato was pitching was true, suddenly had a logical explanation. The 'perfect forms' of everything exist on a different plane, the one from which the soul comes - hence, the soul knows what everything should look like, and be like - in the past, now, and in the future. All of which explains why it is that learning is remembering, because our souls knew all along. Very cool, very cool indeed.

It demonstrates how smart Plato was, in that he can take this rather far-fetched abstract idea and make sense of it. How he came up with the idea that the only way we recognise anything is because some proto-form of that thing exists in a metaphysical reality that we can't see - and turns it into something else entirely by saying that this realm of forms is only available to the soul, is anyone's guess. Maybe he was inspired, perhaps it was something whispered to him by one of those earlier philosophers convinced they'd been touched by the gods, or maybe he just had great insight. Wherever it came from it was a terrific explanation of how the soul brings with it, out of the *realm of forms,* this knowledge into every one of us.

He was certain that we all have a soul, hence, equally certain that everything we needed to know was already inside us. That's the valuable point here; the fact that by having a belief in the soul it does something that results in us all being able to access everything we need right when we need it.

Hm, it sounds like a stretch, but if you think about it, has every big decision you've ever made been based on everything you needed to know, or that you didn't know? Did you ever take a leap of faith just because it felt like the right thing to do? Plato would say that if you assume you don't know enough, then the result will be that you don't.

But, if you believe that the soul gives you access to all you need then something interesting happens - you start to act as if you do - and if there's something technical you don't know, then you act like you know how to find it. That then ends up in you DO knowing what you need to know. A leap of faith might be simply to trust asking a better question.

I think if he'd been around today he'd maybe describe it as your soul is like a kind of metaphysical iPhone, streaming data from the 'cloud'. Bosses assume that they know more than their subordinates, and even if they don't know, that they're in a better position to make a design because they are, well, the boss. Whereas leaders assume that everyone has it within them to reach their own potential; therefore, if a person has been hired because they have the required potential, they are best helped and supported by suggesting they CAN figure things out and that they WILL learn all they need to know as long as they believe they can. Leaders might call it a Positive Mental Attitude, but Plato simply called it the Soul.

The similarity between the things we've heard before about the soul being 'celestial' - and everything else just a made-up reality is obvious, isn't it? The same message from a different perspective. The great thing about Plato is that he's put so much meat on the bone of this metaphysical idea that it no longer sounds 'spooky'. He has made the big picture relevant and useful to our everyday lives. He makes it sound much more like the soul is some kind of source-code from which everything else evolves - and it's a concept we will hear again and again throughout the history of philosophy.

Again, I'm minded to ask 'how cool is that?' I have to admit, I found myself making 'hm and ah ha' noises when I read this for the first time. It makes sense that if you believe in a soul - it must have a purpose, and such a purpose could well useful in providing a *standard of judgement* with which to interpret a complex world. In leadership terms it might men having a set of values that are immutable. Values that provide strength when the going gets tough, when bosses crumble under pressure.

Perhaps my iPhone analogy was simplistic, it's more like that source code in a computer programme -it kicks things off, and has embedded within it a 'map' of all that *can* be within that programme. Then, once it's let loose in a it can almost have a mind of its own - growing, developing, and recognising the programmed world it inhabits. If that's a bit too Sci-fi for your tastes then stick with the values analogy. Either way, Plato had it nailed, because, if this was his thinking then it's fair to say he thought-leading was very advanced for the time.

It's perhaps a shame that ideas of the soul were hijacked by religious zealots intent on securing power through the manipulation of beliefs that brought with it the dark ages. I can only imagine what kind of improved world it might be now if his thinking had been allowed to progress uninterrupted by dogma. Can you imagine what kind of business world we'd have if the dogma of old-fashioned and out-dated hierarchical know-all management bosses was replaced by insightful, dynamic Leaders?

Another thing he believed that was incredibly insightful was the polarity of aspects of life; in his writings he talks of repaying debt, which one might think is good - but, if that debt is the borrowing of an axe and the person you borrowed it from has turned into an axe murderer - then clearly, returning the axe and paying off that debt may in those circumstances be a bad thing. Therefore, repaying a debt can be both good and bad at the same time. He talks of Helen of Troy (she of launching 1000 ships fame) and how compared to human women she is most beautiful, but compared to a goddess she is not - so, Helen is both beautiful and not-so-much at the same time, not merely human but not quite a goddess - two ends of the same spectrum at the same time. You get the idea?

In our world, and particularly in the world of business, one polarity he would have had great fun with is the work-life balance - as if anything can be both good and bad at the same time depending on the lens you use to view it, its balancing the need to work and the desire to have a life. Plato might have appealed to our 'souls' to find the correct balance for each of us.

His Identity: Knowing that knowledge is 'perception' must have meant that Plato was well aware his identity was not fixed, but a choice of whatever he wanted to present to the world.

It might help understand how he saw himself if I'd read everything he wrote; the trouble is, it'd probably mean this book wouldn't be finished for years! If I ever get to do 'Desert Island Discs' (not that I'm expecting an invite any time soon, but if I did) then as well as the complete works of Shakespeare that are provided as a matter of course, as my 'luxury' item I'd ask for the complete works of Plato - because I'd never be bored: The 'Republic', the 'Apology', Gorgias', 'Cratylus' are all works I'd happily read again, never mind the rest of his back catalogue that are just waiting for the day I have time.

I'm not suggesting that Plato was a saint mind you; don't forget, he fought in the war, albeit only for a short time, and he was young but he also must have colluded with uncle Critias when this ruthless relative sided with the Spartans. His uncle wasn't just a collaborator, he was the head of those thirty tyrants. Of course, it's possible to sympathise with people who do what they need to, to survive. However, it's where they draw the moral line that counts – there's that soul thing again. For example, I wonder if his story in the 'Apology' of Socrates being sent to arrest a man, knowing he was bringing him back for execution might have been one of those stories actually about himself? It would certainly explain his deep conviction about addressing wrongs in this life by doing good and living the best life possible, if an incident like this affected him emotionally. It's a story that some leaders will recognise. I have no idea how many good leaders were once bad bosses, who made changes because of a pivotal life experience - but I'm betting there's quite a few.

Like some of those reformed leaders of today who might end up shaping the way we think in the future, I don't think that Plato saw himself as the person of extreme influence he'd end up being. Instead, I imagine him as that person with something special to say - the person who when they start to speak captures the attention of anyone in earshot.

His combination of a rational explanation for the mysteries of the world, combined with a practical recipe for living a life of harmony between the soul and everything else must have been irresistible. In fact, he made things simple by separating the soul into three malleable parts - its reason, its spirit, and its appetite. Logic, enthusiastic energy, and heartfelt desire. He suggested when a person combined the three so that they are in balance, a person could live a good life on this plane - and set themselves up for whatever comes next. I can't say if good leaders are interested in whatever happens after this plane of existence, but I can point out that when a leader balances logical action, great energy and enthusiasm with absolute passion - they become a great leader rather than just good.

His Purpose: There are some things we can be sure were not his purpose; he didn't want to be a politician, that's for sure - he had the opportunity but turned it down in favour of being a teacher in his Academy.

He also didn't want to be an advisor and 'king-maker', because having detailed in the 'Republic' his ideal scenario for a well-run state, there wasn't an opportunity for him to turn those ideas into a reality. If he could have helped create his idea of the best political system, it would have been one where most people lived as merchants, farmers, traders and the like. They would be protected by a caste of people given responsibility for the running and protection of the state. They would live without worries of money but would not be allowed to own property or goods of any kind as their sole purpose was the protection and administration of the state, unencumbered by desire.

The idea was that from this caste of special people an overall 'leader' would be chosen on merit, and that this person would be respected as the ultimate decision maker and a *philosopher king* but not lauded as a regular king or emperor.

It's a pretty good idea – if maybe a little impractical unless starting society from scratch. When Plato was in his sixties, he was coerced into trying to help a dictator set himself up as a philosopher-king, something that Plato must have known was doomed to failure from the outset. But, he went ahead with it because he had no choice, and the guy wasn't the at all the kind of philosopher king Plato had in mind. The long and short of it is that the plan failed, and poor old Plato was blamed – he was put under house arrest by the dictator until he could convince him to let him leave. It's a good job he was a convincing character.

I'm one hundred percent certain Plato would have been a Leader and not a Boss, because I can't help believing that his true purpose was to influence his society to hang onto, and make good use of the wisdom already known. Sure, he developed some of his own wise ideas, but he was happy to acknowledge that his bold new theories could not have come about without what had come before. Many years later, scientists like Einstein would make it clear that they 'stood on the shoulders' of those who came before. I think Plato knew that he was doing the same.

How might he be thought of by his employees, if he was a manager in today's business world?

He has a plan – a plan for everything. He knows that when a well-conceived plan is combined with a team who have passion and energy, then the chances for success increase significantly. He knows that no plan is failure-proof, and is always willing to talk about what's truthfully happening.

He's not interested in people who try and say the 'right thing', he wants to hear the 'real thing'.

Some have called him a Renaissance man because he gives the impression he's good at everything. He somehow makes time to lead the team, paying attention to anything that get in their way of success – be it work related or personal. He knows every member of the extended workforce by name and something relevant to them about their life – no one ever has a superficial conversation with him. He has bobbies he appears to take as seriously as his work, and finds the time to be every-much a leader to his family as he is to the business.

But, he's not perfect. Sometimes, his desire to engage team members in the big-picture as well as immediate actions leads to confusion. Some people need to know what to do, and aren't ready to open up to how that might fit into his understanding of the 'celestial' - it's more than just a stretch for them, their confusion can leave them frustrated. It's a blind spot he has that other senior team members need to step into and fix. Luckily for us, he recognises it too and is grateful for the support.

One of the best things about working with him are the stories he tells. Often, we're not sure if he's telling a true story or is taking liberties with half-truths – but, it doesn't matter -they're always useful, meaningful, and helpful. The stories cause us to participate in decision making without either feeling that we are in a leaderless democracy, or a dictatorship in which we play lip service to participation. It's a clever way to get the best out of us, and we in turn do our best to use the same approach with our teams.

Like him, none of us are perfect either - and just like him, we have our blind spots. Under his leadership we've been encouraged to focus on our strengths and use them to help each other. One person's blind spot is inevitably another person's strength – the trick is to be aware of them to avoid the false belief that there's nothing that can be done about it, and he's good at helping us make that happen.

Coaching questions he might ask: The big theme in Plato's philosophy has to be the recognition that false beliefs are easy to acquire, and even easier to emotionally buy into even when the intellectual part of you has a pretty good idea that those beliefs could be wrong.

i. *"If it is true that the measure of a person is not their power but what they DO with that power, what for the benefit of you and those who depend on you is the right thing to do?"*

ii. *"Put out your hands, palms up and imagine closing your eyes so that the all the complexities of 'now' can place themselves in your hands; those in your true interests in the right, and everything that is not in your left to be left behind...which one do you choose?"*

iii. *"From whom have you learned most, that if you were able to ask for help now and receive it, would whisper something only you can hear?"*

iv. *"If something more important to you, caused you to seek a resolution to your situation immediately, what would it be?"*

v. *"If the things you have seen and experienced are not as you see them, but merely a reflection of something more, what might you ask that could help you?"*

vi. *"If there were to be some good in the challenges that face you today, how might you use that good for an even greater good?"*

vii. *"In this situation, what power have you consciously or unconsciously sought that may not be a necessary part of your solution?"*

viii. *"What do you long for more than anything else that is being prevented in some way by an action you are taking?"*

ix. *"What wrongdoing might you have contributed to in ignorance that isn't helping your situation?"*

x. *"When you think of what you once accepted as true but now know is false, what previous truths about your situation might you now wish to review?"*

CHAPTER 23: #19 ACTIONS SPEAK LOUDER THAN WORDS

CRATES

His Claim to Fame: If you've instantly doubted anything, refused accept things at face value, or sought the simplest answer when faced with complexity, then you know how to be cynical –and you probably have Crates to thank.

By the way, if you're wondering how to pronounce his name, just think Socrates and miss off the ´So´. I absolutely loved learning about this guy - not only was he the teacher of another of the great thinkers of antiquity, none other than Zeno of Citium - another Zeno believe it or not. This Zeno was the most important of the Cynic philosophers - a tradition of thinking that is probably as strong today as it was then.

Remember the story I told in the introduction, the one about the guy who lived 'dog-like', wandering around either naked or in rags and sleeping in a bath-tub - then rushing in to a meeting of philosophers with a plucked chicken crying *"here I have a human!"* He was Diogenes, and it was Diogenes that Crates sought out to teach him about the way he viewed life – and by adopting the dog-like ´way´ he gave it the name cynicism – the way of the cynic. Cynicism was adopted as the ´way´ followed by many seeking a simpler life. Cynicism allowed them to step away from the politics and stress of everyday society. Crates adapted the idea so that it didn´t necessitate living in the street and divesting yourself of every material possession - instead you could become a cynic by simply keeping your life as simple as possible, questioning everything, and being true to yourself.

If that sounds familiar, it should. It's why the idea of being minimalist and living with 'just enough' to get by is as popular now with some people as it ever was.

If Crates and his brand of cynicism questioned the need to ´keep score´ in life by accumulating more money than you need. He knew that owning vast wealth does not guarantee anything other than the responsibility to manage that vast amount of cash – and that there´s no happiness or satisfaction in that alone. Crates knew what you do with opportunity that matters and not simply having the resources to create opportunity.

Then, like now there was no guarantee money would bring happiness - in the same way that being flat broke, supposedly without a care in the world wouldn't guarantee happiness either. His brand of cynicism was more pragmatic. His true claim to fame is that he articulated this difference both by the example of his own life and the way he shared those experiences with others looking for a similar level of 'peace' in their own lives.

He exemplifies that difference between a boss and a leader when it comes to the making of assumptions about what is important. Crates might suggest a boss makes assumptions based on their own experience, fears, and frustrations that they then project onto their team. They might even make decisions about what they believe a person might say or do in a new situation based on these, mostly erroneous assumptions. There have been many occasions when I've heard bosses say things like *"She wouldn't want to do that, it's just not her strong suit"*, or

"He shouldn't even be considered for this position because he would only leave us after a few months for a higher paid job anyway, - best to keep him where he is."

If you haven't experienced this level of arrogance yet, you are lucky. Crates might have said that being unaware that a boss you know may have been talking about you or someone you know like this is to ignore a possible or even likely reality. He'd suggest you question everything and draw your own conclusions.

He'd also suggest that leaders do instead isn't necessarily as narrow-minded, but they are not immune from making assumptions - it's a natural thing to do. However, what they do differently is 'fess up' when they're making those assumptions. They will have the thought and then engage in an appropriate discussion to question their own assumption. In other words, the leader will ask themselves better questions, and when handled well will get far better outcomes.

His Environment: He was rich. This is getting to sound like a pre-requisite to be a philosopher and maybe it is, because Crates like many others was born into a wealthy family. However, unlike others who either used the family fortune to pay for a gap-year or ten, he used his inheritance very differently.

To get into the head of Crates, think about what it must have been like living in this hugely prosperous central Greek city of Thebes. It was a city with a powerful history, engaged in successful trade in every direction. They were a hub of wealth making activity and Crates family had benefitted from it greatly. Indeed, by the time he was born it had become the most prosperous city in Greece, with even more wealth than Athens - and he belonged to one of its most wealthy families and probably inherited more than most people could spend in a lifetime.

However, he did spend it, and quite quickly. This is his story; Crates inherits a large fortune and can now do whatever he wants, whenever he wants, with whoever he wants. He decides to go and watch a play called *'The Tragedy of Telephus'*. If, like me you've never heard of this play, it's about this guy King Telephus who was the son of Heracles, - he of Iliad and Odyssey fame who was wounded in the thigh by Achilles. In this play, the wound of Telephus wouldn't heal no matter what the physicians tried to do to fix it. Eventually, running out of options he consults the 'Oracle of Apollo'. Usually this is an old woman high on psychotropic drugs who allegedly see's the future. She tells Telephus that the only way his leg's ever goingto get fixed is if he convinced the one who inflicted the wound to now heal it. In other words, he had to track down Achilles and get him to heal the wound with the same spear that inflicted it.

Telephus didn't fancy his chances of convincing Achilles if we went to him as the King, so instead he figured out a plan to fool him: He knew that Achilles hadn't got anyone who knew the way to Troy by sea, so he disguised himself in rags and begged Achilles to help him, promising in return to show him the way. Achilles bought it, and used the spear to cure him - in return Telephus gave him the information he needed and it was happy ever after for Telephus. Not such a good result for Troy, but that's another story.

Quite why Crates was moved by this pedestrian play isn't clear; perhaps it was the fact that no matter how much wealth or how many riches the king had, it didn't help his health and happiness. Maybe it was because he only got better by letting go of all that wealth and using his head to develop a plan that influenced his hitherto enemy to cure him - albeit while in disguise. Whatever it was, the play had a powerful effect on him, because shortly afterwards he took all his inheritance and shared it out among the poor of his city until it was all gone, leaving him with literally only the clothes he was standing in.

His family freaked, which probably led to his move from Thebes to Athens, or it could have been that he'd heard of Diogenes and was convinced he needed to meet him. Whatever the cause, he left with nothing but ambition and commitment and went to Athens. I laughed when reading that Crates then 'studied' under Diogenes - that's be like going to school with one of those trolley-and-tin-can people - not quite the perfect teaching environment or teacher methinks. Anyway, he obviously befriended Diogenes and got to know him well enough to extract from him the essentials of what we now recognise as the tradition of Cynicism.

His Culture: The traditions and myths of Thebes go back some hundreds of years before Crates was born. This was a culture with a strong identity of its own.

There are a couple of conflicting accounts of how Thebes was established, but as both include the same central character within them - I'm going with this one. It states that in mythology the city was founded by none other than Oedipus - yes, the fall in love with mum and kill your dad guy. The story goes that as well as being the birthplace of none other than Hercules himself, it also had a clash of the titans-like beginning:

Thebes had this cool riddle associated with it, *"What goes on fours in the morning, on twos in the afternoon and on threes at night?"*

This riddle was posed by the Sphinx - not the one in Egypt but a being with the head of a woman, the body of a lioness, the wings of an eagle, and the tail of a serpent. Unlike the big stone monument in Egypt, this Sphinx was alive – and she had a mission. Her job was to rule Thebes and guard it against strangers. She asked everyone who wanted to enter the city her riddle. Inevitably they couldn't answer it, so she did what any self-respecting tyrannical Sphinx would do - she ate them. That is, she did until Oedipus came along.

He was a smart cookie and got the answer to the riddle straight away as if it were obvious; he answered, *"It is a human being, because a person walks on all fours early in life, on two legs as an adult, and with a walking stick when in old age"*.

Apparently, the Sphinx was so upset that a mere mortal had figured out her riddle that she killed herself. A bit extreme, but I'm guessing she might have had stress issues and was a one riddle pony. Anyway, the Sphinx's passing meant the tyranny of her rule was over. The suffering Thebes had endured in its early days was replaced by the benevolent rule of King Oedipus.

The place clearly had a culture where people were proud of where they came from. It must have had some impact on Crates as he grew up because he took account of his history and attempted to learn from it. He may have wanted to live without material possessions but he valued knowledge - particularly knowledge that people in the past had worked hard to acquire. After all, why waste hard earned knowledge that simply requires a little effort to learn?

Bosses in business today would do well to take a leaf from Crates´ playbook. For example, a recent business study amply demonstrates what happens when you don´t value historical knowledge: The study included more than 70 car parts suppliers in the UK. It found that their ´Quality Managers´ had *forgotten* nearly two-thirds of past quality-related skills, tools and techniques from their company archives. Sadly, bosses like to feel important by making things their own and they confuse massaging their ego with managing success. Without meeting any of the people concerned or knowing anything else about them it's abundantly clear that the men and women in charge of that aspect of production were not leaders but bosses – potentially either with fragile ego´s or appallingly unaware of their leadership responsibilities. They were ego -focused rather than outcome-driven. They may have been the boss of their department, but as we can see, that doesn't in any way entitle them to the title of leader.

His Skills: Clearly, Crates was no fool - he didn´t just waste his fortune - he was measured in his approach and patently successful in helping people resolve difficult issues. He was utterly committed to a way of life and of using whatever he had at his disposal to help others. He wasn´t just well meaning - he had the skills and commitment to genuinely make a difference.

The learning he extracted from the 'wild and woolly' Diogenes must have been teased out over many conversations. I can only imagine how committed to learning Crates was, to spend time quite literally squatting in the street and listening. Therefore, patience must have been as much a skill for him as a virtue. He will have known that Diogenes himself didn't come up with his ideas out of nowhere - but had himself learned some philosophy from somewhere. In fact he´d learned about philosophy from a chap called Antisthenes, himself a student of the great Aristotle. Antisthenes was known to have emphasized the rejection of material wealth, social status, and 'things', in favour of a life free from the pressures of possessions. The Cynical view was that there's no need to hang onto anything because you'll only lose them eventually anyway. They believed that possessions distract you from the act of living your life as best you can.

They do have a point, don't they? My first thought was when you get a new car - and how paranoid some people (like me) get, about parking it to avoid even the slightest ding. It's like the joy of having the car has been sucked away by the tension and worry of the possibility that another car door opening onto mine. Of course, Crates never had to worry about a car ding, but his idea that what at first appears to be a benefit, but that in reality causes you worry and stress about it is something worth thinking about.

His Beliefs: Crates commitment to the 'cynical' life approach must have been contagious - so much so that he attracted a mate who shared the same ideals. She was a lady called Hipparchia, who also came from a wealthy family. She married him and committed herself to this have-nothing, need-nothing life by also giving all her money away to the poor.

My favourite part of this story is that Crates wanted there to be no doubt that she was marrying him, and not 'possessions' that he arrived at Hipparchia's house, without a stitch on. He stood there in front of her wearing nothing but a smile and said, *"Here is the bridegroom and these are his possessions, choose accordingly"*. He´s the only guy I´ve ever read about that turned up naked to demonstrate that ´this´ is what his wife to be will be getting! #kudos

Of course, she did say yes, but the weirdness doesn´t end there, as they are then reported to have consummated the marriage on the porch of a public building - in full view of anyone caring to look. They reasoned that if there was nothing unnatural about copulation in private, then sex in public should be okay too because it's simply natural. I know that´s illegal now, but I don´t think they were breaking any laws back then. However, I'm pretty sure this would have caused at least a little bit of a stir in Athenian polite society, as did the shedding of her own wealth. She made sure every penny she had was spread to those who needed it more than she did. To me, that sounds like a terrific thing to do, but not so in ancient Athens. It wasn´t seen as a good thing at all because it implied other rich people should do the same thing – something they were not keen to do.

Their actions seen as outrageous in Athens - not so much him turning up starker's and then the outdoor hanky-panky(they were a pretty liberal lot), but the giving away mum and dad's hard earned cash was definitely frowned on. It might have been a step too far for most people who were not already rich – their life was all about chasing the Athenian dream of making their own wad of cash. So, they probably found it as difficult to get their heads around as anyone might in similar circumstances today. Can you imagine the Kardashian's or Posh and Beck's having a bit of a naked frolic in public, then giving all their money, houses, cars, and vast amounts of 'stuff' away to the people of the world - leaving them with just the clothes they stood up in?

I say go for it if it appeals, especially as according to Crates they'd earn themselves a way more positive attitude to life. If they did, I think two things would happen; firstly, Becks would probably get canonised and become *St Becks of Leytonstone,* and secondly the world of social media would probably go mad with the stories racing around the world at the speed of light - and incredulity being voiced in every language on the planet. On the one hand they'd become instant hero's – on the other hand they'd be brutally criticised by plenty of other high profile rich people who might be less keen to give away their stuff!

Back then, Crates and Hipparchia may not have been quite the equivalent of social-media royalty, but there were a big enough deal to raise eyebrows as if they were the 'Posh and Becks' of ancient Athens. However, their shenanigans in public and the giving away of their goods wasn't the full story - their marriage was also remarkable because it was based on mutual respect and equality. This was strange in a society where women were definitely considered inferior to men. It was totally unheard of, and raised more than just an eyebrow - some might even have viewed it as a threat to their way of life – even more so than threatening social attitudes to wealth.

It really was a massive social step in a different direction back then. Yet, it shouldn't be a big step for the modern workplace to be a space where people treat each other with mutual respect and eschewed hierarchy in favour of human equality, but I'm afraid it often is. No matter how many signs and posters a company puts up on their walls declaring their commitment to these things, it takes leaders with an attitude like Crates to make it happen. It takes a belief in equality to create equality – and it has to be something that a leader has to 'live' and not just talk about or be compliant with. Sadly, in the world of politics and business this difference between belief and compliance is seen all the time. Unfortunately, all too often the spotlight shines on bosses that are simply complaint – they get caught saying something, or photographed doing something that evidences their true belief. When they fight back by going on camera claiming whatever they did was a mistake, and they now know better, might be seen by Crates as a weak response. He knew that actions speak louder than words.

His Identity: If neon signs had been around in his time, I'm betting he'd have a portable one with Cynic and a big arrow pointing at himself. He wasn't shy about sharing his beliefs.

The man took the idea from Diogenes and ran with it - Cynicism permeated every aspect of his life. He took the idea of facing the reality of life *'how it is now'* rather than how it was or how it might be. He had no problem making up his own rules regarding morality, and no issue with acting in ways that were contrary to the social norms of the time.

For example, when his son reached that age where his body was telling him he was a man - even though his mind might have needed to do some catching up, which let's face it is the same for any boy - Crates didn't just do the 'birds and the bees' speech with his boy. Instead, he took him to a brothel to make sure he learned properly. If that caused you to blink, then listen to what he did with his daughter. His approach with her was even more down to earth - and maybe even a little bit shocking (well, it shocked me anyway).Instead of doing what most families did in those days and matching her up with a suitable husband, he allowed suitors to do their thing to impress her. Then, and only then if she thought 'this was the one', he allowed her to have a month's trial 'marriage' before deciding whether or not to go through with the real thing. I´m tempted to call it a *try before you buy´* approach.

My first thought was that he was an enlightened dude, because as father to one daughter and step-father to two more, they all have done exactly what he allowed his daughter to do, even though I did my best to be a protective dad — they still tried before they bought! And, just like Crates allowed his daughter to do, mine too tried out more than one young suitor. Therefore, as protective as I may have wanted to be, the fact is that all three girls in my family have settled down with fine young men, so it was clearly a good strategy. Crates was simply ahead of his time.

He is said to have been a really good guy. Apparently, he had a gentle, rich, humour about him and was self-effacing with everyone he met. Crates isn't necessarily pictured as a handsome man, but that didn't stop him having a wonderful relationship and a terrific life. Everything I've read indicates he loved his wife and loved his life - despite being born lame and with hunched shoulders. His marriage of equality and respect was successful and yielded two children, a boy and a girl.

He was known as the 'door opener' because wherever he went people readily opened their doors to him. He was known for being of service to families who might have been having problems and engaging with them to make it easier to sort things out, all without being asked or without the need for payment - joining them for a meal would have been payment enough. What a guy. Summing him up, Crates was a happily married man -so happy, that according to reports of him he would laugh at everyday things as if he 'were at a festival'.

He lived his whole life making life fun, never compromising his beliefs for anyone or anything. He may have given everything away but he never regretted it, nor did he take himself too seriously. He just lived life the way he thought he could make the best contribution as a human being. In the summer he was content to walk around in just rags, and in winter he'd use a cloak or blanket - but nothing else against the cold. He did that because he said every winter taught him how to better deal with the next.

He lived his life out on the streets of Athens with his wife - teaching his brand of philosophy to anyone interested, and engaging with students and working with his wife to help other people. She didn't just support him in the traditional ways of a wife but she too took to dressing in male attire and teaching philosophy alongside him. Theirs was a genuine partnership – they were equal partners in every endeavour. Furthermore, it's thought that when he dies from natural causes at the ripe old age of 80 (a great age at that time) she took over his teachings.

I have to say, out of all the worthy people included in here, I admire him the most. Crates really is my favourite, and if I could choose a leader to work with, he would be high on the list.

His Purpose: It's no secret that Crates had a vision; one of a world based on justice, nonviolence, and simplicity of living.

His favourite way of explaining to people how to live a better life was to ask them to *clear the fog* – he asked them what it would be like if they were living in a fog. The word he used was 'Juphos', but I think broadly speaking that meant to suggest either fog or foggy. He wanted people to think about bettering their life as if they were clearing the fog - seeing what matters most more clearly. Thereby allowing them to focus on those things that added value to their life while letting go of the things that did not.

This approach of clearing the fog wasn't solely applied to material things - a great example of how he applied this same thinking to very ordinary experiences. He helped a young man named Metrocles, this young chap was an enrolled student at the Lyceum, the Athenian school of philosophy set up by Aristotle. One day when it was his turn to stand up and speak publicly, the poor guy got a little nervous and couldn't stop himself from letting out a bottom-burp that everyone heard. It was a mega-fart made even more noticeable by the expectant silence.

He was mortified, and so embarrassed about passing wind out loud that he had a bit of a panic attack - he shut himself away from everyone and escaped to the privacyof his room, and the seriously considered starving himself to death. That might sound extreme, but I guess the feelings of self-esteem for some young people were as fragile then as they are today.

Crates heard what happened and decided to help fix things. Without needing an invitation, the great man arrived at the boy's room with a cauldron of soup. He talked to the boy about the necessity for people to pass wind, and that an accidental fart was as natural as an unexpected cough, sneeze or any other natural bodily function - especially one that seems to have a mind of its own.

The soup was purposely packed full of beans - and after they'd finished eating and Crates had completed his exhortation to just accept a little farting as being natural and nothing to be ashamed of, he let out the biggest, loudest, and most amazing rear-end trump the boy had ever heard! Obviously, they both laughed. If it had been me, I would have been in stitches - I mean, what´s funnier than a fart joke, especially when one appears to order like that? The point was made, and the boy 'got it'. He let go of the angst and embarrassment, and went back to his studies without further problems.

I think this story really does sum up his purpose; to enlighten by removing the fog of unnecessary worries, and to laugh at life - because most of the time there's plenty to find that's funny. What was even funnier about this story is that Metrocles introduced Crates to his little sister, Hipparchia - his future wife. #wonderfulkarma

How might he be thought of by his employees, if he was a manager in today's business world?

This is a guy most of us would love to work with every day. He is a leader who keeps his eye on the ball and isn't worried how many times he goes back and questions people on what they think the outcome is or should be.

He takes the facts about 'reality' and uses them to support the achievement of success by focusing only on those things that matter to being successful. He doesn't ignore barriers and challenges, but merely sets them in the context of the greater desire to overcome them. He helps us focus on taking action where it matters most. His leadership makes it easier for all of us to avoid being constrained by the fears of what might 'be a problem'. His catchphrase is ´clear the fog´ - we all know what it means and the more we use it, the more of a difference it makes. It´s amazing how many times clearing the fog is as useful at home as it is at work.

The social or cultural 'rules' that might hinder another leader don't seem to hinder him at all. He rises above them and keep everyone's attention on the greater good. He´s mastered the skill of presenting information in a way that captures both the hearts and minds of us all. He makes no secret that 'facts' in any context can be 'spun' to make almost any argument seem plausible, but then proceeds to create his own position and proposals with such power and credibility that few ever experience the need to question him - even though he's made it clear that they are welcome to ask him anything.

He is a leader who is trusted because he is pragmatic. He knows that whatever might be the best thing to do 'in theory', may not be possible right now in the current circumstances - therefore, he relies on three things to be a great leader; clarity of the desired outcome, choosing those aspects of reality that support the outcome, and helping each individual apply the same pragmatism to their own situation and their own personal reality. The alignment of these three factors makes him a formidable leader.

What matters to us probably even more is the fact that he treats us all as equals. He makes it clear that all of us are leaders of our own role. We get whatever we need to ensure our job is done, nothing more and nothing less. Each of us knew from the moment we joined the organisation that this was a place where material gain is not our overriding purpose - that doesn't mean profit isn't important, merely that it's a necessary part of the process of meeting our overall goals. This is an organisation that makes a difference for our employees as well as our end users. We are paid well because our leader recognises that this is an important need for us, but we do not waste resources on unnecessary costs in the workplace when we can use those resources more effectively elsewhere. It might sound like it's a pious, downbeat place to work – but it's quite the opposite. It's a fun place to be, and a fun loving leader to be around.

Coaching questions he might ask: Crates was all about moving forward in life from wherever you are, being true to yourself, and not letting anyone or anything become an artificial barrier to that achievement.

When his own family came to Athens to try and bring him back to Thebes, (probably because they assumed he was one can short of a six-pack and needed help), he made it very clear to them that he was fine - and that there was nothing wrong with him. Crates made it clear that he was staying put. He's said to have got quite forceful with them and *'drove them away with a stick'* when they attempted to draw him back to a life of luxury.

Therefore, his questions would be all about the direction and needs of the person, unencumbered with the useless clutter of social etiquette, unimportant facts, status, and wealth. His questions were all about helping his team clear their own fog;

i.   *"Are you so in love with your position that you would act like the love-committed couple unashamed to make love in public and uncaring of the feelings of onlookers? as opposed to taking other's opinions and views into consideration?"*

ii. *"Have you considered the minimum you need to be able to move on to more important and better things in your life, rather than being concerned and weighed down with arguing merely to try and 'win'?"*

iii. *"If you were the best, most fair, and compassionate 'judge', what verdict and advice would you deliver in your current situation?"*

iv. *"Imagine a doorway that must be passed through if you are ever to progress, but that will allow you through only if you take with you only three things dear to you... what would they be?"*

v. *"Is it not true that we are all to some extent influenced by people in our past - sometimes without even realising it.If so, how do you know it is to your benefit?"*

vi. *"Of all the choices facing you now, which are those that may appeal but may also might lead you into the fog and away from the things you really want?"*

vii. *"When you recall those painful moments of your life when you realised that you had been wrong, do you feel like inviting more of them in, or being careful not to make the same mistakes again?"*

viii. *"When you remember a time when you had much less than you have now of the thing you are looking for more of, what would you have given to achieve even some of what you have now?"*

CHAPTER 24: #20 IS THIS AS GOOD AS IT GETS?

ARISTOTLE

His Claim to Fame: Okay, how long have you got? Aristotle wrote over 1.5 million words during his 62 years on the planet that we can still read today, and that was just a tiny percentage of what he must have written because the words we have are merely his teaching notes from the Lyceum, - goodness knows how many words he really produced.

To put that in perspective this book is around 100,000 words, so the small amount we have is still almost nineteen books of this size. Don't forget, these were put together during a time without word processors and on-demand printing –and no Mr Google to use as a research tool. That is an unbelievable amount of thinking to commit by hand to a mountain of wax tablets.

I have a couple of personal favourite things he left us with; firstly, he is the inventor of the 'syllogism' - a logical statement fit for Mr Spock[xxxiii] himself. It was pretty basic stuff but is as useful today as it ever was. If you're not familiar with a syllogism it goes like this;

'All authors have something to say, and Martin Goodyer is an author, therefore, Martin Goodyer has something to say.'

It only works if the first two statements are indisputably true, and when they are, the third part of the syllogism works.

The second thing I'm grateful for is that he's the first of the philosophers to ask the *'big'* question of an individual; what's it all for, or more palatably in today's parlance *'what's your ultimate goal'*. I love him, not for the fact that he asked the question, because I'm pretty sure that human beings have been asking that question in one form or another since we were able to think, but because he made a typically impressive distinction.

He realised that the people of his time would agonise of what would be the best goal in life, or the best outcome, or the best achievements - all of which implied that one ending would somehow be 'better' than another. Aristotle obviously had thought about this a lot over his lifetime. It didn't make any sense to him that one outcome would be better than another, just that different people would want different things. For example, I might want my life to be a journey of learning, ending with something close to wisdom left behind for whoever follows to discover. However, my neighbour might also agree she is on a journey, but that hers is of acquisition of material goods and money, ending with a legacy of wealth to pass on. Is hers better than mine, or is mine better than hers? Well, I suppose it depends on if you are her or me, doesn't it? Aristotle was the first to talk about the fact that neither is intrinsically 'better' than the other, merely that each will appeal to differently depending on who you are and what you value. Here's one of the things he said about this:

"...that wishes for the end have already been stated; some think it is for the good, others for the apparent good. Now, those who say that good is the object of wish must admit in consequence that, that which the man who does not chose aright wishes for is not an object of wish. For if it is

to be so it must also be good but was bad. While those who say the apparent good is the object of wish, must admit that there is no natural object of wish but only what seems good to each man. Now, different things appear good to different people and if it so happens, even contrary things."

Apart from being one of the great threesome he was the most pragmatic in his approach. His message was that everything a person has done, is doing, and will do is one of two things; it is either an end (in itself), or it is a means to some end. He was the first to make the distinction between things that help get us moving closer to our ultimate goals, as opposed to those that lead us in the other direction. He called the first, *virtues* and the second, *vices*. He was way ahead of his time, not only with his labelling but the idea that a vice can be turned into a virtue by simply changing behaviour. I think among all the other things he's credited with, he could also be responsible for kicking off the self-help industry.

His Environment: Aristotle's notion that living well is an end-goal for life shaped his environment, or at least how he adapted to it. He was born in a small town of Stagiros (later called Stageira) that's about eight kilometres north of the similarly named more modern village of Stagira, close to Olympiada. This beautiful, picturesque part of Greece sits on a plateau that's part of the Chalcidice peninsular.

I think he might be surprised to find that a statue of him still sits to this day in the ruins of the ancient town. His father was the village doctor and had good, solid social connections that were probably useful people to call on when he left home for the big city. It is possible that dad was more than just a local MD, and that he also had a role serving at the Macedonian court. His father's 'other job' may have been the connection that later in his life got him the job as tutor to the thirteen year old Alexander the Great - when he was just a young Alexander.

At seventeen he packed his bags and travelled the 700 kilometre journey to Athens where he joined Plato's circle at the Academy. I don't think there was any formal enrolment process - he just pitched up started listening and talking with Plato and his followers. He spent twenty years as a student and follower of the great philosopher and playwright. However, after two decades of listening he'd developed ideas of his own, ideas that were so at odds with Plato's that it caused them to part company. It was the combination of learning about science as a boy with his father and then a further twenty years in the learning environment with Plato that shaped him into the man he became.

However, he wasn't content to just move 'up the road' and open his own place to compete with his old teacher - he had more integrity than that. He did stay in Athens until Plato passed away, but then travelled to Assos in what is now Turkey, then on to the island of Lesbos where he joined up with a group of thinkers who shared Plato's philosophy. It was here that Aristotle fell in love with the group-leader's niece. It's likely that this time in his life was as fulfilling as it got – he was in love, living on an idyllic island with fabulous weather, studying things that he loved - does life get any better? Tragically, the good times weren't destined to last and his life changed forever courtesy of the warring Persian's .

They invaded and killed his wife and love of his life. The heart broken Aristotle left Turkey and made his way to the Macedon court looking for some purpose in his own life. It was here that he was appointed as tutor to the young Alexander. No one knows the true influence he had on the boy who was soon to become a young man and Alexander the Great. However, I have a bust of Alexander in my office (and a statue of Aristotle) - because it reminds me that Coaching-Leaders who become that way because they've studied with Aristotle-type teachers, can quite literally change the world. There is one surviving tantalising fragment that refers to his time teaching Alexander, a fragment in which he talks to Alexander about being leader of the Greeks but Master of the Barbarians. We can only wonder what questions he might have posed to the developing young masterful mind. Aristotle was no Rasputin[xxxiv], planting seeds that the boy might then perceive as his own, but an adherent of the Socratic questioning approach. So, I think he would have asked the boy great questions, and the developing young man would develop his own thoughts and his own ideas. Exactly the approach that effective leaders in business still apply today.

His Culture: By the time Aristotle came along, the notion of using the best philosophical, well-read, intellectual teachers to support the children of the great and the good was well established.

'Schools' of thinking and learning were by then well established and his own *'Lyceum'* was one in a long-line of quality learning environments. Although to be fair, his was somewhat different - he would hold his lectures while walking through the cool air of the colonnaded walk near the shrine of Apollo Lyceus (from where they get the name), holding his more difficult lectures in the morning, and then spending the afternoon giving his more popular talks on living life well to those who would follow him around. Yet, as much as he was the person giving the lectures and shaping thoughts, he can't have helped but be influenced himself by the Greek culture of the time. I'm sure he tried to question 'everything', but you just try it - it's hard because some things just slip on by without you noticing - they just seem so, well, obvious so why would you question them?

One of these, slippy-on-by things was the way they thought babies were made. No, they knew that mummies and daddies had to do the 'deed', it wasn't that - but they thought that mum was a passive human baby incubator and that dad supplied ALL the goodies to make the baby become the person they would become. It was this 'understanding' that caused Aristotle said some pretty dumb things about women.

Now, point of order here; Aristotle wasn't a misogynist, neither did he have a low opinion of the contribution women made to society. It's just that he was a biologist doing the best with the information that he had at the time, and well, bluntly some of it was simply wrong. So, when we hear that he said men were superior to women because they were stronger and had male character traits of, say, courage – which meant that men were superior to women, he was talking about what he could see from his understanding of biology. It has, I'm sad to say given him a bad reputation in some quarters, where he's portrayed as the chauvinist he was not. Don't forget, his main source material was from the study of animals- and it looked obvious that in the wild females were the one's protecting the young and males were out there being brave and courageous.

Today, we know how misleading the 'obvious' really is, but we are talking about a long, long time ago. Just for completeness - he did call women 'incomplete men', which doesn't go down well now for good reason. He also posited that some people were better off being destined to be slaves because their 'soul' was not at the forefront and they lacked the ability to learn.

Oops. That was biologist in him speaking and not the philosopher. By the way, back then they hadn't figured out that consciousness was a function of the brain and so thought that the mysterious 'soul' was where all awareness came from. Again, he wasn't condemning anyone to slavery - he wasn't an Ancient Greek Nazi, nor did he mean anything damaging by what he said. This is honest to goodness cultural affect in action, simply because he was surrounded by slaves (which was normal at that time), and just like the plants and animals around him he was looking for ways in which to understand them, and created categories within which to collate his ideas together.

It's another of those slippy-on-by things - he didn't question if slavery was a good idea, it was simply one of those unquestioned aspects of life. Hence, it sounds way worse today than it would have done back then. There's a ton of things to take away from this when thinking about moving from boss to leader; firstly, to cut yourself some slack - sometimes with the best will in the world you're going to screw up, but as long as you are doing the best with the information available and asking the best questions you can, then forgive yourself, apologise and move on. Secondly, recognise that it isn't only arrogant bosses that take things for granted unquestioningly - because we all do it, but the difference between a leader and a boss is that the leader admits when they're wrong and gets on with putting things right, rather than blundering on, too afraid to put the outcome before their ego.

His Skills: There's no doubt he had an amazing education at the Academy, but equally the man had a towering intellect.

He used himself as a model - a tough thing to do because it's much easier to preach a philosophy than demonstrate one through your own actions. It's as if he wanted to make use of every aspect of his life and the way he went about things to get closer and closer to living his own life well, and achieving whatever it was that was his own ultimate goal. It's even suggested that his penchant for walking around while giving his lectures was to instil in his listeners the idea that knowing about something is not enough to get closer to living your life well, but that you must DO something with what you know, take action, and keep moving dynamically toward your goal if every day of this pitifully short life is to be a life well lived.

He said, *"We deliberate not about ends, but about means. For a doctor does not deliberate whether he shall heal nor an orator if he shall persuade, nor a Statesman if he shall produce law and order. Nor does anyone else deliberate about his end. They assume the end and consider how and by what means it is to be attained, and if it seems to be produced by several means they consider by which it is most easily and best produced. While if it is achieved by only one, they consider how it will be achieved by this, and by what means this will be achieved."*

Aristotle had the skill to recognise that all the things people hold to be good, or the 'best' way of doing anything were simply the personalised paths they'd created to take themselves closer to their own ultimate goal. He recognised that the only thing we can take away that's transferrable was the fact that a *'life well lived'* was at the heart of it all for everyone. For him to live his own life well, he spent his time learning - his writings cover aspects of physics, biology, zoology, metaphysics, theatre, music, rhetoric, psychology, linguistics, economics, politics, government, and of course, philosophy.

His contributions to society are enormous; let's start with his biological classification system that's hardly been improved on even now, he created the first 'scientific method' and the mathematical variable, he correctly figured out most of our bodily functions to the respective organs, he set out the first formal system of logic, his ethical approach to life was a huge influence on the founding fathers of the United States as detailed in the Declaration of Independence - and he was a great teacher whose approach is as fresh today as it was fifteen hundred years ago. Phew!

He also came up with a very simple way to classify and figure out just about anything. He called this method his *'four causes'*. These four causes caused him to ask four questions; Firstly, the material; what is it? Secondly, the shape; how is it arranged? Thirdly, the efficiency; how did it come to be? Fourthly, the Purpose; what is it for? He used these questions to sort out and figure out all manner of problems. I can imagine him strolling through the Lyceum picking a topic, and then leading his students through each question. I can also imagine leaders using similar questions to help their team avoid premature evaluation and jumping to conclusions.

His Beliefs: He said that *"An unplanned life is not worth living"*, sort of moving on from the words Plato put into the mouth of Socrates when he said, *"the unexamined life is not worth living"*.

The belief that examining life is not enough, but that planning a life by understanding your own values was central Aristotle's thinking. I love the fact that there's a direct correlation to this and the difference between a boss and leader - because how many successful leaders do you know that run from meeting to meeting, always late, always stressed, and always failing to complete what they set out to do in the time they set out to do it? Not many I'll wager. Yet, isn't that just typical behaviour for a boss? Okay, maybe not all bosses, but be fair, there are plenty who spend more time telling the world how busy their life is than actually getting on with achieving something in the time they've got.

As far as Aristotle was concerned there was only one plan a successful person needs to follow, and that was one leading to the ultimate-goal in life that all of humanity could share - 'living life well'. He made the distinction about things that we do in life necessary for us to survive, and those that are choices about the kind of survival we want to experience. I'm sure just about everyone who's attended any management training will recognise the name Abraham Maslow and his 'hierarchy of needs'[xxxv]- when in the 1940's he urged managers to recognise that without helping employees to 'live', there was no way they were going to be able to 'live well' and hence, serve the needs of the organisation more effectively.

Aristotle didn't concern himself with organisational psychology (it´d be a long time before that term would be coined), but did start the ball rolling with the distinction that 'living' and 'living well' were divided by choice - the first was a basic necessity, and the second was then necessary to think about if the chance to live well wasn't to be wasted. He didn't believe that making this distinction had anything to do with status or resources but was a choice any human being could make - one that reflected their personal priorities.

A fair translation of the Greek 'living well' may be what we consider as our understanding of 'happiness'. I've seen some translations that call it success, but as success has so many trappings attached, 'happiness' is a more meaningful way of describing a life well lived.

I believe that he would believe leadership to be about creating a business environment that supported people being happy. I believe that he would held discussions (probably walking around) about anything that might be getting in the way of that happiness – whether it be directly related to a business issue or not. All of which sounds to me remarkably like he´d be holding coaching conversations.

His Identity: Scientist, philosopher, teacher, and friend to one of the greatest leaders in history - so how did he see himself? I guess no one will ever know for sure, but I'm going for a collection of all of them under whatever made-up title you think is appropriate, because it doesn't matter what he's called - it just matters what he did.

Like, there can be little doubt he made an impact as a teacher - people say that he only spent two years with the young Prince Alexander, but those two years were between thirteen and fifteen, and by then the super-keen young Alexander was taking up a full military role in the Army, so was like a teenage sponge. Those two years were probably the most valuable and impactful of his life - until then he'd have learned the basics of life, and along comes Aristotle teaching him about virtue and vice – it must have been quite a shift in thinking. Not only did he teach him about life, but also about the way that animals and plants could be characterised and that learning applied so as to make better use of what was discovered.

Aristotle's taxonomy of plants and animals is the foundation of what we still use today, and it made such an impact on Alexander the Great that on his travels to conquer the known world, he ordered his men to gather samples of things he didn't recognise and send them back to Aristotle for cataloguing. I think it's fair to say that he and Alexander became old friends and Aristotle would have seen himself in that light. Which by the way was no bad thing to be mates with the most powerful man on the planet, that is until of course he stops being that - at which point his old buddy Aristotle was banished for having such close ties with the Macedonian Court. #politicssucks

His Purpose: Aristotle wanted people to analyse things a little deeper than the hectic hurly-burly of life seemed to allow for. Okay, a lot deeper than they otherwise would.

Now, some might imagine that in his time life was a breeze, that time to achieve things could stretch and stretch, and that with the absence of mobile phones and the internet, how could it possibly be as faced-paced and stressful as today. Ah, all that fresh air, lack of pollution and global warming – no rush hour, metro, or tedious train journeys. Well, to us maybe it wasn't, but people judge things not by what they don't know but what they do know - and as far as they were concerned *their* generation was the most stressful ever, as would be the next, the next, and the next, and so on. Aristotle realised this, and by attempting to teach people to think more deeply, hoped that they could use whatever time they had to make better choices, and achieve better decisions in their life.

Now, doesn't that sound a lot like a coaching-leader to you?

How might he be thought of by his employees, if he was a manager in today's business world?

He is a leader who believes in the latent potential of his team. His fundamental belief that there is 'more' within every person means that in every aspect of his leadership he asks deep and far reaching questions of people.

Every person following him can feel themselves growing in confidence and stature - as they are supported in finding ways to overcome the daily challenges facing them. We'd all admit that he's a bit of a hero to us - it doesn't matter how stressed we become, he remains calm and logical, but still cares how we feel.

He's not like bosses who 'blame' when something goes wrong, he is a leader more interested in helping a person get up when they stumble, and then go on to achieve more than they had initially believed possible. The results he and his team achieve go far beyond the levels that 'blaming boss' might have demanded, simply because each person wants to achieve more - they feel 'good' about achieving more.

He is on the one hand a kind leader and on the other a most demanding one. His restless spirit seems always to be seeking ways to help us collectively climb to greater heights of success by digging deeper and deeper into our own potential. The performance appraisals in his organisation don't seek to grade people on their past performance as a boss might grade an employee, but to ascertain from each of us what undiscovered potential is dormant or is still to be discovered within us. He's okay with the fact that not everyone has the same potential, and talks to us logically about the best way for us to get the most out of ourselves.

His team come out of their one to one management conversations feeling energised and enthusiastic - because his managers lead as he does and follow his example. They don't need to wait for formal situations to talk about performance development or addressing difficulties - they do it as part of the ordinary day to day activities and off-the-cuff conversations that happen anyway. We've all learned his ways and apply them within both the workplace and at home - and are the happier and mentally healthier for it.

Coaching questions he might ask: I can imagine Aristotle teaching as he walked through the Lyceum in the fading afternoon sun, inviting new students and those who wanted to learn some of the easier life lessons he had to teach - saying to his students that they need not concern themselves with 'living' because they are already doing that. Yet, they were unlikely to be 'living well' without some understanding of what that might mean to each of them.

i. *"A universal truth is that everything has a purpose, therefore, what is the purpose behind every one of the barriers standing in the way of your happiness?"*

ii. *"As nothing in this world is ever the 'finished article', what happens to your own thinking if you accept this is as true for you as anything else?"*

iii. *"If it is true that the achievement of all goals are the result of a cause set in motion, what were the goals relating to the causes of your barriers to success?"*

iv. *"If the shared characteristics of something make them what they are, and the only way to experience them is through our senses, what do you sense about your current situation and its characteristics that's helpful?"*

v. *"If you accept that logic is the foundation of understanding, what is logical about your situation that is undeniable, and what does that suggest you must do next?"*

vi. *"If you were to believe your intuition, your senses, your feelings... knowing that there is no choice but to face the goal, what does that suggest to you?"*

vii. *"If you were to mentally fly over your situation, how are the barriers to your success arranged?"*

viii. *"Imagine that despite your age, experience, or anything else that might be in your way that you've been tasked with delivering the outcomes that must now be achieved... what's the first thought you'd have if you were in charge?"*

ix. *"Think about classifying each aspect of the problem facing you into a taxonomy, and then listen to what it suggests is necessary for you to do and ask yourself, what next?"*

x. *"What is it that's materially affecting your situation and acting as a barrier to your happiness?"*

CHAPTER 25: #21 THE 'GREATEST JOY' COMES FROM THE MIND

STILPO

His Claim to Fame: In short – he´s the master of mind over matter - and without Stilpo the saying *'you are the architect of your own future'* might never have come about.

That's not quite how he said it of course, although it would have been pretty cool if he had. His version went; *"People are the architects of their own sorrows and evils, because desires can never be fulfilled completely"*. Close, but no cigar.

In fact, the underpinning thinking from Stilpo was that *'the greatest joy comes from a mind that cannot be dominated'*, - and by that he meant not dominated by anything; not dominated by imagined desires, not dominated by imagined fears, and not dominated by the threats or actions of anyone else. He was the very first to realise (and write down) that *what* and *how* a person chooses to think, leads directly to the actions they take.

While Socrates looked for innate wisdom in people, Plato tried to find people who'd escaped from their 'cave of illusion', and Aristotle would argue that a person can't argue with their biology, this guy was in many ways a huge leap ahead of all of them. His thinking can be directly linked to the hundreds of books from self-help gurus who talk about the *power of the mind*. It may look like they've made breakthroughs in the understanding of human behaviour, but in fact Stilpo got there a long time ago.

He's one of those Greek philosophers that goes under the radar of most popular books on philosophy because he didn't start this or that school. He also wasn't the founder of this or that philosophy, nor did he do something that kept his name on the lips of those of us interested in philosophy today. Yet, had we been alive twenty-four hundred years ago in Greece it's likely we *would* know his name - because he was something of a legend in his own lifetime.

He may not have started his own philosophical school, but he was the teacher of a then young, Zeno of Citium - he of Stoic fame. He was also great mates with Crates, who as we know was one of the masters of Cynicism. However, neither of these two great thinkers could compete with Stilpo in the eyes of the public - because Stilpo was able to communicate his ideas with a story. In this, he had even more in common with the big-time self-help gurus of today.

His was not just any old story, but his own story – one of a life initially lived in the fast lane before falling from grace, then picking himself back up again by his bootstraps. In his early days he feasted on an all-you-can-eat buffet of life choices, before finding his own enlightenment and then making one of those strange-but-true choices that were poles apart from where he'd imagined he'd be - but one that gave him a life of true fulfilment.

So, while other great thinkers set up their schools and hoped their students would learn, Stilpo influenced thousands of people to change their ways by telling a good tale. The obvious boss to leader message here is that it's not being 'right' that causes a person to agree to change their ways, but it's by being emotionally engaging. His story was something that most people could related to, even if their own life experiences were different. They could empathise, they could find resonances, and they could find real similarities in their own lives. Leaders that use authentic stories to communicate (and by that I don't mean boring personal anecdotes, but properly well-crafted Hollywoodesque scripts), will engage more people on their journey than those who do not. Engaging someone in a story versus lecturing them on what's the 'right thing to do' is the difference between being successful and popular versus unsuccessful and tooth-achingly painful.

His Environment: While bosses are apt to say that people are a product of their environment; they are slyly dismissive of people who might not have attended one of the 'best' universities (even if they didn't either), and often secretly some kind of 'ist' - like racist, fattist, tribalist, you get the idea. Leaders are not like that -leaders know that like Aristotle said, once a person turns from vice to virtue they are virtuous from that moment on. Only then do they give people a chance and don't hold their upbringing, address, education, accent, or any other environmental factor against them.

By this definition Stilpo provides some great leadership insights. I love the fact that a chap who ended up a model citizen, preaching moderation in all things didn't start out that way. In fact, he was far from it. Stilpo was in fact one of those well-to-do offspring of overindulging wealthy parents, he had a splendid education and was given every opportunity to live to excess without censure. He didn't need to do a glassy-eyed 'gap year' and then spend mum and dad's hard-earned in the Student-Union bar over the next three to eventually emerge with a degree of dubious usefulness. He could pretty much do what he wanted, when he wanted, and how he wanted to do it right where he was.

This young man wasn't worried about a world in turmoil or the future - life for him was simply idyllic and at first he had no care in the world. Not only was money, booze and girls not a problem, but also his home sat on the most picturesque hill overlooking the Megara Gulf in what is now Greek West Attica. It was probably as wonderful and calm then as it is today.

If it had been only this environment that'd shaped his future, I doubt he'd have made even the tiniest footnote in history. As it happened, it wasn't, and he did. He had money, he had a good education, he had a quick keen mind, he had the natural skills to communicate and the quick wit to make his communication effective, so when midway through his life he turned his back on heavy drinking and womanising, the world started to look very different; he ditched his old thinking and started again from scratch, and proved to anyone who'd care to look that no one is the product of their environment. I'd like to think he started to notice what a wonderful location he'd had the great fortune to be born into, and that he reflected on the nature of whatever 'happiness' he'd achieved with his excess thus far, but there must have been much more to it than a pretty view. The mind boggles at what else he must have reflected on when his idyllic world fell apart. He lost the lot – everything. Then, with growing insights he climbed his way back to an even better life, but more of that in a while.

His Culture: Coming from Megara, there's little doubt that the culture in the town would have been influenced by one of their most famous sons, none other than Euclid. Not the one we are familiar with, that was Euclid of Alexandria, but another Euclid who'd founded the Megarian school of philosophy in the years before Stilpo was born. This Euclid had died before Stilpo came into the world, but as Megara isn't a huge place it would be odd if Stilpo's education hadn't included either attendance at or influence of this philosophical school. The school was founded on the teachings of Aristotle, using logic to translate actions into those that might lead to a greater good. All of which is reasonably standard stuff, but what comes next has nothing standard about it at all.

Okay, I know you know that I'm doing my best to align with each one of these guys and step into their shoes, bronze plated sandals, scruffy tunics or whatever - and in every case until now that's been all about using imagination. However, this is closer to home and at the risk of giving away too much information it felt somewhat familiar. If that's just me then forgive me, but I don't think it will be - which is probably the reason his story resonated with so many back then just as it does today.

You see, I imagined what it might be like to be the young Stilpo and wondered what his school reports might have been like – I´ll bet they said something like, *'has talent but needs to pay more attention'*, *'must try harder'*, *'Stilpo is a sociable and popular young man who would do well to pay as much attention to his studies as he does to having a good time'*. Of course, I'm making these up, but it wasn't lost on me that these statements weren't far off the one's that appeared in my own school reports. Not only that, but as the young Stilpo reached that age when women, wine, song became the young man's priority, it looks like all the attention and effort that had been missing in his school work came to bear on these new, more interesting topics. Isn't that almost always the way?

Now, come on, I can't be alone in resonating with his experience, can I? It can't be just Stilpo and I that were seduced by too many glasses of vino-collapso, too many night's partying, and too much snogging in dark corners, can it? No, it can't be just us. Yet, Stilpo must have taken things a lot further than most of us because he didn't just make a few waves, he created a tsunami. He was so extreme that he was almost exiled from Megara for his overindulgence and his propensity for mistresses. However, maybe because his parents might have been influential, he wasn't actually banished in the end - just severely told off for his behaviour.

Apparently this near-banishment acted as a useful wake-up call and he had an epiphany that changed his ways. It was something that might have been an innocuous event that many people could shrug-off and put behind them, but for Stilpo it changed everything - because he started to think differently. However, it was a far more devastating event that turned his story from one of straightforward bad-boy-turns-good into a spell binding thriller.

It speaks to the culture of his home that a young man considered a wastrel could turn himself around and eventually become one of their hero's. Thank goodness they didn't have social media back then, or he may have had to spend his remaining days defending his early youthful misdeeds rather than getting on with life - and eventually becoming someone his town could take eventually pride in.

His Skills: Clearly, his biggest and most useful strength was as a communicator, but he was also enthusiastic about making them most of the way a person controls their mind, and creative in how he applied that thinking (as we shall see for the way he handles complaints about his daughter).

Any story worth being retold has some basic elements; first, there's a hero, then, the hero's life gets turned upside down and forces the hero on a journey. Next, the journey gets blocked by unforeseen barriers, and tragedy might ensue, but the hero finds a way through, the hero overcomes the barriers and finishes with the flourish of a happy ending. It may sound a bit 'Disney' but hey, look how successful the formula has been for them. Stilpo's story is like that.

One of Stilpo's favourite subjects was politics. He was fascinated by the way a person thought had a direct effect on that person's behaviour and the results they achieved. He became something of an analyst, and developed the skill to immerse himself into the psyche and thinking of an enemy army so effectively that he could predict with uncanny accuracy the outcome of an as yet un-fought battle. This unusual and undoubtedly useful skill was much sought after. In fact, Ptolemy the 1st, he of 'The Alexandria Library' fame and builder of the 'Lighthouse' in Alexandria port, was so keen to hire Stilpo that he offered him a small fortune to predict the outcome of his upcoming battles.

Later in life he proved himself to be eloquent and clever, which earned him offers to work with the great and the good as well as making him a target for others to try and 'get him'. In one altercation with a particularly difficult character trying to make a name for himself by bringing Stilpo down, he was accused of denouncing one of the gods. When called upon to defend himself he smiled and repeated that what he'd said about the gods was precisely true. Apparently, his detractor had called upon him to agree that a female member of the pantheon of gods was a 'Theo', - Greek for 'god', and he had quite accurately replied that this was untrue. He then explained that Theo applies only to male gods. Therefore, the correct means of expression was 'Thea', or goddess! Apparently, his hapless detractor was fuming while Stilpo left with a smile. #cooldude

His Beliefs: Stilpo wasn't a drug-taking oracle, he was just a smart guy.

He had developed a belief that to be truly happy a person must free themselves from all unnecessary desires and wants. It was the reason he turned his life around from drunken debauchery to becoming a philosopher, and it happened when in a drunken state he'd seen a young lad playing in a field without a care in the world, just having fun with his innocent imagination and so it occurred to him that for anyone to be free to enjoy such unfettered joy they must become like that young boy. In other words, free to just use their mind and be happy in that moment.

No matter how positive his attitude, it didn't take him long to figure out that even though his boss Ptolemy was a good man, his success against his enemy Antigonus wasn't just unlikely but that he was destined to lose – and badly. However, realising it wouldn't be smart to tell any king (especially this one) that he was about to get his backside kicked in a battle, he gave back most of the small fortune Ptolemy had paid him for his services, and hightailed it to somewhere safe until the dust had settled. Being a good man, he didn't neglect to share his thinking with Antigonus (without the bit about it being a lost cause) - who thanked him and guaranteed that in the coming battle the ancestral home of Stilpo and his family would be safeguarded. That was nice, but sadly, in the mayhem and complete defeat, Antigonus's soldiers failed to follow orders.

Stilpo's family were all murdered. His ancestral home was burned to the ground. Everything he owned was lost. When Antigonus found out, he angrily ordered that the soldiers concerned be beheaded - and apologised personally to Stilpo. Somehow, I don't think that will have helped - but I do think it was in this moment that the legend of Stilpo was born, because his response to this devastating news is reported as being; "*I have lost nothing. All my possessions are safe.*"

Now, I for one can't see how anyone, no matter how high-minded or controlled, when being told that their nearest and dearest have been murdered and all their worldly possessions have gone, would come out with this. So, let's get real here. Let's imagine instead that he went through the shock, the pain, and the grief, and only then at some time later came back to Antigonus and made this famous statement. I may be wrong, but no matter how powerful his legend, he was human and to me that makes much more sense.

His Identity: I am as certain as I can be that he was a heck of a charismatic character. Why else would hard-nosed Athenians turn out onto the street to welcome him when they heard he was in town? He didn't need Empedocles'-like bronze sandals and sassy purple gowns. He just stepped up to speak whenever he came out on the streets, and people flocked to listen. Let's not forget that these were Athenians - something akin to modern-day New Yorkers. They would not have been impressed easily, but were impressed by Stilpo.

I think he must have seen himself as an educator as well as a politician's consultant -here's something he's reported as saying when attempting to explain why assuming predicates and jumping to conclusions is a mistake:

"To be a horse differs from to be running. For being asked the definition of the one and of the other, we do not give the same for them both; and therefore, those err who predicate the one of the other. For if good is the same with people, and to run the same with a horse, how is good affirmed also of food and medicine, and again (by Jupiter) to run of a lion and a dog? But if the predicate is different, then we do not rightly say that a person is good, and that a horse runs."

If that all sounds strange to our twenty-first century ears, he's saying that the essence of a thing can't be understood by assuming what you see explains it. This example demonstrates that he was not afraid to deal with multi-layered concepts rather than stick to straightforward linear statements. What a guy.

He is also known to have been astute and aware, something that can't be said for a good many of the philosophers we've looked at. While many would speak their mind regardless of topic or audience, simply because they believed what they said to be true – and didn´t give any thought to where or who their next meal was coming from, Stilpo was more cautious. He spoke up only when he thought it useful, even if what he was saying might be 'close to the bone'. Managers and influencers please take note -leaders make what they say count, unlike bosses who just want to be heard. For example, in an encounter with Crates the master-cynic, Stilpo is reported as commenting on the fact that the old guy could do with a new set of threads. Clearly, he was being a bit cheeky. Even so, he would have only come out with that if he had some solid rapport with Crates ahead of time. They were mates, so it would've just been said in jest because of existing rapport. What he is actually reported as saying was something like, *"Hey Crates, you need a new dress!"*

Rapport is the key here - it allowed them to have a bit of banter. Without rapport it wouldn't have been banter, it would have been offensive. If Stilpo had been Crates´ manager and said the same thing without rapport it wouldn´t just have been offensive, it would´ve been an abuse of position. Leaders recognise this fact, they know they can say things with a smile and glint in their eye, but if a boss says the same thing without rapport would it´d be a bad thing – a very bad thing indeed.

As it happens, even if Stilpo had great rapport with Crates, in this instance he misjudged the situation and the comment went down like a lead balloon. Apparently, Crates got the right hump. It just goes to show that even the best of us can get it wrong, but the point of the story is that it didn't destroy their relationship - they just got over it and remained good friends in a similar way a leader doesn't allow a situation that's gone wrong to become a mountain made from a molehill.

In another instance when engaged by Zeno to speak publicly about religion, he just smiled, and avoided saying anything that might cause an offence to anyone overhearing by suggesting that such matters are best only discussed in private. Again, how many times do bosses insist on airing dirty laundry in public while leaders do just what Stilpo did, preferring to smile and set it aside for a more private conversation. He really was a smart chap.

His Purpose: Out of all the guys we've looked at, I think Stilpo is the most *'outcome driven'* character of them all. He was a results-oriented coaching-leader to those he loved, and those we worked with – despite the crappy hand the universe dealt him.

If losing his parents and his home earlier in life, he got on with life and had a daughter. Unfortunately, his bad run of luck hadn't ended, his daughter had a problem - she suffered from nymphomania. This might have been a problem for some father's in today's supposedly more enlightened world, never mind way back then when people gossiped in the market places (well, they didn't have TV or Instagram to keep them amused). When challenged about his daughter's libertine behaviour he replied *"She is not more a disgrace to me than I am an honour to her"*. In other words, he accepted 'who' she was, and like all good dad's, he had her back.

I'm as certain as I can be that his purpose was to live the happiest life he could despite whatever was thrown his way, and without retreating to some 'fake' hermit status after trouble struck. He did not go on the defensive when some small-minded busybody stuck their nose into his business. His attributes and skills are like a potpourri of great leadership choices, after all, wouldn't we all like a leader who had our back like Stilpo. He was politically astute and could engage people and spur them on to even better things in their lives just by changing the way they think - with his words. The best, most inspirational leaders are just like Stilpo.

How might he be thought of by his employees, if he was a manager in today's business world?

Following a leader who knows from his own experience that no one is ever a 'lost cause' is wonderful. His is an organisation of second chances, but also one where once the second chance has been given, the expectations of the person being given it are very high. Everyone following him know his 'rules' and are more than happy to follow them.

He is more ´real´ than any leader most people have ever worked with. He knows that not everything goes as planned, works as well as it should, or ends up the way it was planned, no matter how good the people are that made the plans. All of which means that he doesn´t get angry when it inevitably happens, he simply becomes more determined - and more determined to help the people concerned get things back on track.

It´s like working for a genuine philosopher who knows all about the philosophical big guns, but who applies his knowledge with such a light touch, it always sounds like he´s having each thought for the very first time and making it useful to whoever he´s speaking with. It´s like he just knows the right thing to say at just the right time. There are people in the organisation who have risen through the ranks because he has taken the time to mentor and guide them. The team are inspired by him, not just by his wise words when standing in front of them, but by the way he speaks to them individually. He has a depth of character and caring that goes beyond what is usually expected from a man in a leadership position. He is special.

Coaching questions he might ask:

i. *"Has your journey to get here been in a straight line, and if not, what might you anticipate that until now has been obscured from view?"*

ii. *"How do you know, in this situation you are in what is a genuine concern and an authentic cause for celebration, and what does that thinking suggest if you are to be the architect of your own happiness?"*

iii. *"If the perception of loss of anything were to be an illusion, what thoughts come to mind now that are fresh, clear, or simply new?"*

iv. *"If you chose to redefine everything that's happening right now so that you found some benefit or potential joy in each and every aspect, what would that look, sound, and feel like if you were to explain it to me now?"*

v. *"Perhaps if passions and strong emotion is not always linked to the achievement of the outcomes we desire, there might be a case for thinking about things differently, - what does that suggest to you?"*

vi. *"Should it be true that experience is our greatest teacher, what might you have already learned that has of yet, not been applied to your current circumstances?"*

vii. *"What aspects of your past behaviours must you let go of now in order to be free to make the most of the current circumstances for you, those close to you, those who may depend on you, and those with whom you've yet to meet but can ultimately be of service to?"*

viii. *"What worries are you holding onto that cause you to fear taking action you might be pushing against, and yet perhaps recognise is inevitable?"*

CHAPTER 26: #22 TAKE PLEASURE SERIOUSLY

EPICURUS

His Claim to Fame: Epicurus may be the best source we have for saying something like; *'you don't know what you don't know, but you do know what makes you happy'*. He didn't say it, but his tag line could have been ´Don´t worry - be happy´.

Contrary to popular belief, the legacy of Epicurus was not to indulge in good food until your body is fit to burst - and be the cheerful fat person on a food label. Like plenty of the philosophical heroes in here, one aspect of his life has been seized on by popular history and then (excuse the pun) blown out of all proportion.

True, Epicurus is known for preaching that the goal of life is happiness, (and as we know he was by no means the first to articulate life in that way), but there's no evidence that he took this to mean stuffing your face until your belly was sore. In fact, his approach was more 'spiritual' than materialistic. He took pleasure *seriously*, because his belief was that death marked the end of all sensation. The end of everything, no more chance to have fun – no chance to enjoy anything, ever again. Therefore he pondered, why wouldn't a person take every opportunity while in life to experience pleasure?

He even argued that we shouldn't fear death. He said, it won´t hurt it´ll just be just lacking in pleasure. The thing I said earlier about not knowing what you don't know, is that he argued that death couldn't possibly be painful because no sensations occurred once it happened. He said that as none of us know what sensation takes the place of pain then how can we even comment on it? He had a point I suppose.

However, he was a realist - he did accept that the *process* of dying could well be painful - because that's a different thing entirely. He suggested that this is even more reason to remove all barriers in life to sensual pleasures. He'd be the business leader confessing to NOT knowing what might be around the corner, but then helping everyone in the workforce to do the best with what they've got - and enjoying that journey in the process.

We all know what a typical boss does, and that's the polar opposite of that - they pretend to have all the answers to everything. Then they treat the workforce like they would a mushroom farm - keeping them in the dark and tossing the occasional bucket of manure over them from time to time.

Rather than quaffing gallons of wine or eating to excess, Epicurus taught that the most fulfilling of pleasure was in fact the search for knowledge, and the taming of desires. He saw the constant grasping for whatever fleeting pleasure might come your way as sickening, and that left untamed, desires can be much like an illness. They can cause extreme harm. The search for knowledge and the taming of desires so that something he called 'Ataraxia' was achieved (a freedom from anxiety) were his principle legacies. Sadly, they seem to have been forgotten.

His Environment: Epicurus was born in Athens but was raised in Samos, another one of those fabulous 'Mama-mia'[xxxvi] type islands off the coast of mainland Greece, glistening in the clear blue Aegean sea.

He stayed there until aged 18, at which time he went back to Athens to study at 'Academy'. He lived in the fast-lane of the big city for 10 years, being influenced among others, by the likes of Democritus before moving back to one of the islands.

This time it was to Lesbos. He set up camp both there and on the mainland, running two centres to attract interest, and flip-flopped between Mytilene on the island and Lampsacus on the nearby mainland coast. Like every philosopher before him, he preached his message in the market squares to anyone who'd listen. It was normal for people to be talking about philosophy and it's where they all found their initial following. This two-centre approach to gathering followers clearly worked. He grew in popularity so much, that when he returned in his 40's to the capital he was able to open his own successful school.

He called it 'the Garden' and it became a place where people came to learn how to find optimism in every circumstance and happiness in everything. His next 30 years were spent there until his death, and he was known as the most 'humane' of people, even by those who disagreed with some of his approaches.

His Culture: Think about the culture he was born into and the expectations of behaviour as a little bit like today's competing approaches to leadership.

Just like today there were 'old-school' approaches to thinking, approaches that people were drawn to because of their history and experiences. Today, we still have people talking about leadership as if true leaders are born to it. Then there were various grades of progressive thinking about how to engage with the world around them in order to live the 'happiest' or 'most successful' life. Much like we then have theories about leadership that can be traced back to the decades they became popular - from structured hierarchies, to a structured approach to categorising people based on traits and behaviours, to fitting people into organisational puzzles like pieces on a board game, to theories about leadership teamwork and collaboration, to transformational leadership, to servant leadership, and all the way to what people still consider a bit 'out there' - like spiritual leadership.

The truth for us is that most of these ideas have some value in some contexts, but only a few can apply across the board. Something similar was true for Epicurus when he studied for that decade in Athens. He could see how to pick the best from each, but didn't want to be accused of plagiarising from his fellow philosophers – his ego was big enough to want his idea to be *seen* his own.

Hence, the move to a new location and the freedom to develop his own ideas and approaches without anyone 'looking over his shoulder' was just what he needed. It allowed him and his followers to develop their own very happy culture.

His Skills: He, like some of the stoics he'd studied with wanted to offer people a way to achieve a tranquil state of mind. Of course, his very positive and happy outlook was poles apart from the Stoics. While the Stoics were characterised as uptight and dour, the people Epicurus attracted were more easy going and willing to take life as it comes. They had a much less serious attitude, although he would argue (and I see no reason to doubt him) that they were just as serious about achieving the goal of happiness as anyone. Their lighter approach and acceptance that sensual pleasures weren't a barrier to having a serious approach to life served them well. He was able to get people to collaborate and work together to attract even more people looking for a happier life. His commune was all about living a simple self-governed life that allowed them to feel pleasure right now - and not have to wait for 'someday when'. I must admit to struggling to find any problems with his approach, either in society or at work.

He had the courage to talk about living life in search of pleasure, whereas the Stoics were all about living life more virtuously. It's funny, but conceptually they really weren't very far apart, it's just that Stoics started to confuse virtue with piety - much like some religions take 'the word' and turn it into their interpretation of how that means to live.

Epicurus was skilled at articulating things like *'peace and tranquillity'* and realised that there may be more than one way of expressing the goal. He taught that living in peace and tranquillity didn't necessarily mean living the life of a Hericlitus-type hermit - somewhere up a hill in a cave away from any interference, just so that you experience peace and the environment is tranquil. He knew that following that route won't guarantee any peace and tranquillity in your mind, even if there's nothing but rolling fields and tweeting birds in your environment. He successfully argued that if the experience of something gave you pleasure, and this pleasure leads to mental peace and tranquillity, then it may be part of your journey to happiness. He realised that successful achievement of happiness really is, all in the mind.

I mean, come on - this MUST have been a big attraction. Which commune would you be more attracted to - the one that wants you to live a life of quiet virtue, or the one that wants you to seek out pleasure in the search for mental peace and tranquillity? It's not a trick question, I promise. It's like asking what kind of leader you'd prefer to work for – the pious and virtuous type, or the seeking out of pleasure in search of peace and tranquillity kind?

I hope it doesn't make me shallow for choosing the latter. Seriously, it's a good analogy for a workplace run by a boss and one by a leader; the boss takes perfectly good ways to run a business and forces them into an interpretation that conform to his or her narrow view of the world. Everyone who works 'under' them is then required to adhere to those rules of behaviour. Whereas the leader in search of ultimate peace and tranquillity focuses on the ultimate goal and the requirements of the business, then sets about encouraging each individual to find their best way to achieve that goal most effectively while enjoying the process. Now, forgive me for saying so, but there's nothing shallow about that.

His Beliefs: For once there's an easy way to unpack his beliefs and the things he's best remembered for because he wrote them down and they survived. So, in the words of the man himself– well, not quite as I've somewhat shortened them and made them more (how can I put it) accessible - here's what he held to be true;

Agreements that are mutual are the only ones that bring happiness
All you need is easy to acquire, wanting everything will never be acquired

Anything that doesn't hurt you leads you toward pleasure

Be prepared to change if you want to be happy

Being able to sleep easy is necessary to be happy

Being true to yourself is necessary not just desirable

Being wise, honourable, and just is a precursor to happiness

Death means nothing because once it happens we are not there to feel it

Don't be too quick to declare happiness as you don't know what's around the corner

Effort to be happy doesn't necessarily equal success in being happy

Embrace all sensations so you know what to enjoy

Everyone loves a quiet life – when they want it

Fame and status are no guarantee of happiness

Fear is a pain we all have to deal with – for life

Friendship helps us feel secure

Friendship is the most important route to happiness

If being profligate was truly the source of pleasure then those people wouldn't be miserable

If you are incapable of agreement you're incapable of happiness

It is impossible to be happy without being certain

It's not possible to be happy without being fair

Know what you want if you want to be happy

Knowing necessary from opinion is a route to happiness

Laws need to be good for everyone

Mutual destruction can be a recipe for lifelong happiness

No one can protect you as long as you are running scared from everything

Pain and desire leads us to learn

Pain doesn't last, but memories of pleasure can last a lifetime

Pleasure doesn't increase just by the removal of pain
Pleasure needs to be dynamic for it to provide a lifetime of enjoyment
Recognising your own limits means you know how to get what you need
Success doesn't happen by accident
The best and most lasting pleasures are in the mind
There's no such thing as a bad pleasure – only bad things that some pleasures lead to
Uninterrupted pleasure can only take place in the absence of pain
When everyone is family, there's always family to find
You don't need more time to be happy, just enough time
You have to give to get
You're good enough just as you are

His Identity: Although he argued he didn't get his ideas from Democritus, he clearly did. At least, he got some of them from him – he was a big advocate of the universe being a matrix made up of 'atoms'. The same Democritus atoms, not the atoms we think of today. Those atoms that have hooks and crevices allowing them to come together to make up other bigger materials - that in turn go on to make up other stuff and eventually results in all we see around us.

So, he definitely saw himself as a scientist first and a philosopher second. While he's known for advocating the search for happiness by taming desires through pleasure, he was also an early proponent of the many-worlds theory. He thought that this matrix of 'stuff' was so complex, it must result in the creation of other types of worlds - worlds that may be very different to our own. He had an open mind, and was prepared to think things that others discarded without proper thought. He accepted that the 'universe' as we know it is infinite and as such there's likely to be an infinite number of 'things' that atoms come together to form. Therefore, there's no doubt at all he was a deep thinker - an aspect of him that's missing sometimes when people talk about the superficial aspects of Epicureanism.

One thing he was sure of is that everyone has a life-force that he (like many others) called the soul. Yet, unlike others he thought the soul too delicate to survive after death, and that its atoms would return to the void to be redistributed into something else. This then supported his view that people must make the most of what they have while they have it. It's a view that's unpopular with any alternative group that sought to control the actions of their followers by promises of what might come next after death - like Pythagoras among others, and let's face it, there are plenty of contemporary comparisons in contemporary religions that seek to do the same.

If there were to be an Epicurean movement today they'd be all about the freedom to find pleasure (responsibly) in all they do - to search for happiness in the form of mental peace and tranquillity, in the sure and certain knowledge that while they have a 'soul', it's job is to help them in this life and will not go on in its existing form into the future. However, it will still exist in its constituent parts and so doesn't really ever go away. I suppose he was trying to pitch the best of all worlds. He wasn't an agnostic in religious terms because back then the soul and religion hadn't been bound together as a package. Neither was he someone who advocated personal pleasure at the expense of others. Indeed, he supported belief in the gods in a way that supported a more disciplined approach to life.

In many ways it's the 'Carrot and Stick' approach bosses use to try and motivate their team into ever higher levels of performance. They use the *'put the pain aside you're feeling now because you'll feel even better tomorrow when we achieve these results'* approach. We all know that it may work once or twice, but it soon wears thin.

The Epicurean leader wouldn't do that - they would be clear about what's required because just like the ticking clock of time, or the inevitable wilting of a cut flower, things are what they are. Then the leader will work with each person in their care to help them 'rock' their performance by being the best they can be - reaching their full potential, and enjoying doing it so that they do it more and more without needing to be asked. Epicureanism isn't all about chasing frivolous pleasure, it's as serious as any other philosophy and has the potential to produce great results.

His Purpose: I think he wanted people to be mindful of where they are today and what they doing that's either taking them closer to their ultimate goal or further away.

Epicurus was the kind of man who probably didn't sugar-coat the reality of anything but told it as it was, so that the person he was speaking to had the best chance right from that very moment to think about what they are doing, and alter it right now if necessary.

His purpose was clearly to make it clear that success or happiness and pleasure along the way are not mutually exclusive. He knew that, in his words *"The greatest benefit to self-sufficiency is freedom"*. In fact, to those who've taken the time to understand his purpose — he's a revelation.

How might he be thought of by his employees, if he was a manager in today's business world?

He is a leader of apparent contradictions; he works so hard himself that it appears there is no time or energy for anything else, and yet he does find time to play, have fun, and both give and receive love from those he cares for - which includes all of his followers. He has his own moral compass and accepts that not everyone will share his values. However, he believes that to be successful in any organisation, everyone within it must be absolutely clear of the 'mission' - simply put, if the mission is to be successful and they are to truly experience joy along the way then they must be gaining pleasure both along the way AND when the mission is achieved.

He doesn't tell, he asks. He is always clear about what's necessary but then makes an agreement with each member of the team about how they'll fulfil their part. Everything he sets out for us to achieve requires us to grow both personally and professionally, and often causes us to set aside preconceptions and develop new ones. That being said, he does his best to keep stress to a minimum — he always wants us at our best and knows that sleepless nights won't help with that. He's quick at making decisions but thankfully, not so quick to judge. None of us in the team take anything for granted and are encouraged to keep an open mind — about everything. He wants us to be happy at work and at home, to embrace whatever happens and find something good about it – even if that's simply that things could always be worse.

He wants the best for us all and wants to be our friend, but none of us are in any doubt that he's still in charge – that's because he keeps us on track. He checks in with us, makes sure whatever has been agreed is still agreed, and reminds us that even when things are painful, that this too will pass.

Another great thing about working with him is that he knows our limits probably better than we do, which means he pushes where it'll create the most benefit, and supports where it'll help us all achieve a better result. He is a remarkable leader 'he sort of makes us all feel like family. His mantra is not 'if it's not fun then don't do it', but *'there's always joy to be found in anything you do if you look for it'*.

Coaching questions he might ask:

i. *"As you think of an experience where logic and pleasure came together for a successful outcome, what are you learning that might be useful for where you find yourself now?"*

ii. *"If nothing was stopping you from having some fun while doing something new that's also difficult, what might you do differently?"*

iii. *"If you fight against yourself, who is going to lose, what is going to be lost, and who might then win?"*

iv. *"If you were to see any anger or personal agenda in this matter as a weakness preventing you from moving forward to something better and more pleasurable, what would you do?"*

v.   *"If your choices are always between that which is painful and that which is less painful, what might you change about the way you think about your challenge so that retreating from doing what's necessary is more painful than creating positive change?"*

vi.   *"Should you be a judge rather than participant in your own situation, what verdict on your own performance would resonate with a jury?"*

vii.   *"The prick of pain that saves you from lasting affliction becomes a pleasure, so what about this situation might have been seen as difficult but in reality is just a little prick?"*

viii.   *"What is your ultimate goal in relation to the outcomes of this situation, and what might thinking about that cause you to do?"*

ix.   *"When have you been pleased to have changed your thinking, and how might such pleasure manifest in your current situation?"*

CHAPTER 27: THE VERDICT?

WHAT DID YOU THINK, MY SCEPTICAL FRIEND?

That's it, twenty-two of the greatest thinkers from the sixth century BCE right up to about twelve hundred and fifty years ago. Twenty-two doesn't cover all the great thinkers of that time by any means, but I hope I've laid out an interesting mix.

Did that help with your formulation of coaching questions? Questions you might use to help someone change who might be 'stuck'?

It certainly has made me think, - which I suppose was the point! Of course, I've learned more than I thought I was going to along the way; each one of them was fascinating, and I can't believe how many I hadn't heard of, or how many facts I didn't know about who thought of things long before now!

I was the same. The big realisation I had in putting it together is that we assume people from long ago weren't very bright because they didn't have the same advanced technology that we take for granted, but if you strip that away from us we are much the same as them. So, quite why any of us should be surprised that they came up with great ways of thinking about things doesn't make much sense. Their words are like a freezer full of ice cream in the garage that we forgot about. Finding it again, especially on a hot day during a party can feel like winning the lottery; and that's how I feel about these guys, they are the ice cream in my freezer, my forgotten lottery ticket in the crease of a wallet! So, what have you gained most from hearing all this?

Now that's a big question. I loved the story about the olive-presses, - I've already started thinking about what patterns I'm recognising and how to make them useful. The Chinese stuff makes so much sense when you break it down into simple bite-size chunks, and I want to spend some time thinking about my own expectations of myself and other people, - that's very useful to think about, and all that stuff about the Buddha, who knew? Okay, I know the Buddhists knew, but I didn't. The commitment to making sure about yourself before trying to fix anyone else rang loud and clear to me, - plenty for me to do there! And the stoic approach is going to stick with me too, - by not trying to control things that aren't in my control. I've heard all that before but had no idea where it came from and how pointless it is to push against things that aren't going to give. There's so much to choose from!

Well, let me ask you in a different way; now you've heard all their stories and their questions, what do you think you'll immediately do with what you now know?

You know, that's another good question... anyone would think you've written a book about them! Okay, the truth is that there really is so much in here that I honestly don't know where to start. As I was hearing the questions at the end of each story I found myself thinking of situations where I can most definitely use one or two of them.

Just the one or two?

Well, for now anyway. There's something else; I hope this doesn't disappoint, but there are some that I'll never use, - they just don't sound like they could come out of my mouth without me feeling fake.

That's great!

Great? Why? I thought you'd be disappointed?

Not at all. It's great because you are imagining yourself asking the questions. Of course, some are going to sound more like you could ask them than others. I'd urge anyone to do what you are doing and figure out what makes sense for you. In fact, I'd go further and say you might want to think of getting a highlighter and marking up the questions you can use, and then ignore the rest. It could be that someday they'll come in useful, but better you focus on now and what makes immediate sense.

Thanks, that's great and I think I will. I know I'll be coming back to these questions time and time again even if I don't use them exactly as they've been written or in precisely those circumstances. The best things about the whole book are that it's both entertaining and useful. I can see it becoming quite dog-eared!

If you've enjoyed this then drop me a line at martin@martin.coach to say you want more and I'll oblige, but for now all I have to say to finish is thanks for reading the book. I hope it was fun.

WHO IS MARTIN GOODYER?

'BLURB' ABOUT THE AUTHOR

Building trust, creating a safe space and recognising that no leader has all the answers but always has strengths to build on, are hallmarks of outstanding senior executive coaching. Martin has an exemplary and extensive track record of coaching built on the solid foundations of a business career, qualifications in business management and as a psychologist, and now more than two decades as a full time coach and coach educator.

An author on books on popular psychology, coaching and productivity, a teacher of coaching philosophy and skills at the highest accredited level, and a coach of vast experience working internationally with C-suite clients from India, the US, Africa, Scandinavia, Central and Eastern Europe, The Middle East and Far East, Martin is a genuine, authentic, and successful world class coach who has also undertaken the role as personal coach to a number of high profile clients in the public eye. He is an engaging presenter on seminar platforms, with extensive television (ITV & Channel 4) and radio (BBC) experience. When coaching clients in business the vast majority have been members the C-suite and senior individuals from a vast variety of situations and contexts; they include gaming executives, communications professionals, private equity investment company chief financial officers & directors, investment banking executives, utility company directors, local authority strategic directors and senior managers, directors of private and public companies, senior executives, partners and entrepreneurs in a variety of sectors including architecture, banking, construction, chemical processing, property development, brewing, recruitment, healthcare, hospitality, higher education, interior design, insurance, IT, logistics, legal practice, manufacturing, pharmaceuticals, professional sport, retail, utilities and venue management.

At the time of writing Martin is in the process of completing a research PhD at Birmingham City University into the effectiveness of coaching in the workplace, achieved an honours degree in psychology, graduated from Guelph University in Canada on their Advanced Management Programme, is an NLP Master Practitioner, holds a raft of training & coaching certificates gained with international hotel companies and began his career by graduating with honours and a Diploma in Management. In addition to being a coach himself, Martin is also Head of Coach Training at an international training academy and a long serving member of the coach training team delivering executive and operational coach training to the highest qualified level. The methodologies applied by Martin are based on solid scientific foundations and delivered with practical business acumen. In summary, he is a media savvy, highly skilled change director, author, and coach.

NOTES:

EXPLANATORY REFERENCES

---

[i] Research into the effectiveness of coaching in the workplace. Supervised by Birmingham City University.

[ii] Emotional Quotient or Emotional Intelligence

[iii] Goodyer, M. 2014. *How to be a Great Coach; Brilliant Coaching Conversations.* iABCt, Santa Cruz de Tenerife

[iv] The 'friend' is in fact a synthesis of sceptical questions actually asked during my career. The conversation is not fictitious because all of the comments made by the 'friend' were made and the questions asked over the course of my career. For ease of explanation they are presented as a single conversation from a single 'friend'.

[v] While this conversation is a synthesis for illustrative purposes, it is representative of many conversations I've had over the years with people after they've learned what coaching is, how it 'works', the science on which it is based, and after they've had time to go out and practice using it themselves.

[vi] Goodyer, M. 2016. *WTF Just Happened; how to make better decisions by asking better questions.* Crown House Publishing, UK. www.crownhouse.co.uk

vii Originated from "logical types" of communication and learning-which he called the "most important" criterion of "mind" in his book Mind and Nature (1979). Bateson derived the notion of different logical types of communication and learning from Bertrand Russell's mathematical theory of logical types-which states that a class of things cannot be a member of itself. According to Bateson (Steps to an Ecology of Mind, p.202): Our approach is based on that part of communications theory which [Bertrand] Russell has called the Theory of Logical Types. The central thesis of this theory is that there is a discontinuity between a class and its members. The class cannot be a member of itself nor can one of the members be the class, since the term used for the class is of a different level of abstraction-a different Logical Type-from terms used for members. This was then developed by Robert Dilts In a November 1976 paper published in Roots of NLP, 1983 he distinguished between logical types and logical levels, resulting in the now widely used model known as 'logical levels of thinking', a hierarchy of factors that influence thinking, normally presented in the form of a pyramid. Starting at the base with the environment, stimulating questions about where the person was or is at the time of thinking, and the time the events took place. The second level refers to influences on the person's behaviour, including what they were doing and what was expected from them in that context. The third level refers to the person's capability and skills, including how they know to do what they were/are doing.

Fourth in the logical sequence are the person's beliefs and values, stimulating questions about motivation for their behaviour. Fifth out of six levels refer to the way the person views themselves, otherwise known as their identity, suggesting questions about who they see themselves as, how they might describe themselves to another person, and what priorities come to mind in respect of the way they wish to be perceived. The final, highest level on the pyramid of thinking levels is the 'purpose' the person attributes to their existence. Sometimes referred to as a person's spiritual purpose, but equally relevant are the ultimate desires a person has for their life. The concept is that the higher up the hierarchy a person thinks it affects the way a person experiences thinking at the levels below it. Reference: *1990, Dilts. R., Changing Belief Systems with NLP, Meta Publications, CA.*

[viii] From 'A Minimalist Translation' of the Dao de Jing by B R Linnell, PhD, 2015

[ix] The Law of Conservation of Energy states that the total energy of an isolated system remains constant.

[x] A change in global or regional climate patterns

[xi] a gradual increase in the overall temperature of the earth's atmosphere generally attributed to the greenhouse effect

[xii] Indiana Jones is an American media franchise based on the adventures of Dr. Henry Walton "Indiana" Jones, Jr., a fictional professor of archaeology
[xiii] The Babylonian creation story known as 'Enuma Elish' was prominent in the twelve century BC

[xiv] Temple, R.K.G. 1976. *The Sirius Mystery*. St Martin's Press, London.

[xv] Using ultra-precise analysis of ice from a Swiss glacier, a team of researchers from Harvard University found the year 563 AD to be the worst to be alive. The team led by Mr McCormick, chair of the Harvard University initiative for the science of the human past, and glaciologist Paul Mayewski, of the climate change institute of the University of Maine (UM) in Orono, found an enormous volcanic eruption in Iceland was likely to blame, leading to a volcanic-ash winter causing global crop failures and freezing temperatures.

[xvi] Two epic poems forming the central works of Greek literature; the Iliad is the Trojan story of their Queen Helen, she of 'launching a 1000 ships' fame, and the Odyssey starts from the fall of Troy and tells the story of the Hero Odysseus and his struggle with the gods

[xvii]Since the 1940's Oklahoma City has been known as the capital of the bible belt. The term ' Bible Belt' refers to the region of the southern U.S. states stretching from West Virginia and southern Virginia to southern Missouri in the north to Texas and northern Florida in the south, where Southern Baptists, Methodists, and evangelical Christians are the predominant religious groups.

[xviii]*The 4-Hour Workweek: Escape 9-5, Live Anywhere, and Join the New Rich (2007)*a book by Timothy Ferriss spent more than four years on The New York Times Best Seller List. It has been translated into 35 languages and has sold more than 1,350,000 copies worldwide. Ferriss proposes "lifestyle design" in favour of a traditional "deferred" life plan in which people work long hours and take few holidays, to save money for a better life in retirement.

[xix]Hogwarts is the school of witchcraft and wizardry invented by J.K. Rowling in the Harry Potter books. Most of the action of the novels takes place in Hogwarts and it the place where the student wizards and witches learn their spells.

[xx] The four laws of thermodynamics define temperature, energy, and entropy at thermal equilibrium; The Zeroth (which is actually the first but not called the first) law states that for two systems to be in thermal equilibrium with a third they must be in thermal equilibrium with each other. The law called the First (but comes second) states that when energy passes in or out of a system, the system's internal energy changes in line with the law of Conservation of Energy and stays constant The Second (that comes next) law states that in a natural thermodynamic process the sum of the entropies of the interacting thermodynamic systems increases. Finally, the Third law states that the entropy of a system approaches a constant value as the temperature approaches absolute zero.

[xxi]New International Version (New Testament) Luke 6:31

[xxii] The book series by J. K. Rowling

[xxiii]EQ relates to five factors; Firstly, self-awareness; the ability to recognise an emotion 'in the moment', thereby affecting emotional awareness of self-generated emotions and the emotions of others, self-confidence, certainty regarding self-worth, and personal capabilities. Secondly, self-regulation; relating to the exertion of control over the experience of emotions such as anger, anxiety, depression, self-control, the management of disruptive impulses, trustworthiness, standards of honesty, integrity, conscientiousness, the taking of responsibility for own performance, adaptability, handling change, flexibility, innovation, and being open to suggestion. Thirdly, motivation; specifically, the movement toward the achievement of clear goals and a positive attitude, the consistent striving to improve, commitment to alignment of stakeholder goals, initiative, a readiness to act on opportunities, optimism and the persistent pursuing of goals despite obstacles and setbacks. Fourthly, empathy;

meaning the ability to recognise how people feel, anticipating mood, supporting the meeting of other's needs, people development, bolstering abilities, leveraging diversity, cultivating opportunities, being politically aware, understanding others, and discerning feelings behind the needs and wants of others. Finally, social skills; including the development of interpersonal skills, influence, effective persuasion tactics, effective communication, empowering leadership, inspiring and guiding groups and people, becoming a catalyst for change, initiating or managing change, conflict management, understanding, negotiation, disagreement resolution, building bonds, nurturing relationships, collaboration, cooperation, working toward shared goals, developing team capabilities, creating group synergy in the pursuant of collective goals.

[xxiv] Probably most notably in the writings of William Blake

[xxv] Greek for 'indivisible thing'

[xxvi]The Matrix is a 1999 science fiction action media franchise created by The Wachowskis about an imagined reality in which the earth has been overtaken by machines that keep humans in pods as 'batteries' to supply them with power. The premise being that humans are maintained by placing them in a virtual reality, indistinguishable from any 'real' experience.

[xxvii]Intelligence Quotient - IQ refers to a score derived from a test rating the subject's cognitive ability as compared to the general population. The test uses a standardised scale with 100 as the median score where a result of plus or minus 10 (90 to 110) describes average intelligence. A score of 130 may be indicative of exceptional intelligence, or below 70 of indicating reduced cognitive ability. The test may employ questions relating to spatial ability, mathematical dexterity, memory, and language application, that are collated to provide a generalised score. Therefore, IQ is not influenced by the learning of facts, but potentially might be positively influenced through the practice of improved thinking effectiveness.

[xxviii]James Warren Jones - an American cult leader who, along with his inner circle, initiated and was responsible for a mass suicide and mass murder in Jonestown, Guyana. James Jones born May 13, 1931, died November 18, 1978.

[xxix] 'Drinking the Kool-Aid' is a United States expression referring to a person who is coerced through peer pressure to go along with potentially dangerous or outrageous behaviour. It originates from the tragic 1978 death of over 900 members of a cult group known as the 'People's Temple' who were followers of the cult-leader Jim Jones. They committed mass suicide by drinking a mix of Kool-Aid and Flavour-Aid flavourings with cyanide, valium, phenergan, and chloral hydrate.

[xxx] Anthony Robbins is a writer and presenter of personal development material, known for hosting large-scale educational seminars in auditoriums, characterised by high-energy participation and the positioning of the host in a manner not unlike that of a cult-leader.

[xxxi]See the works of Zacharia Sitchin

[xxxii] www.quantumgravityresearch.org

[xxxiii] Character from Gene Roddenberry's 'Star Trek', known for a logical approach to everything

[xxxiv] Grigori Rasputin is best known for his role as the mystical advisor to the court of Czar Nicholas 2nd in the early eighteenth century. His alleged abilities made him a favourite of Nicholas's wife Alexandra, and is rumoured to have unduly influenced her who in turn influenced the Czar, although historian experts suggest such influence was minor.

[xxxv] Born in 1908 in New York, Abraham Maslow published a motivational 'hierarchy of needs' in the 1940's; it suggests that at the most basic level people need their biological and physiological needs met and that once fulfilled they move up to the level of fulfilling their safety and security needs, then once they are secured they seek out the fulfilment of their emotional needs, then after that may move up to the fulfilment of their needs for self-esteem before finally reaching a state referred to as self-actualisation, - in which a person achieves personal growth and ultimate fulfilment.

[xxxvi] In 2008 the film mamma-mia became the 5th largest grossing movie of the year, was a juke-box musical featuring tracks by the musical act 'ABBA' and filmed on a picturesque Greek Island

www.ingramcontent.com/pod-product-compliance
Lightning Source LLC
Chambersburg PA
CBHW072011230526
45468CB00021B/1188